ALSO BY JIM PAUL

Catapult

WHAT'S CALLED LOVE

WHAT'S CALLED LOVE

A Real Romance

JIM PAUL

VILLARD BOOKS • NEW YORK • 1993

LIBRARY OF CONGRESS CATALOGING-IN-PUBLICATION DATA
Paul, Jim.
What's called love : a real romance / by Jim Paul.—1st ed.
p.   cm.
ISBN 0-679-40971-8
1. Paul, Jim, 1950–   . 2. Biography—United States.
3. Biography—20th century. 4. Love. 5. Courtship. I. Title.
CT275.P4789A3 1993
818.5403—dc20   92-56837
[B]
Designed by Fritz Metsch
9 8 7 6 5 4 3 2

FIRST EDITION

But let us leave the forest
and return to Paris.
—Stendhal

ACKNOWLEDGMENTS

First to L, with love, thanks for everything. I'm grateful as well to the other actual people sketched herein, who are larger than life and so certainly larger than art. Thanks, too, to Jennifer Dowley, Barbara Bratone, the La Napoule Art Foundation, Kajsa Agostini and the French Government Tourist Office, whose material help made this book possible; also to Carl Dennis, Fenton Johnson, Beth Kriegler, Christian Marouby, Peter Gethers, Stephanie Long and Chuck Verrill, who contributed to the progress of *What's Called Love*.

—Jim Paul
San Francisco

CONTENTS

WHAT'S CALLED LOVE

1

C'est l'Aube

....

I woke up naked and alone in the strange bed, the light from the other room leaking in around the door. It was still night, if you could call it night. We'd been in Paris only a few hours, but the trip was already different from what I'd had in mind. Nothing was going according to plan, but then nothing had, with L. France wasn't going to provide any instant magic, obviously. She seemed to want to sleep in the other room.

I got up and went out there, wincing. L was sitting in the single stuffed chair, low and white, which alone made that bare swept corner into the living room. She'd been reading, maybe; in any case she sat there in her plain white T-shirt holding her book. A blue book, Colette—that name on the cover in tall slim deco type, orange—with the title *Flowers and Fruit*. L looked up at me and I stood there for a moment, trying to see and having no idea what I was about to say, how I was going to do this.

"It's dawn," she said, pronouncing it so before I had a chance to say anything. At least she wasn't sleeping in the other room.

She was wishing for the night to be over, for it to be morning. I just gestured at the blackness beyond the shutters, meaning it wasn't dawn. Both windows stood wide open in the warm night, their shutters swung out, and beyond the iron balustrades lay the dark, or what passes for dark in big cities. In the canyon of apartments beneath us—the middle of a block—no light shone. Over the rooftops and chimneys, the city night glowed across the urban horizon, and the moon was setting there, almost horizontal, a flat, coppery crescent, like the rim of a bowl. Out there perhaps the quietest night of the year lay over Paris, a Sunday night gone to a Monday in August.

"Have you looked at the watch?" I said, posing in the helpful interrogative, this pose, as always since I'd fallen in love with her, completely transparent. She sat there, knowing everything, in her white chair. I didn't feel that I could simply say what I wanted, and so had to proceed despite my transparency, clinging to the business of the time. My wristwatch, as it happened, was the only timepiece in that spare, barely furnished place. The apartment's absent owner, Phillipe, a bachelor and a light traveler, didn't even own a clock.

"I couldn't find it," said L. Her long hair, chestnut, still ringleted from her sleep, lay around her shoulders. With L, I always had to be paradoxical, to go sideways, having sensed from the start that demanding anything was the worst thing I could do. She balked under pressure, simply refused. She wanted possibilities, always. Oddly, that was what I loved most about her. I certainly wanted to possess her though, and so my touch had to be so light as to seem to be no touch at all.

So we'd gone to France, but only as writers. Even though I might have called us lovers already at home, we'd be writers, a pair of writers on the road. I wasn't thinking about writing anything at that point, though. At that point I was too busy being Mr. Delicate, and praying it would work. And after all, I'd gotten most of what I'd wanted—I had gotten her all the way to Paris, alone, six thousand miles from her answering machine. And for three whole weeks.

I found my watch. It wasn't hard to locate. Other than the white chair, only a table and two wooden folding chairs graced the room, nothing else, not even a carpet. Phillipe had a place to eat, a place to sit, a place to sleep. He'd streamlined his modern urban French life, never allowing any moment to accumulate and clutter up the place in the form of some useless souvenir. There was something appalling about this spareness to me, as if it were evidence of how little I might actually need. My theory was that he had another place somewhere, a whole house stuffed with things, with books and records and knickknacks and pictures and dried flowers. L had liked this apartment from the first, though. Sitting there, she, too, looked essential.

I picked up my jeans, which were draped over one of the folding chairs, and felt in the front pocket for my watch, a heavy scuba-diver's chronometer, capable of resisting pressure to a depth of 150 meters. I pulled it out by its black rubber band. I'd set it to Paris time before we'd left San Francisco, and now it was right.

"It's two A.M.," I said as flatly as possible, trying to rid my voice of need.

From the white chair, L looked at me brightly, blue-eyed and nonchalant, as if time didn't matter. What was she going to say? That we'd slept all evening, since we'd arrived exhausted in the afternoon? That it had been eight hours since then, an ordinary night and time enough to reach an ordinary dawn? I couldn't have answered that. There would have gone my pretense with the hour.

But that wasn't her look. She had on her why-not-just-stay-up-all-night? look, her everything look. When she was seven, she'd told me once, she'd made up the Everything Dance, which you did by jumping around a lot, shaking everything you could shake, and shouting out the names of all the animals you could think of. This dance—I knew it when she described it—she was still doing. It was in her look at that moment, that readiness for anything that might happen at any time. Being with her, I had to be prepared for everything, which to tell you the truth I didn't want to be. I wanted to be one thing—in love with someone who was in love with me, but with L, I never knew. I might be up in the middle of the night, naked, in Paris, France, standing before a woman I adored but who didn't adore me, for instance. Essential L in her white chair and her T-shirt and her readiness.

It made me ache, this wanting and not wanting to want, feeling my need to possess her, nevertheless, all the more. And that, I knew, too, was really why she was up, out here in the living room, not just because our bodies were out of tune with the movement of the earth, but because in there with me she was defined. She was Alone in Paris with Jim. That was something, after all, not everything, and that had pushed her out of bed and into the other room. That had turned the lights on.

"We should try to sleep," I said, not feeling sleepy. "Otherwise we won't adjust." Pathetic. Transparent.

"What time is it in California?" she said, just now getting around to practicality.

I had to think, subtracting nine from two. "Five in the afternoon," I said.

That was dawn enough, apparently. She went casually and absolutely back to her book. I could see that there was no rejection in her, but part of me still felt crushed. Oh, get a grip, I demanded of myself. But there was no grip.

So far, in the course of this romance, I'd had to refrain, to let us be as autonomous as mountains or something. But stay up and read? I considered it as she went back to her Colette. We'd brought French books for our French trip, and I'd brought the first volume of *Remembrance of Things Past*. From the start, Proust had been horribly perfect, even seeming to anticipate my jet lag. He'd begun his vast memoir with descriptions of those dislocated thoughts that occur between sleep and waking, and with that sense of awakening in a strange room, which you finally recognize as foreign after you have discarded, one by one, the details of places you've known, until you're left, new and mute, amid the unfamiliar. This I didn't need.

Besides, L had the one soft chair, and lovelorn though I was, this defeated me. I could not sit in a hard folding chair in a bright empty room in the middle of the night and go back with Proust into his incredibly sensitive childhood. The book was like some condensation of Europe itself, old, elaborate, gorgeous, intensely personal, petty yet profound, rich as foie gras, dense as Latin. On the plane I'd read some of it out loud to L and she'd said good grief.

But it was Proust or the dimness and anxiety of the other room, in which I wouldn't sleep, either, not without her, and not in any case, probably, since she was certainly right about being awake. I wished I could just sleep, adjust instantly to Paris time and sleep, as if it were a normal night. Sleep would give everything meaning. But wanting sleep was nothing like actually feeling sleepy. Jet lag was profound, I'd decided earlier in the dark. Imagine Proust jet-lagged, I'd thought. He'd have hated it. When you woke up jet-lagged, you had to toss out even the passage of time, as you went through your memories to come up with the present.

Oh hell, I thought. I just wanted L back in bed, her long body back in bed. That night could have been so great, our first warm summer night after chilly, astringent San Francisco. Paris's darkness seemed perfumed. Maybe we could pull the mattress out here—to be in this room if she wanted to be in this room—and lie there, delicious and strange in the dark, naked to the night breeze, the empty town outside quiet as the country, and the night and the two of us in it perfect, in Paris finally and perfect, but no.

I had to be cool; I didn't want to seem to be obsessed. Why not just ask anyway? a voice in me pressed, but I held back. If she said no, I'd go back to bed hurt; and even if she said yes, I'd go knowing I had to ask, and it wouldn't be perfect. Ask anyway, ask anyway, said the voice, but, in her chair in the light, she was beyond all that, and watching her turn back to her book, I knew I'd be going back into the bedroom alone, into Phillipe's bedroom, where his festival poster was pinned above the bed. My demands would only send her further into her inviolateness, which this white chair and blue book stood for by now.

So I could do nothing, just drop the timepiece back into my jeans and turn back into the darkened bedroom by myself, quietly, as if I bore a chalice I dared not spill. I spilled it anyway, of course. As I left the bright, empty room, some vagrant impulse rose into my arm and shut the door too hard behind me. It didn't actually slam, but it confessed. Out there in the light, she knew everything. She'd known everything all along, I thought, cowering a little as I lay down again in the strange bed. What was happening to me? What were we doing in France?

We were there, for one thing, because I'd heard that strangers, asked by psychologists simply to gaze into one another's eyes, tended to fall in love. So I had arranged this trip for us, that we might be alone together for almost a month, gazing into one another's eyes in romantic France. We'd started in Paris, which—even more to the point—L had loved since she'd lived there as a child. I had to be patient; it still might work, I prayed. Proximity, proximity—I called on it like a mantra—mere nearness would bring her to me. And France would hasten her approach. I was still hoping she'd say she'd marry me, at the end.

·   ·   ·

After a while I sought refuge by thinking about other things, imagining the night sweeping westward like a wave, long crested over France and just now falling on California, L and I beyond the break, deep in its dark wash. Actually, the darkness was motionless, the earth turning beneath it, as if away. "Sunrise" was a misnomer, since Copernicus anyway. Even the light from the sun itself was only relatively still by comparison to the dark, I realized. The sun washed around in the spiral of the galaxy, but the dark was always there, always still. Even when things were illuminated, it stayed at the heart of things, calling out, ready to resume. I wished it would.

Things had been illuminated a lot in the twentieth century. The one window in the room opened on an air shaft, and even in there the backwash of city light, Paris light, poured thinly down. In the darkness of his century, Proust might imagine himself in the bedroom of his childhood or the boudoir of his youth, but streetlights were unromantic. I could tell that the room was unfamiliar even with the lights off. Another Venetian festival poster was pinned at a jaunty angle to the wall beyond the foot of the bed. It was the bedroom of a strange man. His French change and big business cards lay on the nightstand.

L had known Phillipe from before, from the time she'd lived in Paris on her junior year abroad from college. What they'd been to each other then—which hadn't been that long ago—I didn't know, and didn't want to know, and had to know. They'd met on the train, was all she'd said. I couldn't stand thinking about it and couldn't stop thinking about it. What had they done together? I wished the dark would blot everything out. I wanted the real dark, disorienting and for the same reason rich. What was she doing out there?

After a while I heard a noise in the other room, a book popped shut. I thought I heard her get up, and then the light went off out there. The door opened, and she came in, shadowy, slowly, so as to go silently. Her body darkened as she pulled off her shirt and got gingerly beneath the sheet, staying on her side.

It was enough. She was there. I hadn't had to ask, and she hadn't had to answer. We might still be anything. I didn't move.

2

Morning at the Opéra

In my dream I'd become homeless somehow and had decided to live in the airport. It was a good ruse: I could walk around all day with my belongings packed in a suitcase, shave in the men's room without attracting too much notice, sleep for an hour at a time in the gates. All this worked for a time, but finally I aroused the attention of the security guards, who began tracking me with their walkie-talkies and finally trapped me in an alcove. I protested that I was simply on a long layover, but when the guards opened my suitcase, they found it loaded with dynamite. Somebody switched it, somebody switched it, I pleaded. But nobody would listen. I had one phone call, they were saying, as I awoke in Paris. Still night, I noticed in disbelief. One phone call. L slept on, innocent, beside me.

This trip to France, which I'd been imagining as a romantic triumph, I suddenly saw from her viewpoint, as a problem. I knew what she felt about me—that I was unlikely. She'd thought of our relationship at first as an arty fling. She was surprised, the first time we made love, when I got deer-eyed, serious, quiet. It wasn't that she didn't like me—I could even think this thought, thinking with her mind for a minute. She might have even loved me a little. But I was probably not The One. I'd known that all along, though until that moment, with the shock of the dream leaving me clear-headed and feeling released, it had only made me burn with aspiration, ready to seize any opportunity to be with her. If she wanted just to be writers together, we'd be writers together, reading our journals, discussing the meaning of things. It was all fine with me. Granted that avenue, I went to work for us as writers. I came up with an idea enlarged by my own big romantic ideas. I'd get the French government to give us a trip to France, as travel writers. I'd project us into France. Until that moment, it hadn't dawned on me that this might be too much.

I couldn't lie down anymore. Creeping around the bed, I stubbed my toe hard against the post. When I yelled, she sat up, wide-eyed but uncomprehending, then, when she finally saw me—gesturing I'm sorry!—at the foot of the bed, she flopped back down into her pillow. I dragged my wounded foot out of the room. In the living room, I found the white chair and sat in it, waiting as the pain died down.

Idiot, I thought. This trip has put her in a horrible position. It was a gift she could not refuse, but I'd set it up on my terms. The Paris she'd cherished as a child was not really available to her, for it wasn't France she found when she'd gotten off the plane, but me, disguised as France, as if I'd laid the cape of my interpretations over the whole country.

That seemed to explain everything, to clarify the way she'd acted since we'd arrived. Sitting there in her white chair, I could feel her resistance, could recall it in a hundred details of the evening. Being in Paris with someone who was in love with you meant something, I could feel her feeling, even if you didn't intend anything yourself. She wasn't in love with me, and so couldn't just relax and be in Paris. So she'd been miserable—being in Paris and not being in Paris was worse than being in San Francisco and not being in Paris. What had I done? I'd thought. Why couldn't this trip just be whatever it was? If I truly loved her, I could let her have Paris the way she wanted it. I resolved to try to release her from any sense of obligation to me.

Some part of me took up this self-effacement with a good heart, while another part took it up as a ploy. I knew it was probably the only chance I had of getting her to fall in love with me in France. If she feels free about it, I reasoned, maybe she won't mind me, and the old proximity might get a chance to work. Of course, releasing her might simply be releasing her, but it was a chance I had to take.

I got up and looked out the window. The sky beyond the horizon was dark, though I recalled the moon setting there and knew the day would begin behind me somewhere, though I couldn't yet get a sense of it. I felt annoyed at all this turmoil, at a life requiring a strategy. Why did I inflict this stuff on myself in the middle of the night, when I couldn't resist it? Then I went back to bed, thinking that I was probably wrong, anyway. I'd watch in the morning and see.

When finally it grew light, neither L nor I had slept for what seemed like hours. I'd felt her attempts to settle. She knew I was awake, I thought. But we maintained the semblance of sleep, as if that might engender it. And as the light rose—the airshaft growing pale—so did my hope that she might say something reassuring, though she did not.

She didn't say anything. I lay there gauging whether her silence was empty or full, and as it became day, and language more and more likely, her silence seemed fuller and fuller. She lay there, gazing at the ceiling, saying nothing, until Paris and our presence in it was reassembled without a doubt. Finally she said, "Let's find a café."

We rose and dressed, mute as long-term residents—those lucky beings, their silences emptied by habit. She remained quiet as she put on her loose, dark smock, quiet as we left the apartment, heading downstairs to breakfast on the avenue. I held my own silence against hers, trying to make it into nothing, and we descended the six flights, turning the tight squared spiral and following the red runner down. There seemed to be no one in the whole building. The floors below opened to us, each silent and almost identical. I looked for the subtle differences, as for life. At the third floor, a piece of an envelope lay on the red carpet of a stair about halfway down the first flight from the landing. I looked at it, recalling it from the evening—or the afternoon—before, when we'd rested there with the luggage. That the little piece of paper had spent the night in the hallway gave me hope, as evidence that the world might hold its own without our holding it.

At the bottom of the stairs was a dark, marble-lined passage where the mailboxes were. It was dark there still—as it was always, I guessed. L found the *minuterie,* a spring-tripped light switch, and pressed the button. When we'd arrived the night before, L had shown me how to use this switch and told me its name. You had to know about it or get caught in the dark, she'd said. You set it when you entered the hall and a timer shut off the lights just as you left. The hall stayed lighted just longer than it took to cross. In my frame of mind that morning, it seemed symbolic: of the mind illuminating whatever passed before it, of all things dim without some hope or fear cast upon them.

L flipped the latch on the thick oak door at the end of the passage with the same experienced calm. Then she went briskly through it, and I plunged after her into the coppery light of the avenue, the Rue de Maubeuge. Paris seemed like an exact, incredibly detailed copy of itself, out there. It was a moist summer morning, the traffic light on the boulevard. The scale of apartment buildings on the avenue seemed perfect to me, as large as things could get with grace, the upper stories elegantly graduated so as to retain their domesticity. A sort of fanfare broke over my reverie. Just let go of all this, some sane voice inside me yelled. I was in France, after all! I loved to travel for this reason, for this fanfare, this sense that everything might be special, that anything might reward my attention. I surveyed the mansard-roofed façade; the occasional tricolor; the balconies, which I loved especially, shiny black gates hanging on the creamy walls of the avenue. And everything *was* interesting on this ordinary, everyday street: the haberdasher's window with its display of suspenders worth looking into, the chiropractor's shop fascinating. It cheered me even to imagine a whole nation of people thinking about back pain in French.

I followed L, who in her black dress patterned with red roses strode to the corner, waded into the cluster of brass-rimmed tables at the cafe there and dropped into a wicker chair. The tall waiter knew to speak to her, rather than to me, and she began conversing with him in her other tongue. She ordered simply *"Deux crèmes,"* as I rehearsed to myself the way she said it, admiring. Then the two of them talked, seeming to exchange pleasantries. Her French was thrilling, unweighted, liquid rhythm.

She looked like a different woman when she spoke French. She pursed her mouth for the French vowels, but this minor shift didn't wholly account for the change. Maybe the year she'd spent in France as a child had been a really good one, I thought. Maybe the person that she had become that year, speaking French in a French school, could only reappear when she spoke that other language. *"Tartine,"* she added at the end.

The first time I'd felt myself in love with L, I'd been watching her speak French, seeing her illuminated by it, and feeling that delicious pain, of equal parts exclusion and desire. As she ordered breakfast, I felt that want and hurt again, and gave in to it, noticing that light around her face. It stayed around her as she tore her bread apart. Then I had to eat, to calm myself down.

I've never had much facility in other languages, perhaps because my family has spoken American English for centuries. While young I was trained in Spanish by rote, and though I still remembered those dialogue sentences, the main effect of this training was to encase my sense of endsounds and ruin my accent for French. So when I learned French in college, I learned only how to read it, and forever after it had remained on the page. I couldn't understand anything that L had said to the waiter, for instance, though if she wrote it down I could puzzle it out, translating it word by word. And when I tried to speak in French myself, I had first to imagine print before my eyes. I'd never learn to speak French that way, L had told me. I should think of music.

But it was all text to me. And always by the time I might compose it and read it out loud, the opportunity to converse had gotten away. So in France I was placed in the presence of things before I had a chance to name them, and with L still in her luminous French self from speaking with the waiter, I felt as if I peered out into a wordless realm. Being mute made life intense. Or more so, anyway.

"What do you want to do today?" I asked, as if from my little tent of English.

"I don't know," she said, reverting to her own American self. "A lot."

"Oh," I said. I knew what that meant. She was selecting everything at once. It was typical of the way she was back home. When she watched TV, for instance, she was an inveterate channel flipper, sampling a station for thirty seconds at most before racing on to what might be a better show: "Star Trek" to "Entertainment Tonight" to a nature show about baby penguins to the horrifying news. If she had to watch a whole program, she would often take it too seriously, and have to leave the room. It's actors acting, I would cry, frustrated, not wanting her to go. But even if she fled—as the good guys rode into the ambush—even this choice could not be final, and she would call from some hiding place to ask me what was going on. It's not so bad, I'd say and she'd peer in from the hallway, peeved. Movies were worse. When we saw *Europa Europa,* about a Jewish boy hiding his identity among the Nazis, I had my arm around her, and realized at one point that she was quaking. When it got worse, she went to the lobby, and quizzed the popcorn vendor about which parts would be the hardest to watch.

I watched her crush apricot jam into the bread and return to this American ambivalence. She planned to do everything that day in Paris: to see friends, to go shopping, to visit the museum, and all this before lunch. She would fly ahead to the next thing, skimming, not wanting to rest a moment and be defined.

"Are you mad about something?" I asked.

"No," she said, and after a pause, added, "I'm not angry."

Actually I hadn't thought it was just anger. She could get angry with me—it would flare and go away. This was more complex than anger; a larger thing than reluctance. I didn't want to name it either, and I didn't press her. I'd only wanted to let her know that I thought she was holding something back. In any case, we seemed in that moment to have shared some understanding, and when afterwards she said nothing again, the quietness was even deeper as we finished our coffee.

"How about if we just go to the Opéra first and see the Chagall together?" I said. "Then you can go off and do everything you want."

She said "okay" a little too quickly, I thought.

．　　．　　．

So I put it off until we got to the Opéra. We walked down the avenue to the Métro, which was beneath the blackened and ancient church called Notre Dame de Lorette. In the vaulted underground, a group of African women waited for the train, draped in robes of rich, intricate patterns, in siennas, greens and gold. On rubber wheels, the train arrived, and my legs ached as we climbed aboard. Calculating the hours—a mistake—I found it was two A.M. at home, and suddenly felt that it was still two A.M. in my body. We didn't just *have* a place on the earth, I thought, but *were* that place, and like the bougainvillea with its tiny capillary roots, we didn't tolerate transplantation.

We rode a few stops and ascended again, to the plaza in front of the Opéra, which had a flat green dome and green-winged muses. The words *Poesie Lyrique,* among others, had been carved into the stone.

In the square a big-breasted woman, who'd painted herself gold, stood on a platform and danced to rap music with the jerky simulation of a machine approximating human movement. The crowd that had gathered to watch her seemed somehow mechanical, too. One man watched as he listened to his own music on a small CD player hanging on a cord around his neck, the spinning disc like a robot's heart, visible through a little window.

The tourists looked quite out of it. A woman tried to put her hand in her pocket and missed, then didn't bother to try again. Another pulled her exhausted husband up the steps by his slack arm, as if it were a leash. It seemed like a shame to go all this way and then visit the Opéra in what felt like the middle of the night, in which even great works of art appeared at the numbed distance of jet lag, as if on late night TV.

Inside the Opéra, which was a palace of overstatement, the tourists seemed meeker than ever, before the bewigged statues, scaled to the heroic, enshrining Haydn and others whose names I did not recognize. We paused at the foot of the ornate stairs to look up at maidens, each upholding an enormous candelabrum with ease. I looked at the guidebook, to see exactly what it was I was seeing. The Opéra had been an enormous undertaking, begun by Napoleon III and interrupted by the Commune. Its construction had taken fourteen years and cost ten lives, I read. Five hundred homes had been destroyed. The building had a steel skeleton, one of the first of its kind.

Thus unenlightened, I followed L up the grandiose staircase, beneath crystal and mosaic, white marble trimmed black and gold, feeling as if we were climbing into enormous petticoats. Surveying the baroque lobby from above, L said she thought it was a bit much. Official as anything, she added. She was right. All the bellowing about art seemed finally to flood the place with denial.

But we hadn't come to see the Opéra so much as to look at the painting by Marc Chagall on the dome. At the top of the stairs, we were bunched with others and pressed though a doorway into a single opera box, where we emerged beneath a vast vaulted interior. Above us, four tiers of boxes, their wooden façades carved with angels blowing trumpets, lined the walls of the chamber. The seats below were upholstered in crimson and red and gold, and each had a silver scroll bearing a number.

We gawked at the dome, a double-circled rotunda beyond an enormous chandelier. There on the vault Chagall had painted in primary colors and washes his own simple twentieth century versions of characters from symphony and dance. The Firebird was a big chicken. The lovers in the Berlioz panel looked like Kissin' Cousins. A winged cello played itself. On the dome, too, he'd painted scenes of Paris—the Eiffel Tower appeared there, and the flat beretlike exterior of the Opéra itself. I liked the painting, though it was funny to see it on the ceiling of that place, an irony out of Tolstoy, a Russian peasant triumph like a last echo of Napoleon's debacle in Moscow.

We were crowded closely in the opera box, and L's back was pressed against me as we looked up. We lingered that way when the other tourists left the balcony. By then L was looking at the stage. The curtain was up, and behind it the mechanical elements of the stage were exposed racks of gray steel from which cables ascended. On the apron stood a single thick-legged chair and a table, and on the table a hammer. It was like a Beckett set. Some man was shouting French in the wings.

I spoke quietly into her hair. I said, "This trip doesn't have to mean anything."

"What do you mean?" she said.

"We're going to be whatever we're going to be." I said. "There doesn't have to be any obligation."

She turned around and put her arms around my neck, smiling and seeming already released. "Sometimes," she said, "you're the greatest. How did you know I was thinking about that?"

"I divined it," I said, "in the middle of the night."

"Well, thanks," she said. "That makes me feel better."

I had been right about her silence, and having been right made everything fine. Part of me dedicated myself to the task of being whatever. We would be writers and friends, colleagues. Whatever we had been in San Francisco—to say lovers might have been to put too fine a point on it—we'd be what we'd be in France. *Qué será, será,* as it were. Maybe we wouldn't even have sex.

As a ploy it started to work immediately. She didn't have to run off into Paris to do her everything dance for the rest of the day. As long as we weren't anything, she could just as well be everything with me. The spell seemed to hold as we left the Opéra, and as I followed her through the splendor and plenty of the shopping mall called the Galeries Lafayette. It held as we ate a lunch of bread and cheese and fruit on a bridge over the Seine, held as the day went on and held—barely—that night, when we slept as colleagues.

By then we'd spent a whole day together, night to night, something, I realized, that we'd never done in America. All day, and all I had to do was pretend not to be in love with her. So in France, until the illusion wore off, we were together, after a fashion. We were not, which seemed to allow us to be.

3

A Madman in Love

....

Later, when the trip was over, when I could see how fully possessed I had been, I went to my books for refuge, and found—this is often the problem with books—the truth there instead. Hoping for solace in the company of romantics, I found others with my disease. I found Henri Beyle, for one, he who was known, among some three hundred other names, as Stendhal. Protean Henri introduced the word "tourist" into the French language. This was fitting, as he lived his early eighteenth century life at a distance, as a sort of tourist, an original romantic, a prototypical modern man. In him, as in his English contemporary William Blake, the period's insistence upon rationality—upon thinking making the man—took its fuller dimension: a preference for the self-created universe, for the world within. "How many precautions," wrote miserable Henri, whom I knew as I knew myself, "how many precautions are necessary to keep oneself from lying."

Stendhal would title his last autobiography *Memoirs of an Egotist*. By then he understood the paradox of egotism—that the seeming certainty of internal reference radiates into everything and finally admits no limit. By then he had discovered a crowd of pseudonyms within himself, and had been forced to take precautions against his own lies. "I don't know myself," he wrote in this last book, "and it's this that distresses me sometimes when I think about it at night."

He discovered slips in his earlier drafts. He'd look again and find lies, as if someone in the crowd of selves within him had shouted out to the recorder, over the objections of judgment, some irresistible falsehood. Rereading his previous autobiography, the fictionalized one called *The Life of Henri Brulard,* Henri found that he had claimed to have been a soldier under his beloved Napoleon. It was a slip of vanity, portraying himself as a warrior—though this portly and reflective dandy was hardly suited for soldiering. True, he'd gone to Moscow with Napoleon, but as a quartermaster, a chief of supply working in the rear of the battle, and towing an extra coach that bore his books and wardrobe.

He was not a man of action; he was, as he put it mildly, "not clever at the practical details of life." He suspected his own sensitivity even while young. "With my inward faculties and senses so ardent, and so painful," he wrote in a youthful journal, "it is very possible that I may go mad." By then he already was. Especially in his youth, he looked through himself into the world, eager to find his own ideas in its myriad forms, and as usual this had disastrous results, especially in love. His affairs with women composed a lifelong fiasco. Again and again he mistook some real woman for an aspect of himself, and rambled, lost in thought, off the cliff.

Still—of course—he thought himself expert in the fine art of love. He even wrote a sort of guidebook of love, his first great work, called *De l'Amour,* which almost no one, even his close friends, understood. Henri himself predicted that his work would not be popular for many years—that it might even be the twentieth century before anyone appreciated his mind. Henri couched *De l'Amour* in some of the language and forms of the French encyclopedists of the previous era, such as Diderot, and the work begins as a "physiology" of love, a term both scientific and vaguely titillating, though he gives the briefest of treatments within it to what he calls *amour-physique.*

De l'Amour is, as Matthew Josephson writes, "in no sense an orderly treatise." Its scientific format soon gives way to a sort of internal travelogue, in which what seem to be descriptions of the world—of the differing sensitivities of women in the various countries of Europe, for instance—turn out upon examination to be descriptions of Henri's need. "You hear," he writes, "of a traveler speaking of the cool orange trees beside the sea at Genoa in the summer heat. Oh, if you could only share that coolness with her." So we find in the book more of charmed Henri than of the Andalusian women he finds so charming, more of Henri ravished than of the ravishing beauties of Italy. And he knows it, furthermore. "I do not pretend to picture things in themselves," he admits, "but only in their effect upon me."

And so, all in all, *De l'Amour* seems cool, as if written from a great height. He cast the book that way to insulate himself from what he was experiencing at the time—his ultimate fiasco and excruciation in love. Only when his friends finally learned of this love affair with the dark lady Métilde did this book begin to make sense to them. Like Donne, he had populated the world of the book with figures for his love and himself so that he might stand as if apart and seem to explain. Therefore the book's pronouns proliferate, flying away from the local first person. "We were all wondering '*Fara Colpo*'? (Would she succumb to him?)" Thus he frames his obsession, as if he were a mere tourist, peering into a gorge. Lord Byron, who met him, called him "a human curiosity."

. . .

Henri was a plain, plump child, precocious and commanding, his mother's boy always and an enemy of his father. His mother he loved "criminally." "I returned her kisses with such ardor that she was sometimes obliged to run away," he recalled as Henri Brulard. "I wanted to cover her with kisses and for her to have no clothes on." When this beloved mother died Henri was just seven, but he endured her death without crying. Called heartless by his sister, he was too hurt for tears, gathered already into a world he had begun to compose, a substitute for the large one that had so failed him.

Henri was born at the perfect moment to be able to view the French Revolution as the larger expression of his own childhood rebellion. At age ten, he outraged his Royalist papa by declaring himself a Republican and publicly celebrating the news of the king's decapitation. But when the boy went surreptitiously to a Republican meeting, he was appalled by the real revolutionaries, finding them unkempt in their dress and uncouth in their language.

Nevertheless he remained an inflamed spirit. When he was a little older, he was taken on a picnic into the mountains near his family's home at Grenoble. There a young woman paid him some attention, kissing and fondling him. When she abandoned him for a handsome officer, little Henri flew into a rage, pelting his adult rival with stones. The nonplussed officer put the boy up a mulberry tree, safely stranding him on an overhead branch. From his perch, Henri heaped abuse upon the whole company below. Then, when he had their rapt attention, he made the women shriek by giving out a great shout of rage and leaping dangerously down at them.

This scene may stand as an emblem for Henri's career, though as a grown man he would make his attacks seem witty and systematic. In a Paris salon Henri would hear the naturalist Georges

Cuvier explain how he had overcome his loathing for insects by studying them, by examining their behavior and classifying their kinds. To Henri this was a brilliant stroke. "Why not do the same thing with human beings?" he wrote in his journal afterward.

And so he did, dressing his rage with a gloss of scientific method. So for all of *De l'Amour*'s charm, for its volubility and brightness, it is, like some of Mozart's music, ultimately grievous. His specimen was his own wounded self, finally, and no other. And this makes him seem modern. This self-enclosed universe, this wit with rage within it and grief deeper than that makes complex Henri, who wrote at the end of the age of powdered wigs, seem like somebody we know.

At twenty-one Henri made his first conquest, of a woman slightly his elder named Mélanie. At the time he was a parvenue in Paris—not yet a supply clerk for Napoleon, he aspired to write plays and kept a journal, though the true work of his days was presenting himself. He took elocution lessons. He bought and wore finery—this especially was his vocation then, essential, he thought, for entering society (in this he would prove correct). He racked up considerable bills with tailors and dunned his father, back in Grenoble, for money to pay them. He wrangled invitations and went forth, his big body, which he'd always thought ugly, in ruffles, in yellow trousers and a long, light blue waistcoat. "I looked superb," he writes of one occasion. "Cravat, jabot, two vests—superb, breeches of cashmere, good shoes."

He took his elocution lessons in the same spirit, reading Molière before his ancient, lecherous tutor and several other students, one of whom was Mélanie, tall, thin, blonde and melancholy. Still young, she'd fled to Paris from the boondocks of Normandy, determined to be famous in the Comedie Française. She had big blue eyes. The Pandarus who was their elocution coach put them in scenes together, the fat, flamboyant, serious

Henri on his knees, declaiming away like mad, and at the finale seizing her hands and kissing them.

For Henri, to act the lover was to begin to fall in love. He imagined the figure they'd cut together, "a future dramatic young bard with a future young actress," and soon the scenes at elocution class were real enough. Henri spent all day dressing, and in class seethed in his chair with jealousy if she played a part with another. One night, scanning the audience of the Comedie Française—during a performance of *Les Folies Amoureuses*—he decided he must have her and began to make his plans to "attack," the term he was fond of using for his amorous forays.

Up until then he'd only made plans in love, no point of which had ever touched reality. The previous object of his affections, a woman named Victorine, knew nothing of his great love for her, though he had borne his passion for three years and had written about it at length. He'd seen her one night at her family's home in Paris, where she'd played Haydn for a musicale, and though he hadn't seen her alone or even spoken to her, he'd gone home that night to find the very night air charged with his new love and had proceeded to conceive an astonishingly indirect strategy for attracting her attention. First he befriended her brother, a man he detested, and when the family returned to their estate at Rennes, some two hundred miles from Paris, he wrote letters, the most gorgeous he could manage, not to her, but to her brother, in the slim hope that the dolt might praise his writing within his sister's hearing. This he continued to do for three years, never mentioning his feelings. He got a glance at her on the family's rare visits to Paris, but she showed no sign of having heard of him, much less of having any idea of his passion. Still, he persisted, agonized, in his own world. Finally, her family came to Paris again, and when he called on them, she answered the door. Face to face with her at last, he only managed to ask for her brother, and recording the moment in his journal later could not recall exactly what she looked like, only that she wore a pink straw hat and might have been chubby. Finally ashamed of his timidity, he planned an elaborate attack, even sketching floor plans of her house, but at last could not carry it out. He wrote to her instead, proclaiming his great love but speaking hypothetically, referring to his beloved in the third person and in terms borrowed from Rousseau's romance *Héloise:* "I love her as happiness itself." Embarrassed or simply baffled, Victorine never responded. Finally Henri gave up.

With the actress Mélanie, he was again in love with being in love—it was that role, that idea, that romance, that perfection, that he sought—though with Mélanie for the first time he succeeded in winning a woman over, at least momentarily, to his idea of her. An actress was perfect for this, though she turned out to be a better one than he imagined.

Mélanie had on her own acquired a few features from literature and art. She was, among other things, a damsel in distress. At home in Normandy, she'd been ruined, as the phrase went, left pregnant by a bounder, a married man. She'd given birth to a little girl, but had left the child with a relative and come to Paris to elude the stigma and start over. When she'd made it, she figured, she'd send for her daughter. But she wasn't making it in expensive Paris.

In a fix himself, Henri was convincing himself otherwise. His connections—rich cousins—hadn't yet won a position in Napoleon's government, and his father had cut off his clothing allowance. With his characteristic enthusiasm he determined, despite his utter ignorance of the business of finance, to become a banker. A neighboring family back home in Grenoble had become millionaire bankers, nouveau riche in that time of royal divestiture. Yes, a millionaire banker might be a nice thing to be, he thought, and began acting like one immediately. A friend who heard him speak of his rising fortunes offered him the chance to go into banking by investing some of his father's money in a commercial venture in Marseilles, but he declined. The offer was a little too concrete at that point. Then Fate, or something momentarily resembling it, intervened.

Mélanie happened to decide to go to Marseilles herself. She'd decided to become a star in provincial theatre and return to Paris in triumph. But she couldn't even afford a ticket south. By then they'd gone to first names, and had kissed once at her door. She invited him over to her apartment for a little supper of potatoes and wine, then told him her worries, and finally wept. Henri recognized his cue. He'd rescue her. He'd be a rich banker and have Mélanie, too. He'd take her to Marseilles. She wept at his offer, asked him to fetch her handkerchief, and wept some more. For his part he never mentioned that he had had plans to go to Marseilles all along. For hers, she never mentioned that she knew.

In each other's clutches, they went south by coach in May of 1805. She was twenty-five, he twenty-one and with the last of his own money providing her passage. At the stops young girls proffered flowers and fruit to the windows of their coach, already stuffed with Henri and his snacks and finery, Mélanie in her robe, long gloves and bonnet and the other passengers and freight. When they reached Marseilles he had to part from her for a time and go on alone to Grenoble to beg money from his father for the whole scheme, which had turned out to be somewhat less grand than he'd first imagined—his father would be buying into the grocery business where Henri would be working as a clerk, keeping the books and weighing the loads of oranges and soap.

So they spent an anxious month apart before he could rejoin her in Marseilles. His father—as always—could not resist his son's entreaties. Perhaps he thought a little reality in commerce would be good for the boy. In any case, funds finally in hand, Henri flew to his beloved. He embarked by boat, descending the Rhône for three days to reach Marseilles, where she had booked adjoining rooms in her hotel. She met him at the dock, and they went straight to her performance in a comic opera—a little strained, he thought. Only then did they proceed to bed, though it wasn't until eleven o'clock the following morning that they consummated the affair, when he finally "saw" her, as he put it in his journal. To his notebook, he declared himself happy, in terms that also seem a little strained, lending the affair a continued air of rehearsal. "I am tenderly loved by a woman with whom I am madly in love," he wrote. "She has a beautiful soul."

But reality gathered swiftly around them in Marseilles. An ancient officer, whom Mélanie had befriended in Henri's brief absence, proposed marriage to her, and insanely jealous Henri had to be dissuaded from challenging him to a duel. Worse yet, the prefect of police turned out to have had a hand in casting Mélanie in her part. He took a personal interest in her as well, though Henri could only rail against him in his journal.

These threats to Henri's happiness were as the merest eddies, though, compared to the vast tides of history poised against the lovers. France, too, overextended herself at this time. Soon after their arrival in Marseilles, Admiral Nelson obliterated Napoleon's fleet at Trafalgar. Britain, mistress of the sea once more, blockaded the port of Marseilles, forcing the docks to go idle, and after a brief lag, the theatres dark. Henri and Mélanie found themselves alone, diminished with their nation and no longer in the presence of their careers.

Henri, who had taken up being a banker as he might have tried on a hat, turned back to literature. He read Machiavelli's *The Prince* and began planning his next move. Mélanie fretted constantly for her imagined future in the Comedie Française, and never mind her beautiful soul, Henri grew tired of her, now that their roles had been extinguished. "I begin to find Mélanie stupid," he wrote in his journal. Soon after he noted that their relationship seemed "utterly extinct."

Finally she proposed that they return to Paris, where she could at least get bit parts. He swore his love to her yet, but on the first of March saw her tearfully to the coach depot. He had business he must attend to, he said. She rode north, and he walked from the depot, feeling joy in his liberty. For some weeks he drank, gambled and whored around—mounting, among others, a chambermaid in a darkened doorway. In moments of regret, he wrote Mélanie fond letters. These cooled as the weeks wore on.

Before, he had donned a role from *Héloise,* but now he took to heart *The Prince.* Machiavelli's ruthless tract was good for him, he thought, "a remedy for that instable sensitivity which makes me womanish." He instructed himself in strategies for everyday life: "When I meet a man," he noted in his journal, "ask myself what he wants of me, not 'What do I feel for him?' " Thus he tried to make himself cagey. His degree of success at this is once again obscured by history. For cagey or not, Henri found himself with suddenly improved connections. His cousins in Paris—the acolytes of Napoleon—had become important, their power enlarged with Napoleon's conquest of Europe. Wheedling Henri heard of this and sent them a letter. "I would prefer a thousand times to sit copying newspapers in your office," he wrote, "than to be a rich banker in Marseilles."

On these forces, he was borne up. When next we see him, within a year, he appears as a kind of splendid equestrian statue, on his steed huge and in a gold-braided uniform and a hat with a plume. In New Brunswick the conquered natives cursed him as he passed. But for all of his newly conferred power—he commanded a population of 200,000, he said—he played at the role. "I write letters," he wrote in a letter, "lose my temper at my secretaries, go to formal dinners and read Shakespeare." He, too, found himself enlarged with Napoleon, who by 1808 controlled all of the continent. "Here I am a somebody," he wrote from captive Germany. Later, when great forces reduced him again, making him an exile from his native land, he would recall this zenith of his power fondly, taking full credit for it when he could, and nostalgically choosing for his most durable nom de plume the Teutonic "Stendhal."

So Henri rode gloriously into disaster with Napoleon, following an army that increasingly diluted its commander's intentions, as Napoleon proceeded away from France and had to conscript the locals, who had their own reasons for following him. The troops resorted as never before to looting and plunder, and by the time they'd reached Russia, Napoleon's command had begun to fail completely. Describing this campaign, Tolstoy can only find the idea of strategy absurd, a delusion of Napoleon's ego. And if the Grande Armeé had become unruly, Russia was altogether foreign. There the peasants refused even to recognize their own interest in easy surrender, but burned their grain rather than leave it for the French.

Luxurious and literary Henri, clean-shaven, came along behind the carnage, riding into Russia with his notebook and fretting for his official stores and for the safety of his adored emperor. Tiring of the dirt and the duty, he looked forward to reaching Moscow, where he hoped there would be winter concerts. That gorgeous town contained "six or eight hundred palaces," he wrote in a letter, "as one may never see in Paris." There everything was "arranged for the purest voluptuousness." On September 17, 1812, he entered the city, noticing a fire started by the unruly conscripts in a bazaar near the Kremlin. By dark other blazes roared up as exhausted Henri found an abandoned palace and fell into a feather bed.

He awakened to a palled daylight, to a city on fire. In his nightshirt, Henri went out into the smoky street to witness the melee. There drunken servants brawled over loot; soldiers smashed shop windows to take stupid things like candelabra. Henri deplored the looting—he drew his sword and ordered them, fruitlessly, to stop. Still, as he returned to dress, to put on his plumed hat and vacate the palace, he found some books—a volume of Voltaire, Lord Chesterfield's letters—and carried them out with him to his coach.

Then he attempted to go forth and do his job. He was assigned to oversee the loading of some wagons with sacks of grain, but the streets were sheer chaos, and no one would listen to him, the soldiers interested only in frantically loading their carts with linen and silver, as the fire approached. Henri could control no one, not even his personal servant. "I saw new proof of want of character in the French," he would write later.

Deprived of command, Henri decided, finally, to give up and to repair to a club with some fellow officers, but as they went, a woman approached him and fell to her knees at his feet. He was astonished to recognize her as Mélanie, his old love from Marseilles. In the eight intervening years since he'd seen her, she had performed French comedy in Italy, where she'd met a Russian count who'd married her and taken her back to Moscow. Now, amidst a city in flames, surreal as an apparition, with her children and lady-in-waiting in tow, she begged for his help.

To Henri, it was a scene "of the highest ridiculousness." He had no choice, though, but to take her and her two children and her fat Russian maid into his coach and set off for God knows where, seeking safety and finding none. The avenues were blocked with rioters and debris; street after street concluded in a wall of flame. If Mélanie had expected Henri to take charge of the situation, she was wrong. Henri was enchanted by the spectacle, especially by the the flames. It was, he wrote later, "the most beautiful conflagration in the world," and it made him aimless. All he wanted to do was watch the blocks on fire, the flames hundreds of feet high, devouring the town. All day, Mélanie waited for him to do something, but he had become a spectator, enraptured at the early October darkness falling over the burning city, and at the moon rising reddened, as if by the flames. The only drag on his pleasure was his sense that he alone had eyes fit for the spectacle. "I should have preferred to be alone," he wrote, "or at least in the company of people who had the wit to appreciate it."

At last Mélanie and her entourage gave up on Henri's aid and simply slipped off into the chaotic night, looking for someone competent and leaving him alone to marvel at the blaze. From a ridge outside of town, he watched the separate fires join, rising finally as a single brilliant pyramid, its crown frothing with sparks. It was hours before he realized that she was gone. Later, recalling her at the burning of Moscow, as elsewhere, he found her performance wanting, her expressions of gratitude strained. "There was not a trace of the natural in her," he said.

4

THE POPPIES

Then there was the rain. The second day we were in Paris, the storm had gathered itself all afternoon as we had walked along the river looking for cassis sorbet. I hadn't heard of cassis, and L had decided that I had to have some, the best kind. She grew passionate describing it, its color like crushed violets, almost black—black currant, it was called back home. So we looked over the sorbet stands, seeking the proper purple, and made that quest the business of the afternoon, as towering dark clouds rose over the city. We had to walk down the river to the Pont d'Austerlitz before we found the right sorbet, and she said the word again as the tart, fine-grained ice melted over my tongue: "Cassis," as if I were tasting the word as well.

By five, when we turned back toward the apartment, the day was steamy hot, brewing a violent rain of the sort we almost never saw in California. We shopped in the markets, and in the tiny kitchen L made veal in a Dijonaise sauce, with those small red potatoes called Rosevalle. I was daffy, in love even with the potatoes, with L's French "r" in her throat when she said their name. After dinner, we went to the balcony, just as the storm began to break. Then we turned off the lights, stood at the railing and watched the front cross the city, the throng of thunderheads in the half-dark, like castles, L said. I watched the lightning firing here and there at the bases of the clouds like signals, pulses between titans. Now and then the thunder startled us, made us shout. But we waited for those big ones.

That night, as we lay together listening to the rain roar on the nearby roofs, it was enough that she said, after a time, "When we first went out, I never imagined anything would come of this."

That meant something had, I thought. I stopped myself there, trying not even to consider what we were. Life, one day of it anyway, had been great since we'd released ourselves from such considerations. What we had been, what we were, what we would be, I tried to let go, to make weightless. L fell asleep. Her breath drew deeper and deeper, her face sweet and blank, as I listened and imagined the towers of cloud in the dark above the rooftops, sweeping the city with the rain, and for all their effect and vastness lighter than air.

The next day it seemed that fall had occurred in Paris. I suggested that we spend the day apart, and in the morning we separated briskly at the Métro, L off to shop and meet her old friends for coffee, disappearing into the crowd of working Parisians in their *rentrée* clothes, while I paged through my *Plan de Paris* and found my way north to the cut stone of the riverbank, a bridge of the same pale stone ahead, and the glistening sidewalk pasted with yellow leaves from the plane trees—sycamores, they seemed to me. The Seine seemed staid within its stone banks, black-gray. At dockside was a *piscine,* a swimming pool on a barge, its broad deck empty. Upstream, a long tourist barge barely negotiated one of the arches of the bridge.

I was having September feelings, that sense from school, of hope tinged with dread, of having to begin things at the end of summer. The best thing about school was that it made things finite. You started and you ended. After that no story was as neat. Not that things weren't always finite, of course. I thought with a pang of L, the image of her back as she took off toward St. Germaine de Pres, at home in the crowd, speaking their language, knowing the town. This was her place. Whatever happened, I'd always associate it with her. As I walked, everything I saw seemed to take on some aspect of L, as my feelings for her, groping for their object, had to settle for the world itself. No matter what path I took, she would be at the end of it, like a goddess of the plane trees and the river, the pale stone and wrought iron. Oh, give it up, I thought, as I crossed the street to the museum.

The Museé d'Orsay was once the Gare d'Orsay—the railroad station—and, in spite of everything, remained so. Inside the enormous building, the echoing steps and talk of the crowd blended into a single hollow quiet tone, high in the air above us, a sound produced nowhere but in huge municipal train stations. The place was a vast glass shell, the exhibits bivouacked within it beneath the far girdered roof. One wall of bright frosted glass still bore the huge baroque clock of the train station, which ticked above the exhibits as if to confirm the immortality of the art, second by second. Behind the glass on several levels strolled the clouded images of pedestrians, tourists seeming like laggards beneath that clock.

In marble crypts on the main floor hung French paintings, delicious as cream. I looked at the figures of women, the peachy nudes, seeing L in them all. The first was a prizewinner from the Académie Français, a "Birth of Venus." In the painting she reclined on the green sea, auburn hair spread about her, pale breasts skyward, one wrist draped across her forehead as if in repose. The artist had rendered her peeking out beneath her hand, her glance direct and seductive, the look denying the casualness of her pose. In the azure sky above her head five putti with penises frolicked. Everything about the picture seemed artificial, designed to produce an effect. But as I wandered the d'Orsay that morning, I wasn't in the mood to get critical.

I remembered an old modernist who'd taught me poetry. An original aesthete, he had presented the great poems like bonbons. Such a delight, he would say when he had finished reading one aloud. Any other comment would have been too rude. At the time, I wanted to argue. But just then I felt like thinking he was right, and let the paintings be simply delicious, even this one.

Still, I couldn't help but compare. Renoir's bathers, whose fullness and radiance I'd liked once but had come to distrust, seemed, after the academic Cabanel, more real, less determined. Then there was a hazy nude *couchée* by Millet that was even more like it, and after I had climbed the stairs and had become one of those shadowy pedestrians passing high above the floor beneath the big clock, I found a Bonnard, the figure stretching, nude upon the bed, almost perfect, accidental seeming, so ordinary and casual in its appreciation, as if she had come into his life and yet he had never lost that thrill of seeing her as she stretched in the morning. Nothing about the figure acknowledged that she was the subject of a painting. The Académie would have hated it, of course, as it liked its nudes ideal, exotic, remote, passive, alluding to classical themes. Made to represent something, in other words. Anything but real.

I was thinking about L again, I knew, about her reluctance to give our being together a meaning, which made it sweeter for that. After that I looked at the other paintings to measure their inviolateness. The larger their implications, the less they were possessed, the more they seemed gorgeous to me, and the more they stung. It was a feeling I remembered from looking at the Sierras or the ocean. Then I saw Monet's poppies.

I got married when I was twenty-one, without wondering why. Back then I loved those rosy, fat nudes of Renoir, and all the gooier Impressionists. Early on we had a print of a Monet painting framed for the house. It was his poppies, that familiar picture of the woman and her parasol and her little girl in the scarlet-dappled field. By the end, nine years later, the print had hung in a little house in the Midwest in which we'd chosen everything for years, to express this thing we were together—the books and bookcases, the carpets, the porcelain cats on the shelves. Our meaning lay in these things like a guarantee, and above all of them hung that print of the poppies in its sleek gold frame. By then its subject seemed overdone, sentimental; its vagueness felt just equivocating, offering room for delusion. By then I liked de Kooning and his women, and Rouault with his grief and thick line and captive color.

Then in the d'Orsay that morning, full of feeling for L, I came across the original of that picture, the poppies. It gave me a shock to see it, and I almost turned away, afraid that it might ruin my mood. But the painting wasn't so daunting. Its colors were richer than I remembered from that copy, and in the surface of the paint I could see the strokes implying the hand that had made them. Most of all, the picture was smaller than the print that had hung in our living room. The copy had been enlarged and mass-produced and had seemed like a certificate of some kind, a con-tract—if you did this and felt that, such a life would follow. But the smallness of the original painting made it seem tentative, less sure of itself, as if its richness were merely a suggestion.

How stupid I'd been when I had first gotten married, I thought. We had agreed on which feelings we would have, as if we could

make them to order. Once we had decided to be together, we had
fallen in together completely, each doing whatever the other
couldn't. As a system, we worked perfectly at first, though we
were cut off from others and on our way to becoming parodies of
ourselves, helpless but for the things we'd always done well. I
hadn't balanced a checkbook for years, and had to learn how
again after the divorce. What I hadn't realized then was that some
part of each of us would always go ahead, irresistibly, into what
we weren't. And in the end, we somehow still had our pristine
bubble—the poppies on the wall, our fond names and dual identity, though by then all of that was reliquary and composed, preserved only to honor the other, while the rest of life lived secretly
elsewhere.

On the last day of the last term—we were both teachers—I
pulled off the bedsheets when I got up, then folded and packed
them, too. I had only one thing to do before I left town, to see her
one last time and make some final settlements. By then she lived
across town, in that house with the poppies, which we still owned
together. I had avoided her all that term, though I'd seen our car
in the college parking lot. She'd gotten another teaching job, in
another Midwestern state, and I was leaving that day for California, driving over the mountains to San Francisco. We'd spoken on
the phone to make arrangements for the sale of the house and the
disbursement of the furniture. This furniture had reproached me
for years with its meaning, its steadfastness, and I wanted none of
it and was happy to take whatever offer she made on it, which
came to two hundred dollars after she found various deductions
for things she'd done over the years. I'd put off going over there,
but on this last day I had to, and so I drove the loaded car over,
on my way out of town.

In the interim since I'd moved out, I had shaved, taking off a
beard I'd had for all of our marriage. And when she opened the
door of my old house to let me in, she looked at me differently and

called me by my first name. She looked strange, too, short-haired and new. We'd become new people so quickly in our months of separation, though we weren't really new at all, I realized. The secret people we'd been—for years probably—had finally gotten their chance. And now we were as strange to one another as we had been in our first moment together, and were exiting in the same place that we'd come in. And I knew then that if we could have remained in some obvious way strangers to one another, we would not have had to become strangers in the devious way that had destroyed our marriage.

I found a bench in the museum and wrote in my notebook my feeling about the poppies. I felt good about my suspended state with L. She wanted no definition, and so I had to restrain that impulse to plunge. Until that moment I believed I was enduring this hurt only to please her. Seeing the poppies—small and suggestive, the brushstrokes of a certain person on a certain day, the painting portraying a moment among many, a pretty one perhaps, but one which would soon give way to another—I could feel that in our distance we were leaving room for everything, for whatever we might become.

But by the time I met L by the river that evening, I just wanted her. I missed her by then and didn't want to think about the richness of our distance. We went for dinner at a place her friend had told her about, in the Marais. How was the museum? she asked, and I felt at a loss for adequate words. Besides, feeling the hurt again, I didn't want any longer to understand. Powerful, I said.

"I decided to forgive Monet," I added, and L, who didn't have anything yet to hold against Monet, looked at me ironically and said, "How nice of you," and I left it at that.

5

THE MEADOW

My students, the summer I met L, were a dozen children in that awkward age—nine to thirteen—of awakening from childhood. The camp was up in the Headlands of Marin County, and meeting in the field on the first day, I was amazed at their range, from the tiny, dark-eyed, shy son of the Peruvian consul to the long-legged, sharp daughter of hippies from Bolinas, who wore tight jeans and sat looking insulted among the children. On that first day she took her breaks with the kitchen guys and smoked their cigarettes.

I and the three other artists charged with this mix of humanity had been hired to produce a performance with the children that summer. We worked from scratch, making life-size marionettes, providing them with songs and a story, and building out of beach flotsam an elaborate stage with a balcony. It was a month of loud work. We gave the children percussion instruments, and the cymbals especially punctuated the days of shouting over the din in the workshop and calling out into the wind at the beach.

Each child made a puppet of their own choosing, and I had to put all these random characters—a robot, a ballet dancer, a turtle and others—into a story, with equal parts for everybody. That first day only two fourth-graders, Simone and Julia, had decided on their characters, and so the story began with a gnome selling his soul to the devil for five pieces of gold. Julia, the little blond girl with braces who wanted to be the devil, had already come up with a sound effect for the part, a piercing shriek that she intended to use for her character's entrances and exits and that she practiced repeatedly on her friend the gnome, who carried on beneath the shrieking in equally uproarious gnome-fashion, unfazed. A little boy decided he wanted to be a parrot, and so I worked a parrot into the plot, as I bent and spliced chicken wire into puppet skeletons. I didn't mind the children's uproar. I was cheered by their tumult, in fact, and even grew loud and happy myself, tossed around in it all day.

I had come to the countryside ambivalent. The idea of leaving my apartment and living among other people, even for a few weeks, daunted me and made me shy, but I felt even on that first day refreshed to be out of the narrow city life I had arranged for myself. I had told myself I was taking the job for my cat, who was middle-aged by then and had spent her whole life in a city apartment. Shosha—a pink marbled, green-eyed apartment animal— needed to be in the country, I'd thought. For once in her life she should be able to lie in the long grass of a meadow and go out at night.

I'd taken a room for the session in a big wooden house that stood on the rim of an upland valley above the beach. The house was a former officer's quarters, one of a cluster of old army buildings. From its porch I could look through black-green cypresses to the bowl of the valley, the old parade grounds, long returned to meadow. Across the meadow was the art center, housed in a former barracks.

I'd arrived at the house in the evening, and found as I pushed the kitchen door open three guys drinking coffee. They looked up impassively as I came in, clumsily getting through the door with suitcases and the cat's carrying case, the animal yowling inside. One of the guys—a lively man with bleached hair and a Latin accent—got up and showed me my room, a tiny space just off the kitchen. It was formerly the maid's quarters, the blond guy told me.

I went into the room and shut the door behind me. Inside was a narrow bed and a small desk. I put my bag on the desk and sat on the bed. It creaked. I heard one of the guys in the kitchen say, "He brought his cat?" and I slumped. I wanted to go home, back to the city, to my apartment. But the cat was still wailing in her case, and so I let her out, anyway. She was immediately intent, exploring the place like the animal she was. After a circuit of the room, she found the door and stood expectantly in front of it. I called her quietly, but she would not come. Then I heard the men leave the kitchen, and I opened the door. The cat disappeared into the big house. After a while I ventured out after her, afraid she'd get caught in something.

The big house went on and on. Worn and warped, it felt stately all the same, the rooms and doorways broad, generous, beneath intricate pressed-tin ceilings. In the living room stood a massive hearth, the mantle piled with rocks, shells and driftwood. I went out the screen door onto the front porch, which overlooked the meadow, and found a hammock hanging there, and nearby, a section glassed in as a sunroom. In there, it was quiet; motes stood in the sunbeams. After a while, I remembered I was looking for the cat.

·   ·   ·

Within a day or two, the cat had gone wild, to the degree that her apartment upbringing would allow her. She paid little attention to me. When I noticed her she was often intent on something—some scratching behind the baseboards or trembling in the grass, usually nothing I could perceive. One night she confronted a raccoon on the porch, waking me up with an intense wail and glaring after the raccoon when I had shooed it off. One morning she came up from the basement bearing a dead mouse, bringing it proudly into the kitchen as I ate breakfast with the other men. We gave her a big hand when we saw her, and she dropped the mouse in the middle of the floor, her gift for us.

The guys loved the cat, Rudolfo—our short, blond, hilarious and hot-blooded Brazilian house mother—most of all. The cat went upstairs, to sleep where it was warmer, pushed open the bedroom doors and tried the beds out, finally settling on Rudolfo's, where he doted on her, giving her a new name—something like "Dorianne" pronounced in Portuguese—and declaring that she was no longer my cat. "She is mine," he said, hugging her.

Rudolfo scolded the men in the house about doing the dishes, which we did in return for his elaborate cooking. He wore outrageous and beautiful clothes, most of which he had made himself. He liked ample silk shorts. Rudolfo gave me a shirt—a deep green with a sort of diamond pattern in the weave. In my closet, it looked wild and elegant among my familiar things. Rudolfo sang constantly as he cooked, often crooning in Portuguese, though sometimes he ad-libbed an obscene version of an American show tune. "Fairy tales can come true—it can happen to you," he sang once, "if you're young and hard."

The other men in the house—Ben, Jack, Scott—were semi-young guys in the grad student mode who like me wore jeans and sneakers. We all came to love the wild, fey Brazilian, Rudolfo.

Without him, we might have just passed each other on the porch, remaining friendly strangers for that short summer. But Rudolfo insisted we take meals together, and within two days of my arrival, I had joined this family of brothers, at home at the table with them, roaring with pleasure and disgust at Rudolfo's songs.

Ben, the tall North Carolinian, liked to tell slow, pointed Southern stories. Like the other men in the house, Ben was an artist in residence at the center. He was a filmmaker and a found-art artist. For one of his pieces he'd set out to find an entire deck of cards, one by one, from litter in the street. It had taken him three years. Ben was in the middle of a divorce, or had just been divorced, and didn't care to talk about it at first, though he came around to it, by the end. Jack made animated videos, and had a round face with a crest of black bangs over one of his blue eyes. Scott was a whistling artist. Rudolfo himself created what he called rituals, which seemed to me to be part samba, part Santería, part Venice Beach.

At first we talked a lot about art at the table, then they got on to the subject of sex, and in particular, the possibilities of sex with the women across the meadow. The staff at the art center were all female, and those four women working over there in the big barracks all day became touchstones for our conversation, as Rudolfo chided us. The night after I arrived, Ben, whose divorce made him the most alert to the women, said that they'd hired somebody new.

"She's young," he said. "I think she's just out of school." An expectant pause held the table for a moment, before we broke into that rising cry, that sound of having located some new affection, some new vulnerability, in our friend.

"Look," said Rudolfo. "Again he is in love." He made a mocking, mooing sound out of the vowel in "love."

"She's great," said Ben, shrugging and grinning. "She's fabulous."

That was L.

·   ·   ·

I met her a day or two later. That first week I'd mostly hidden amidst the children's tumult, seeing only the other teachers and the kids. Then one afternoon I went into the main building to wash the flour paste from my hands as the children threw Frisbees and Hula-Hooped out front until their parents picked them up. Inside, in the big hallway, I encountered a young woman carrying a carousel slide tray. Our eyes met as we passed.

I asked who she was and she told me, warmly but a little fiercely, as if I was about to ask her to do something. "Just wondering," I said, adding, stupidly I felt, "You look like you belong here."

"Thanks," she said, "I guess." Then she proceeded, seeming never to have paused. Outside the parrot boy and the frog-or-dog into whom the son of the Peruvian consul had transformed asked me to play Frisbee in the field. We walked down the hill into the valley, spread out across the grass and began sending the plastic disc around our triangle. I felt agitated. As I waited for the Frisbee to come back, I thought of her again, trying to decide I didn't like her. "Young besides," I thought. I wondered, with a vehemence, whether Ben would get her, and that night at dinner, listened carefully when Ben spoke, deciding he was all talk.

The next day the robot boy and the turtle boy decreed that the play would have a combat scene, and I had to accommodate this action to the demands of the ballerina, the nerd, the angel and the other animals in the story about the gnome selling his soul to the devil. Maybe the gnome might win his soul back, I thought, by betting it on the turtle's victory over the robot, the devil's favorite. That way they could fight while everyone else made cacophony with their drums, tambourines, cymbals, triangles and woodblocks. The musician was teaching the children cacophony, or rather teaching them that name for what they did.

It engaged me completely, this production. We spent days rehearsing and making puppets, drilling and bolting puppet supports, and by Friday, after an afternoon of lugging heavy flotsam on the beach, I walked home feeling pummeled, tired but happy. On the meadow, it was suddenly bright. The last of the day's fog had finally dispersed, uncovering a clean summer sky for the close of the day. Squinting, I followed the faint track that the men had trodden from our house—a worn but not yet broken path, our way to work. The field was dry and yellow, the grasses broomy underfoot.

Who chose this path? I was wondering again. It was a question I considered every time I walked it. The house had been occupied only a month or two, and the path had only borne—what?— three hundred, five hundred crossings? Yet the way had narrowed to a single, wandering trace. And not even the most efficient way to cross the field.

Just then I heard my name called from the shade of the cypresses that lined the road rimming the little valley. It was a woman's voice, maybe fifty yards off, but I couldn't see her and wasn't even sure of her direction.

"What?" I shouted back at the trees.

Then L emerged from the shadow from the direction of the studios at the high end of the valley, striding down the yellow slope in blue jeans. She looked long and lean, I thought. She wore black flats and lay her long feet before her as she came down the hill. I watched the little arc of her step. She descended the hill with a steady gaze, watching me watch her, and carrying herself like a dancer, limber.

"Are you living here?" she called as she came up.

"Sure. Right here. In the field," I said.

"No," she said, smiling, "Are you living up here?" She waved both hands, indicating the valley.

I pointed to the house beyond the cypresses. I was staying there, I said.

"Oh, with Ben and those guys," she said. "With Rudolfo."

"Yeah, the guys," I said.

Her big eyes were blue, I noticed as I searched for anything else to say. I was spattered with kid goop. After that moment, she said, "Well," in a friendly tone that nevertheless invited our departure.

"Anyway, see you," I said.

"See you, too," she said. Then we went opposite ways, I on the faint, new path to the house, purposefully not looking back and wondering if she was. What was that about? I wondered. Why was she interested? Why had she been in the meadow in the first place? I walked home, startled by her presence and aware of my longing.

Before the summer ended I glimpsed her again a few times, now familiar enough to say hello, though I didn't try to make anything of it. Then, near the end of my stay there, I was placed in a more intimate situation with her. Rudolfo finally staged his theatrical performance, and since we were isolated up there, he asked everyone to help with some aspect of the piece. L volunteered to play a role in it, and Rudolfo gave her the part called the Virgin, for which she had to wear a tiny and outrageous costume—gold breast plates and a sort of escutcheon with a wild feathery pubic bush attached. He planned to put silk ribbons in her long chestnut hair and to make up her face extravagantly. He asked me to hand out programs, but in the frantic hour before the show found himself short of time and ordered me to help by painting the rest of L's body white. I didn't have to be asked twice.

I went into her dressing room to paint her and found her giggling with another volunteer actress. They had drunk a bottle of wine together to get up the nerve to appear in public in their costumes. She had covered herself with the greasepaint as well as she could. Only her back was still unpainted. So she held a towel over her breasts as I tried to seem casual about the whole business and rubbed the greasepaint over her neck and back, making her skin both luminous and opaque. It was funny, never having touched her and then touching her like this. She bent forward, lolling her head, exposing her longish neck and shaking like a nervous animal. "I don't think I can go out there wearing that," she said, gesturing with her chin at the breastplates of the costume, which lay draped over a chair.

"Don't worry," I said, concentrating on her back, which was warm under my fingers. "You'll do fine." When I had whitened her whole back, I left her in the dressing room.

She did do fine. Her role required no long speaking parts, which would have been inaudible anyway beneath the howling sound track. Rudolfo instructed her to charm the audience by acting seductive. She took this up in a silly, ironic way that I found more seductive than any serious attempt to portray the femme fatale. During the performance she came up to where I stood in the audience and made a goofy come-hither gesture with her finger, which gave me more of a thrill than I showed. In the middle of the performance she had to do a sort of duet with Rudolfo, and at the end she ducked down among the props with the other characters for the finale, as rifle-fire roared on the soundtrack. The piece might have seemed baffling and awesome, even a little sinister to strangers, but because most of the cast and the crowd had worked together and known each other outside of the performance, it seemed burlesque and hilarious, and we cheered it on. Afterward a bunch of us drove down to a tavern in Sausalito, where we squashed ourselves into a booth and drank and laughed about the piece until late. I ended up sitting beside L, her warm thigh pressed along mine.

. . .

Still she seemed beyond me, impossible. Plus I had dated one of the other women in the office where she worked and that made things seem complicated. I thought about her wistfully, though, and made up things to talk about when I saw her, to prolong the encounters. But soon enough the session would conclude, and I would move back to my apartment in San Francisco.

On the last day of the summer, the children put on their performance. The audience, parents mostly with video cameras, perched on a natural gallery of rocks at the beach. L came to watch. Seeing her gave me a vague and anxious feeling, as if I had already done something wrong and might get caught.

The children readied their puppets behind the crazy stage we'd built of beach timbers and driftwood, festooned with Styrofoam and scrap plastic. Manipulating the big puppets—most of which were larger than themselves—was a task that required most of the children's concentration. They could growl, hoot and scream on cue, but they couldn't manage the lines, so I took on the job of providing the words for the action. Behind a pair of puppets of my own creation—an MC and his beautiful wife both in evening dress—I read the narration.

The performance started with a wacky procession to music. The audience laughed just to see it, so varied and charming. When the children had carted their big puppets off behind me, only two remained, presiding over the stage from platforms above it—the tall, skinny girl of Bolinas, who as the angel mostly just shook her head, and the parrot boy, who did a lot of preening and squawking. I announced the devil and the gnome.

The waves slapped the beach beyond the stage, and I had to shout the lines over the roar of the ocean and the wind. "When he said he needed gold," I bellowed, "all the creatures mocked the gnome." I waited a moment for the children to work the strings and make their puppets mock the gnome. The gnome responded with great, exaggerated gestures of dismay. "For there was no need of gold in that kingdom," I yelled.

L watched and laughed at the chaotic performance, and in the pauses, spoke to her friend—S, the woman I had dated—with a conspiratorial air, I thought. What *didn't* they tell each other, I wondered. I carried on with the story, pacing myself carefully so that the entrances and exits might be accomplished with the unwieldy marionettes. I played the tambourine, shaking it like crazy during the cacophonous finale, when the boy in the big turtle shell proved victorious over the raging robot. The women applauded and then were gone, disappearing as the parents descended onto the stage from the rocks and the children rioted, celebrating their play. I was tumbled among them.

Then it was over. I spent the next day with the other teachers demolishing the stage. We untied the logs and the pilings, dragged them down to the surf, and flopped them into the ocean. They didn't wash out, but the waves, which that day broke a little aslant the shore, spread the flotsam, until by day's end the pieces had washed far down the sand, and the beach looked more or less as it had when we'd begun gathering the driftwood for the project. Then we bid each other goodbye and went home, and the summer was over.

I thought about L, but I didn't call her. For one thing I was still sort of seeing S—we hadn't gone out again, but we hadn't officially called it off—and as long as the two of them worked together, I felt I couldn't ask the other one out. But mostly I had no faith in my chances with L. I returned home to my apartment and found it exactly the same as I'd left it, significantly so. My venture into the world hadn't yielded anything, it said.

6

La Tête Américaine

....

That night we rejoined the world again—going out among others as we did at home. We met L's schoolmate, a beautiful dark Algerian woman, and her friends and went to a jazz club in Les Halles. At the club L seemed to move deliberately away from me, and I recalled us as strangers, the night after I'd painted her white, when we were pushed together in the bar by accident, and I'd felt the strange heat of her thigh. Now that we knew each other, we'd go politely apart, to acknowledge the others. L in pale silk and pearls sat across the table, seeming as luminous and cool as the moon.

Everybody yakked in French, and I tried to appear as if I were comprehending it. Finally the man on my left said hello in English. "You are American," he said. Yes, I agreed.

"Try this beer," he said. "It has the taste of what?" Either he didn't know the word or I was supposed to guess. I tasted the stuff, which was terrible I thought, and still had no idea. He told me the word in French, and I called it as a question across the table to L.

"Berries," she called back. I drank more of the berry beer, trying to be polite. It tasted like jam in the brew and masked the bitterness I liked about beer. I thanked my new companion, nonetheless.

Across the table, L had become French again, gossiping with her friend. I tried to dedicate myself to being where I was, without reference to where she was. I'd be present. I'd be cordial, as strangers were to one another. Why was it that lovers treated each other both better and worse?

To avoid the berry beer guy, I turned in desperation to my right and said hello to a big woman who suddenly began speaking to me in English with a broad Texas accent. She'd been raised in Panama, she said, in the Canal Zone. She was a linguistics professor, and she was—the day persisting in its rigorous theme—getting divorced. For the next two drinks, she entertained me with the tale. She'd left her husband in the South, where they'd both taught. He was French, she said, and was having an affair with a student. She just couldn't submit to that.

At first I listened uncomfortably, recognizing her tactic, an attempt to find some relief by placing her grief at the distance of a story. But by the time she finished, I felt kindly toward her and told her the story of Monet's poppies, how in real life they'd simply been a small suggestion.

"How long will it take me to get over this?" she asked.

"Five years," I figured, and she seemed relieved to hear it. The band, a piano trio, had set up while we talked and now began its first number, a jazz waltz. The Zonian woman leaned into me. Had I come there alone? she asked. I'd come with somebody, I said, almost apologizing. I looked up for L, and there she was, looking back at me with raised brow amid the welter of French.

. . .

The late streets were still crowded when we left to catch the last subway. I was a little drunk, and moved swimmingly through the passing crowd of faces I would see only in that instant, and then never again. This sense of crowds was a traveler's feeling, I thought, common now in the late twentieth century, but a great and rare shock in times past, when people stayed put and lived in small places. When the "last wild Indian," Ishi, went to see the Pacific Ocean for the first time, his impression of it had been entirely overwhelmed by his shock, panic even, at the hordes of people—more human beings than he had ever seen in his life— sunbathing at Ocean Beach.

As we waited in the Métro, L asked me about the Zonian woman. "What was her story?" she said. "She was awfully friendly."

"She was getting divorced," I said. "A mess." L hadn't been through this, and wouldn't get it.

At home in the tiny apartment where we'd lived for two days, I returned one last time to my dutiful distance, cheered and rededicated by the touch of jealousy L had shown. The wish to obliterate that distance between me and my beloved had stood untouched within me all evening. When I was younger I had never even seen that wish, so fully and immediately did it find its expression.

I unclasped her pearls, and we undressed like a calm couple who'd been together for years. L was happy to have seen her old friend and to have spent the evening among French people, as if we'd rendered Paris ordinary and belonged there, which was the best. She was still talking about it as we got into bed and turned out the light. So-and-so had a new boyfriend; so-and-so was writing a thesis on embassy security. Someone had said I had a *"tête Américaine,"* she told me, laughing. I laughed, too. It was okay;

I'd have an American head; I didn't mind. Everything we shared was bringing us together, I hoped. It wouldn't be necessary to say or do anything. Still, I had been in my distant orbit all day and was tired of it, and at last gave in, let myself feel bereft and held her, for a moment anyway.

7

SAVING THE SONG

OF SONGS

Afterward I wanted to find a time before romance, to see where I'd gone wrong. Maybe if I started at the beginning, I figured, I could end up somewhere else. Babylon, though different, was worse. There, the day came each year when the young women of the town were simply sold into marriages. They were brought to the marketplace "in a body," writes Herodotus, and auctioned off to a crowd of men. The crier made them stand and offered them one by one for sale, beginning with the most beautiful. The rich men regarded beauty in a wife, notes Herodotus, and these would bid upon the beautiful one until she was purchased for a large sum. Then the crier proceeded to the next most beautiful. But there always came a point when the bidding dropped off, though some women were still left unwed.

Poor men, of course, couldn't compete in the initial bidding. But they did not so regard beauty in a wife, according to Herodotus. So the commoners were allowed to bid on the less beautiful women, and the auctioneer would pay the price for these brides from the purse paid for the beautiful ones. Thus no woman went unbought in Babylon, where the beautiful, as Herodotus concludes, "portioned out the common and the lame." And maybe this was all that love was called, in Babylon.

In Palestine, though, there had always been the Song of Songs, the ancient love poem that eventually found its way into the Bible. The Songs seem to have given a name to love forever, or at any rate since human beings had set down the names for things. As a young man, Akiba ben Joseph had those words for love, when, among animals in the wilderness, he considered his beloved Rachel.

A rich man's daughter, Rachel was beyond him. Akiba was born into the peasant class called the Amme haarez, the ordinary people of the land. As such, Akiba was an illiterate outsider, a peasant in a society run by the scholars, the high priests and the rich, all of whom he resented. Scholars especially aroused his ire: "If I had a scholar in my power," he said later of his youth, "I'd maul him like an ass." Still, he had little choice in life, and hired himself out to Kalba Shebu'a, one of the richest men in Jerusalem. Akiba went meekly to his master each dawn, walking into the walled city and going to the man's house to take charge of his flock. He drove the sheep back out the city's gate and stood over them all day in the flinty hills above the town. He probably filled the time with idle plans and nourished that dark hope of the disenfranchised, that when chaos came, it would bring a windfall.

Akiba's ancient people knew that chaos would come. The Amme haarez had seen everything, twice. They'd seen the rich arrive and leave, rise and fall. When Moses lead his people into Judah, he found the Amme haarez there already. They were immemorial in Palestine, descending in thousands of generations before histories ever came to be written. They came late to Yahweh. Before the arrival of this new god, they had worshipped generation itself in form of the goddess Astarte, she whose name meant both womb and what comes from it, and her brother Baal, whose name meant to possess by sex. The Amme haarez married their sons and daughters simply by singing the Song of Songs.

The Songs too had descended—sung down the generations— from the ancient heart of life in the West. Scholars find in them echoes of the love poetry of Egypt and Sumeria. And what was it about, this song a thousand years older than the Iliad? About love and the mystery of sex, about being fruitful and multiplying. It offers a profusion of images for passion, for longing and joy. "Let us arise early," the singer invites her beloved.

> *Let us see whether the vine has budded*
> *And its blossoms have opened*
> *And whether the pomegranates have bloomed.*
> *There I will give you my love.*

"Thy love is better than wine," sings a voice in the Songs. And this: "If a man offer all the wealth of his house for love, it would be utterly scorned." And simply this: "Love is stronger than death."

These were the words Akiba would have heard, the way he would have had to think of Rachel, his patron's daughter, auburn-haired, perfumed with myrrh. I see her, as if in a pre-Raphaelite painting, at her window or at the well or emerging from a darkened archway, and imagine that one glimpse might suffice to make him forget himself all day, to inspire him to recall her, there in the desert, in the words of the Song of Songs.

But all this we can only imagine. How he proceeded with Rachel, how he turned their glances into words; how he arranged to be alone with her, to touch her; these are not recorded. We know that he was an ambitious man, large-boned, forceful and according to legend so smart he could turn the rage of his class into wit and make his superiors laugh even as he upbraided them; these powers he must have poured into persuading Rachel.

The legend, preserved by the rabbis, also records her father's reaction. When he found his daughter with his hired man, Kalba Shebu'a was enraged, and when Rachel agreed to marry Akiba, he disinherited her. Still, she chose Akiba, raised her desire for him over the whole society that bound them, and to his astonishment and delight, they wed, married by the words of the Song of Songs.

But whatever love was called, it was not sufficient. As a strategy for their social betterment, the marriage was a fiasco. The historical commentators, practical men, seem to see her father's point. The Talmudic tractate called the *Nedarim* only notes, flatly, "Then she went and married him in winter." They had to leave Jerusalem, to live among his people, to sleep on straw in the damp cold.

When the Hebrews first arrived in Palestine, the new religion of these conquerors both purged and adopted the local dieties. The Amme haarez to some degree accommodated Yahweh, and the high priests of Judah overlooked for the time being the old ways of the country people. Even in Solomon's Temple, writes Raphael Patai, Hebrews worshipped Asherah, daughter of Astarte. For centuries after the arrival of the Israelites, her wooden image stood with Jehovah's—as his mother, his sister, his bride. But this period of tolerance did not last. Babylon would change everything for the Jews, even the name for love.

On the sixteenth of March, 597 B.C., Nebuchadnezzar and his Babylonian army entered and burned Jerusalem. Intent upon plunder, not empire, he enslaved the ruling class of the nation— as recorded in Kings, "all the princes, and all the mighty men of valor, ten thousand captives, and all the craftsmen and all the smiths"—and bore them back to Babylon in chains. Only "the poorest people of the land," the Amme haarez who had been there to begin with, remained behind, upholding their ancient ways.

Then a century later these Babylonian captives came back. They had proven valuable in Babylon, and by then were counselors to the Persian Empire, granted finally the repossession of their former home. Back in Judea, however, the returnees were not welcomed, but viewed simply as another wave of powerful outsiders. The Amme haarez resisted the settlers at first, blocking their construction sites. But the workers bore swords against the peasants, and by 445 B.C., the exiles had rebuilt the temple.

Dispossessed in Babylon, these Jews had moved to codify their faith, to make the doctrine strict and the form orthodox, so that they might possess at least this. They demanded greater adherence to the one God who had appeared to Moses as pillars of fire and cloud in the wilderness and, in their new temple, reinstated a religion instructed by the prophets in Babylon. Jeremiah in particular blamed their catastrophe on permissiveness by the old regime and viewed the scourge of Nebuchadnezzar as God's punishment, especially for the people's devotion to Astarte and the idols of fertility. Wicked, he declared, were the women who continued to "knead dough to make cakes for the Queen of Heaven." These old rites were an abomination in the eyes of the Lord.

So when they returned to Jerusalem, the new high priests, the Sadduces, looked askance upon the Amme haarez, considering them less than Jewish, because—for one thing—their marriages had not been officially consecrated. The Song of Songs was not sacrament enough, though it was older than Solomon and had been sung for centuries at weddings and even recited in the temple at Passover. As a document, this erotic poem had been preserved not in the Pentateuch, the first five books of the Bible that composed the Torah itself, nor in the *Nevi'im,* the secondary class of prophetic works, but in a third division, simply known as the Writings, popular among the people, though not considered sacred. To some, the Song of Songs did not belong even among these minor works. Among the high priests, there were those who believed that the Songs "defiled the hands" that touched them.

Delineating his four-fold scheme for the cosmos, William Blake called the lower part of ordinary world—which was neither heaven nor hell—Generation. He believed that in this realm only the plants were perfect and so wrote of Generation as vegetal. And this vegetal perfection, flowering and fruiting, beyond the ordinary fallen state of human beings, was a power both enlivening and destructive to them, healing and subversive, offering a higher world and undermining rationality, order and law. So, too, in the Song of Songs—where Blake may have found his Generation—erotic love is revolutionary, opposed to the daily round, to the economic and the rational. The Song calls from the passionate heart to the quotidian mind that can't deny them. In the Song, the lovers long to escape from the city and the squares of the marketplace; they aspire to the wilderness, to the pomegranates and the wild rose of Sharon.

The universe of the Song is sympathetic to this aspiration. The matter that they celebrate is larger than what we now understand as erotic, encompassing the generation of all living things and viewing human love as expressing and expressed by that broader generation. This connection, which now appears as mere dead metaphor—a bouquet for the date—was living then. The Song may have been a magical incantation, meant to invoke the power of that connection, to induce fertility in the garden and in the boudoir. Some scholars of the Song have identified in them remnants of the liturgy from a Palestinian fertility cult, the original religion of the Amme haarez. Certain specific forms—the comparison of the male lover to an apple tree, a repeated oath sworn by gazelles, and other images—appear in both the Song and the rites of Asherah, whose female, nude, melon-breasted image is found everywhere in the Middle East. "Sustain me with raisin-cakes," sings the voice in the Song, "for I am sick with love." These are the cakes prepared for the Queen of Heaven, the same cakes condemned in Babylon by Jeremiah, speaking for his God.

But if the Song of Songs is subversive, erotic, fertile, female, how did it finally come down to us in the Bible, the document of Israel and Jehovah? There among the mythic, legal, historical, abstract, prophetic and patriarchal tracts, it blooms like no other book. And it appears to have little use there, beloved as it was. The Pentateuch instructs, first of all, telling the story of the origins of the people, delineating the laws and recounting the Exodus and the arrival at the Promised Land. It is both history and constitution, and as Paul Johnson notes, the Song of Songs is "evidently an anthology of love poems," with "no intrinsic reason for its inclusion" in the Bible. There is no mention of God in the work, and even its identification with King Solomon—it is often called the Song of Solomon—may be spurious, the result of a late emendation in its title, perhaps an attempt to give this popular work some claim to protection as a historical document.

The book was an ancient anomaly and a problem, though not an urgent one as long as the canon itself remained an open question. In the tolerant, confident nation of Israel, landed and without undue anxiety about its enemies, a hundred flowers might bloom. But after the Babylonian conquest, the Song would be an irritant, and five hundred years later, after the next fall of Jerusalem in A.D. 70, the question of the work's place in the canon would become critical. Then, amid the new ruins, the rabbinical authorities would have to construct an ark, a lifeboat of law and literature that might bear the Jews intact through the coming diaspora.

Manuscripts require constant recopying to survive, and left out of the canon, the Song would never have claimed such diligent scribal attention. Without preservation in manuscript, the Song would have returned to the oral tradition of a people, whose memories would be weakened by centuries of reading, and whose culture stood in the path of great and crushing empires. Had the Song of Songs not found a place in the Jewish Bible at that point, it would probably not exist today.

Fortunately, Rachel lived then. When she and Akiba were forced to take up the life of the Amme haarez above Jerusalem, Israel's old catastrophe, the destruction of the nation and the scattering of the Jews, was about to recur. By then the unanimity among the Jewish ruling classes had dissolved, and the Romans had taken advantage of the situation to extend their Empire. The nation lurched toward the cataclysm that would destroy it. Again, the Amme haarez would look on, left out.

Akiba and Rachel were safe, if poor, among them. That winter, report the commentators, she had to sell her hair to buy food. Together at night, their breath misted the clear air, while in the valley below, the city sparkled like foil around the Mount with its jewelbox temple. "If I could," he told her, according to the legend, "I'd give you a Jerusalem of gold." But he could not.

One night a ragged, filthy mortal, actually the angel Elijah in disguise, pounded on their door. "Straw!" he cried. "My wife is giving birth, and she must lie upon the bare ground! Give me your straw!" Straw they had, though it was all they had. Still Akiba without hesitation bid the beggar to take it. Left alone again in their empty room, Akiba exulted. "See!" he said to his wife. "Here is a man who lacks even straw."

Perhaps there was a pause, as Rachel considered her response—she who had cropped her hair off for them. "Go," she said at last. "Become a scholar."

Her words in this small rabbinical tale ring to a modern ear with irony, as if this were literally her last straw. But she was serious, it turned out, and made her continued marriage to him contingent upon his taking up the study of the Torah.

Of course he refused. He'd always hated scholars, with their scribbling and their judgments. To learn to read was, in one sense, to betray his people and his past. Besides, Israel was in chaos at that moment, and it must have been difficult to imagine the good of studying anything. The nation was convulsed with the rebellion that would culminate with ruin on an epochal scale, when Roman forces under the young commander Titus would recapture and burn Jerusalem, killing or enslaving most of the Jews there.

Rachel's words, "Become a scholar," proved their deliverance. Scholarship thereafter was the path to power. There was little other distinction after the leveling war, and there was great work to be done. The destruction of Jerusalem enhanced the importance of the Jewish academies, as they became the chief remaining institutions in the country. Here, and not on the battlefield, would the fate of the Jews be decided. Here also might Akiba's mind prevail. The academies had always been meritocratic— places where brilliance would be rewarded, no matter whose, where class and background were of lesser importance than one's ability to debate, to master text, to judge.

Still, Akiba would not be moved from his old hatred of scholars and scholarship. Nor would Rachel relent. The story gives some sense of years passing as they resisted each other. Then one day Akiba stopped at a spring to drink. The light touch of the falling water—a gentle pressure, constantly applied—had cut a deep groove into the stone that capped the spring. When he saw this, he knew he would give in.

So, at nearly forty years of age, he began studying the Hebrew alphabet with his son. As they learned one character at a time, they proceeded as if into a vast city of letters, where all that he knew and felt would take a particular finite form, and where the future—for him and for Rachel, for the nation and for the Song of Songs—would lie.

8

Clefts in the Rock

....

For a week after we'd returned from the camp, the cat yowled at the front door. I'd open it for her to show her only the hall of the apartment building out there, not the long grass of the meadow. But I knew how she felt. The summer had seemed to offer possibilities now vanished. Inside the apartment everything was steady, firm, reflecting the choices I had made for years: that painting in that corner, those books on that shelf. For a long time, that steadiness had been my comfort, but that September it seemed like so much heavy old clutter. Meanwhile I couldn't sleep, at least not all night. I'd wake up at four in the morning and walk around my darkened place. When I'd first moved in alone, I loved the feeling that once I put something down it stayed where I put it until I picked it up again. Nobody would intervene in the meantime. Even in the dark, I could find the smallest thing. But now, eight years later, the thought of nothing moving until I moved it seemed for the first time alarming, implying a lack of possibilities.

Without exactly wanting to, I had begun to remember what it was like to be in love. I remembered M, the last woman I'd been in love with, and for the first time in the years since we'd broken up I began to recall not just the painful end of that affair, but how it had felt in the beginning, and back in my solid, stolid apartment, I began to want to have those feelings again. Of course, there was no one in my life for whom I could have feelings like that. Just wanting to have them, though, gave me a pain high up in my chest. I rearranged the furniture, but the stirrings persisted. Only a lover or travel would disperse them.

In a month I was on the other side of the world, on a tour bus leaving Jerusalem, heading east toward the Jordan River. That fall I was working on a book about siege weapons, consoled by the descriptions of destroyed fortifications, and in October I went abroad to study siege sites. It was travel as I had used it often before, as a way of radically changing things, though I had the sinking feeling, as we left Jerusalem, that I was only moving my solitude around the globe.

The bus crested the ridge to the east of the city and dropped into the Judean desert on its way to the Dead Sea. My ears popped. We drove past the goatskin tents of bedouin shepherds. Over the centuries their herds had carved a filigree of trails across the hills. So this was the land of the rose of Sharon and the lily of the valley, I thought. The country must have had more water then. The bus verged a cliff, and below, in the deep cleft that a stream had cut into the rock, a blue-domed monastery stood, set into ledges in the stone. This road, said the guide, took Herod to his summer palace. Jesus had gone this way also, to and from the wilderness. We drove to Jericho, where Arabs in the shade eyed us warily. It was occupied territory, and we didn't stop, just peered back out the windows at the still and seedy town, where the date palms were taller than the buildings.

The passengers on the bus were young and hearty. This was to be a hiking trip, sponsored by the equivalent of the Sierra Club in Israel, which would include, among other outings, a predawn climb up the Runner's Path at Masada. We'd been forced to introduce ourselves before we'd gotten on the bus. There was just one other man—Roger, from Texas, a big guy with hairy legs. He was reading *Exodus* and said he'd cried five times already. There were two silly English girls, very young and in their own world, and there was Lee, who was silent, tall, big-browed, very quiet, proper, dressed in brown, from Albany, New York. Chia, a wisecracker from Amsterdam, ostrichlike, said anything at all that came to mind, and wore high-heeled pumps to go hiking in the desert. Rachel was a strawberry blonde, an American from Miami, who used the word "ubiquitous," speaking of American TV shows overseas. And Andrea, from Munich, who had no English, and who stung me the most—dark and beautiful in her shorts and big hiking boots.

We stopped to hike around the rubble of Herod's summer palace, the light so explosively radiant on the dry stone that my eyes watered behind my sunglasses. The hard scrabble on the surface of the ground was flint, our guide said. The hardest of the sedimentary stones, essentially petrified algae, the stone had been alive once, capable of nourishing itself from sunlight. We got back on the bus, sweating, and proceeded deeper into the rift valley of the Jordan. By late afternoon the Dead Sea glittered below us, blue and seemingly sweet in the distance.

I'd left the situations at home up in the air. Daunted, I hadn't dared to call L. S, her friend who worked with her at the art center, I had called. S had a big mane of blond hair, a deep knowledge of astrology and was easy to be with. We'd been seeing each other long enough to have reached that point at which we might expect to see each other more, though we continued to act ironical and autonomous, and to be buddies. I was glad to get away before I had incurred any further obligations. She offered to feed my cat, and I'd given her the key to my place, then had left town with a cursory good-bye, hoping a month apart might resolve things. Coward, I thought, though I said nothing.

As the bus descended into the desert, toward one of the lowest places on earth, I felt how effortlessly S and I might settle together, and for some reason that thought made me feel alien and sad in the presence of the young women on the bus. The beautiful German woman, Andrea, seemed especially unreachable, like a galaxy beyond the Milky Way.

I'd befriended Roger, who told me about the things he'd found in Israel that he liked to eat: falafels, Arab bread, pizza in Tel Aviv but not in Jerusalem. The guide announced that the pockmarks in the cliffs above the road were the caves of the Essenes, ascetic Jews who'd fled the wickedness of the city and who'd written the Dead Sea Scrolls. They believed in a final apocalyptic battle of Good and Evil, he said, adding that million-year-old fossil water sprang from the ground near here. How did it taste? asked Roger. Salty, said the guide.

When we stopped again, we hiked up into a dry gorge in the cliff where we hoped to see some ibexes—ancient ramlike animals. A sign read AVOIDING UNPLEASANTNESS WITH LEOPARDS— THROW A ROCK IF YOU HAVE TO BUT DON'T HURT THEM. We hiked up into the canyon single file. I walked behind Andrea, sighing to myself. We saw no ibexes and no leopards, just the precipitous rock and the salt bush, which could live anywhere, said the guide. It grew in the seams between the stones of the Wailing Wall.

By the time we got back to the bus, the October night was falling quickly, and when we finally reached the Dead Sea, we had to make our way down to the beach in darkness. I clambered down to the water with the Dutch woman, Chia. At the rocky shore we stripped to our bathing suits, waded and then plunged into the brine, which burned like acid on my tongue. Chia and I lay there on the surface as if on a bed of bitter gelatin, the stars thick overhead. Then the rest of the group was around us, and suddenly we were all friends, familiar with one another, joking about being pickled, crying out if the brine got in our eyes.

That night we slept in a dormitory on the ridge, at a mountaineering school. In the common room we were given dinner and shown a movie about ibexes, a nature film so corny and anthropomorphic that we hooted at it. For some reason, perhaps fatigue, the ibexes seemed hysterically funny, the goateed males idiotic as they locked horns in their struggles over females while exciting music poured from the cracked speakers. After the battle, the champion ibex male was shown mating, his tongue sticking goofily out as he mounted his ewe. This the women found particularly uproarious. Afterward Roger and I retired to the room we shared. We could hear the women, still laughing, through the cinder block wall.

I couldn't sleep and stayed up, awash with wistfulness. The camp where we were staying was full, the other buildings occupied by a large group of young Israelis, boys and girls, all just eighteen years old, there on a government-sponsored "fun night," their last before joining the army. I went out into the dark and sat on the grass and watched them. They were sweet, tough kids, dancing to records in the dusty yard in front of their dorm. One girl swayed and sang in front of the stereo, her voice as loud as the record, a group looking on. Other couples strolled out of the light, looking for a place to be alone, and once they found one, lay together and kissed in darkened heaps around the bushes. Watching them, I remembered the seamless feeling of being eighteen.

The next morning Roger and I got up in the dark, and were met in the dining hall with cries of greeting. By the time the sun rose, we were atop Masada, having climbed the steep desert walls up to the ruins as the sky slowly brightened above the Dead Sea. We cheered the old flaming orb when it appeared between the crags of the mountains beyond the water, over there in Jordan, and then sat on the rocks as the guide demolished, at length, the heroic legend of Masada, representing the heroes as mere bandits who had terrorized the local villages until the Romans had picked them off. All day the sun hammered us, as we walked over the chalky broken ground, in pairs and trios, joking and telling stories from home, hiking from one vista to another. I walked with Andrea, exchanging what information we could without a common language. "California," I said, pointing to myself.

That afternoon, for our last hike, we walked up a canyon to the spring of Eingedi. There lush reeds filled the cleft in the stone. Our path crossed and recrossed the stream cascading down the canyon. Finally we came to a sheer rock face down which a waterfall dropped into a shallow pool. There was a good swimming place above the waterfall, said Dani, the guide. Dodim's Cave, it was called. But to get up there, we would have to climb back out, to the rim of dry rock, then descend again, and by then the group was tired, and nobody seemed to want to climb this extra leg. They were content to sit at the shallow pool and soak their feet. So I went up alone, out into the heat and then down into the gorge again by a steel ladder set into the rock. At its base lay a small pool that flowed out of a low cave's mouth. Alone, I stripped to my swimsuit and swam out into the pool, which deepened sharply. Across the surface was the cave, and I could see some light farther back there, a deeper chamber in the grotto. I submerged and swam beneath the stone, and when I surfaced on the other side, I found myself in a lush, reedy chamber, which echoed with the rush of falling water. Overhead a lane of sky opened in the stone.

I lay floating in that inner pool, feeling my headache from the sun disappear, until I heard someone splashing in the outer pool. She called some question in German through the opening in the rock. "Sure," I called back, as if I understood her, and as if she understood me, Andrea swam though, her face emerging from the pool. She exclaimed when she saw the inner chamber.

She drew herself up on the little sandbar and sat there, her red nylon suit taut across her breasts. I stood in the waist-deep pool looking at her, then splashed and sighed to indicate how much I liked it. She smiled, and we seemed for a moment intimate, safe and alone, aware of each other's feelings, though we had done nothing to establish that awareness but to be in each other's company for a couple of days.

Nothing happened; it didn't even last long. In a moment Roger surfaced in the pool, then the others followed, until the stone chamber was full of wet girls, rowdy cries and splashing. And Andrea and I weren't alone together again on the trip. She got off the bus in Jerusalem, giving me a hug with everyone else when she said good-bye, and I rode all the way to Tel Aviv, the last one left on the bus. But our encounter in Dodim's Cave filled me with strange, wordless hope. Life still had its surprises. You might find yourself in an ancient grotto—in an oasis in the desert, yet—with a beautiful woman in a red bathing suit. You didn't have to plan anything. You didn't have to say anything. If you waited, the moment would come.

Though not because you wanted it to, or when you might expect it, or when it seemed easy. When I got home I found the apartment spotless, and it made my heart sink to see it. Wonderful S had cleaned it, and it meant that she cared enough about me to do so, and I wasn't ready for her to care that much. There was no standing still with anyone, I understood. Once two people came together, their feelings began to change. Everything had meaning. There were no empty moments. If I refused to choose, a choice would be made for me.

Then a month after I returned from Israel, a friend called to ask if I'd like a blind date. Yes, I said, desperate from celibacy and hoping it would be fate. My friend gave me the number, and I called it. N lived in Marin, and said she'd like to meet. How would we know each other? I asked. We'll be the ones looking, she said. But this wasn't quite enough in the way of description, it turned out. When I got to Squid's, a seafood bar, I talked to two other women before I found her. She was tall—taller than I was, anyway—and wore her long hair curled by a perm. She was pretty and sexy, I thought, also strategic. She worked as an administrator for the symphony. We shared fried calamari, drank hard liquor and talked for two hours about our romantic pasts.

She wasn't entirely divorced, it turned out. Nor did her husband entirely wish to be. But they were separated. He was impossible. He lived in Oakland, across the Bay, she said, as if she were speaking of a vast ocean. She was a mom, too. Her daughter was three years old, named Naomi. I took in these facts as if casually and drank my Irish whiskey. And told my stories, too, conscious that we were exchanging what might be termed sexual histories.

Nothing happened that night—we simply parted in our separate cars—but the next week, after dinner in the city, we went back to the bungalow she rented in San Rafael and went—quickly, competently, safely—to bed. We made love, we spooned up like the long married. Comforted, disturbed, I drifted off.

N had a mother's arms, strong from carrying her three-year-old. That first night, N's daughter had stayed at her dad's. But the next weekend we took Naomi ice-skating in Berkeley, each of us holding one of the little girl's hands as her feet slid crazily beneath her. After two hours my arms ached, and Naomi seemed no better at skating. She's a lot better, N insisted. She's already keeping the skates under her, she said. A couple more afternoons and she'll be skating on her own. I loved N in the moment she said that, showing wisdom and patience and strength and hope in one casual comment. It made me want to take on that family work with her.

"I like you," I told her. "You have life-force."

Still, when we got back to N's house, I felt uneasily familiar again. We had dinner, put the little girl to bed, and lay together on the couch in front of the TV news, then fell asleep and woke up groggily to the end of *Saturday Night Live* and dragged ourselves to her big bed.

The following morning, her husband—he who didn't wish to be divorced—showed up unexpectedly, in the rain. It was my second shock of the morning. The first was awakening at dawn to find the little girl, Naomi, pressed in between us in bed. I'd lain there cramped and worried, finally waking N and asking her to take Naomi back to bed.

"She just wants to snuggle," said N.

"I'm not ready to snuggle with both of you yet," I said. So N took her sleeping daughter into the other room, and returned to sleep heavily against me. I'd gotten in too deep, too soon.

When we woke again, it was raining out—a gloomy Sunday morning—and we turned on the lights in the kitchen to make breakfast. N cut up a banana and put it on Rice Krispies for her daughter, then made huevos rancheros for us. As we were eating, there was a soft knock at the door. N rushed to answer it, but left the chain on the door when she opened it, and spoke though the opening without saying hello or acknowledging who our visitor was.

"You can't come in," I heard her say.

"Daddy?" said the little girl, who by then had gotten up from the breakfast table.

"Honey," said her mother, "you just go back and sit with Jim and eat your Rice Krispies." The sound of my own name seemed to ring like a gong through the little house. "Daddy's not coming in," said N.

"Daddy!" called Naomi.

I heard the unseen husband say, "Who's Jim?" Was there a

back door to this place? I was wondering. Then N took the chain off the door and went out onto the porch, shutting the door behind her.

I sat with the little girl at the abandoned breakfast table, neither of us eating. Naomi didn't move, just eyed me for the first time like a stranger, as if the presence of her father had suddenly made it clear that I was not him. Outside in the drip of the rain, the pair of voices, his and hers, rose and fell, muted by the door to simple tones, one insistent, one pleading. Inside we were so quiet I could hear the Rice Krispies clicking to death in their bowl.

N came back in with a sharp intake of breath that made me wonder if she was going to cry. But as she closed the door, she exhaled sharply, as if to blow the impossible husband off her porch. She looked at me with her what-next? face.

"Where's Daddy?" cried Naomi, knowing the answer.

"He couldn't come in," said her mother.

The little girl wailed, "He never can!" and broke from the table, running into her room.

N sat back down, as if calmly. She took a sip of her coffee. I waited for what seemed like a decent interval, then asked, "What did he want?"

"Just . . ." she began, cheerfully enough, then without having anything easy to say, bit her lip and said, "Just nothing." That seemed final enough. What was so wrong with this guy? I wanted to ask. What did he do to become so impossible?

"He was soaking wet," N said. This she said to herself, I realized.

I got out of there as soon as I could. The situation was way beyond me. Maybe some guys could just charge in, drive off this pathetic wet husband, be the mother's lover and the daughter's father, but, at least for that moment, I was not that guy. I didn't say much to N, just that I had to get home. She seemed to understand. Maybe it was too soon for us to be dating, I wanted to say, but because I thought it would appear cowardly, I didn't. I walked out into the rain myself, half expecting to see hubby-what's-his-name still hanging around out there, dripping water from his hair. But he seemed to have vanished or dissolved.

I drove to the freeway and then south across the Golden Gate in the slosh and the beat of the wipers, second-guessing myself. I went home to my apartment, which seemed chilly and dark, to my unslept-in bed and my hungry cat, who did circles around my ankles as I fed her. I unplugged the phone. The cat slept in my lap as I watched football—the 'Niners hurling themselves onto frozen turf in Chicago. I felt that ache, strong now, in the top of my chest. When the game was over, I went back out into the rain, found a florist, and bought big red flowers for L. A goddamned blaze of glory, I was thinking.

9

A WAY OF SEEING

....

In the end, it was L who had called me. Would I come to her birthday party? she'd asked. She'd told me the date—Ground Hog Day—and the address. She lived on the top floor of a white building on top of the hill on Pierce Street. I had wanted to take her invitation lightly, though her call put me in mind of the summer and its untried possibilities. Once I knew where her apartment was, I seemed to notice it almost every day in the intervening weeks. I'd be on the ridge above Dolores Park, or driving down Oak in traffic, and I'd look up and there it would be, high and white against the trees of the little hilltop park called Alamo Square, her window a tiny dark square on the top floor.

The night of her birthday turned out to be the rainy Sunday of the wet husband. I went to her house with the flowers—a spray of scarlet gladioli—and as I was buzzed in, I felt a wave of dread, going alone to a party where I'd be a stranger and seeing her. In the elevator, the flowers were suddenly too much and too red.

The apartment door had a picture of Madonna beneath a white floral grid over the peephole. I listened a moment to the roar of talk and music inside, then knocked. A dark-haired woman who said she was L's roommate instantly took my flowers, saying that L would love them. Inside I found a foyer full of flowers. Not knowing what to do, I followed L's roommate back into the kitchen and watched her put the gladioli in a vase. I got a beer—which felt like a pass to the party—from the fridge.

The living room was crowded and loud, and in the uncurtained bay windows, the black winter night outside reflected back the party. I found L in the farther bay, wearing a cornflower blue dress, perfect for her eyes. She stood between two women, all three holding red wine in big glasses. I made my way over, noticing as I did several men standing on the peripheries with their beers—three or four solitary young guys, taking notice of me as I took notice of them.

When I got close enough to the three women, I realized they were talking in French. How pretentious, I thought at first. Then I realized I couldn't understand what they were saying, that they were speaking real French, good French, French as a language, not as an affectation. They were talking fast and telling jokes, and their speech was like a mountain brook. L didn't seem like the woman I'd known in the summer. She seemed transformed and cosmopolitan, and I just listened, dumbstruck, losing myself in the incomprehensible lilt of their musical and high-spirited talk as it rose with emphasis that broke like a wave into laughter, or surged around some qualification or uncertainty.

L finally noticed me and said hello. She said something else in French to the other women, and they looked my way, too. Then she introduced me, in English. One of the women turned out to be an Algerian friend; the other, visiting from France, knew no English at all. I raised my beer in mute greeting. I was a little daunted by them and couldn't join in, so I took the first opportunity to move away and perch on the couch, where I tried to seem to be enjoying myself.

The party surged and paused and surged again. Someone turned the music up and two couples danced. I met a guy who was taking the bar exam. Then L's roommate called us to attention, and we watched L unwrap her presents—clothes and CD's mostly. Finally, as the early retirees were already saying goodnight, I spoke to L alone.

"Where'd you learn to speak French like that?" I said. She'd lived in Paris as a child, she told me. I felt a rush of desire for her as she spoke.

I'd been to Paris, I said, for a week. From my trip to Paris, I remembered at that moment almost nothing, only the Eiffel Tower, which I recalled as frightening—vertiginous, exposed, girders and riveted steel beams plunging sickeningly towards some distant domesticated greenery. I didn't mention that.

I'd gone there as a travel writer, I said.

"Really?" she said. "That sounds great." She wanted to travel, she told me, and she wanted to be a writer.

"I'll tell you about it," I said. Then, encouraged by her interest, I added, "Maybe we could go there together sometime."

"That'd be great," she said, idly, just as a large young guy tapped her on the shoulder. He had to go. He just wanted to say goodnight and thanks. She turned to him, asking when she would see him again, as I went as if purposefully into the other room.

On my way home from the birthday party, I decided to try to forget about her. It had stopped raining by then, and I drove down the hill from her building brooding, over streets glistening and empty. She just wasn't like me, I thought. I never went out on Sunday nights, for one thing. But I felt a pang at dismissing the possibility. I imagined her body beneath the loose cornflower blue dress she'd worn, the way it would feel to draw my palm up her warm stomach, that feeling of smooth warmth I'd suddenly wanted while she spoke.

I wasn't in love with her, though, I thought. But I drove home feeling that glimmer, that hunger. She wasn't possible—daunting, pretty L in her blue silk dress—and I didn't want to respond. I could feel my fear of a beautiful woman's power—the power to inspire jealousy, for one thing. Every guy at that party seemed to be wearing the same expression. We'd stood around, mute, careful of our clumsiness, looking slightly stung—especially the younger guys who didn't know what they were feeling yet.

I didn't like younger guys, I thought. My twenties had been occupied by the sense that I was about to become complete as a person: out of school finally and surely by now an adult. The sense of being nearly complete led me to try to act as if I were. That was the smugness of men in their twenties. In my thirties I'd realized that for me at least there was no completion, that I would remain unsure, unclosed, which was okay, I'd thought at last. Just then, though, it occurred to me that maybe I was making a virtue of my own indecision. A writer, a perpetual observer, I was clinging to the ongoing as a way of ignoring the ungotten-to. And then I knew what I was really feeling: jealousy. I didn't need that, I thought vehemently, shifting gears as I crossed Market Street. I wasn't in love with her or anything. I was beyond being in love, and had been for years.

I climbed the hill at Twenty-first Street, trying to put off wanting her. I hit the electric garage-door opener and felt my desire come back. She seemed to like me. She seemed to radiate, before she'd pulled away, with something besides mere flirtation when we talked. Maybe we'd just sleep together sometime, I thought. Have a fond brief affair. Then I'd probably shock her by mentioning something from the seventies—the Carter Era. Might as well be the Cretaceous. I was in sixth grade then, she'd say, with a sort of amazed archaeological expression, then we'd awake to our differences and be off on separate lives, she to some law student, and me—with the memory of her at least—to some artist, a suitable veteran of the gender wars.

When the next weekend arrived, I went alone to see a slideshow by some Northwestern Native Americans, Haidas, who'd been commissioned to carve a totem pole in the Headlands. They presented their work at a gallery across the Mission from my apartment, and though it was raining lightly, I walked over, about ten blocks, getting there late. The lecture had already started. I stood in the back of a full house. The Haidas—three young men, who sat at a table in the front—had come down from British Columbia. They had the sincerity of country people and spoke without irony or qualification about their work. They worked with axes and power tools to make the traditional wooden objects— masks, totem poles, canoes—that had come down to them through thousands of generations of their tribe.

In the midst of this, I noticed L, sitting on the aisle in the second row, her chestnut hair suddenly special among the heads of the audience. I took a seat where I could watch her without her knowing, but she seemed to feel my gaze upon her and looked back, noticed me and smiled. She didn't seem surprised.

I smiled back, idiotically I thought, feeling a little caught. It hadn't occurred to me that she'd be there, though now that I thought about it, the art center where she worked was one of the sponsors of this event, and of course the staff would go to the lecture. It made me feel uneasy, as if I had a smarter self inside me who liked to play tricks. What did I really want?

The Haidas cut the lights in the room and began their presentation by projecting images of masks that they'd carved. The faces, wide-eyed, festooned with hair, were both fierce and funny. When the children watched dancers in these masks, said the speaker, they were scared at first, but then, when they saw that their elders weren't afraid, they came to love them. The fearsome characters were the gods of the enormous world, but who might allow you, finally, not just to survive, but to prosper.

L looked at me twice during the slideshow. The first time she looked, she found me looking at her, and made her cheerful, cut-it-out sort of face, both familiar and slightly mocking. I liked that one. The second time she looked, she looked to see if I was looking, and when I was, looked away so as not to encourage me.

The Haidas moved on to pictures of their totem poles—stacks of faces, their features struck elegantly into redwood: Wasco the Killer Whale, the Eagle, the Raven Stealing the Moon. The speaker described the placing of such a pole, a ritual in which the prostrate pole was first cleansed of evil spirits—one of the carvers circled it, shouting at the invisible demons—then placed in a hole in the ground and ponderously raised by all the men in the tribe.

By then I was impatient to talk to L. I'd been to a lot of slide-shows, and they always went on too long. Each picture yielded much more than a thousand words, as if the art became insolent under the narration, slipping, outflanking and contradicting it at every turn, and finally making it seem like so much vapor. Even these Haidas, speaking directly of their traditional images, couldn't keep up. Mercifully, after about an hour, the projector broke. The pictures would go backward but not forward. The audience was given a break and poured out into the lobby, bur- bling suddenly with their contained talk.

I waited at the verge of the crowd for L, but she didn't come out. I went back into the auditorium, but found only the Haidas, trying out the projector, and L's chair, significantly empty. I wound my way back through the crowd to the door and stepped out on the street. A group of smokers huddled on the wet side- walk, and beyond them, there she was, standing in her coat and looking into the traffic on Seventeenth Street. I walked over and asked if she was leaving. She was supposed to meet someone, she said.

"Oh," I said.

"Nan," she said. "From work. She hasn't shown up and I'm hoping to go." It'd been a long day, she added.

"I was thinking of leaving myself," I said. "But I don't have a ride." She had a car. Did she want to give me a lift across the Mission? No problem, she said.

She had a big, old, roaring blue Volvo. Both inner door panels in her car were damaged, I noticed. On the passenger side, the window crank was missing, and on the driver's side, the arm rest hung by one bolt, partially ripped from the door. "What are you," I said, "hard on handles?" I guess so, she said.

I couldn't think of anything else to say, and the trip across the Mission was too short to tell me anything, and in the end, when she pulled up in front of my building, I just had to take a chance and ask, on faith.

"Want to come up for a minute?" I said.

"Sure," she said. So we went up. I felt a little breathless climbing the stairs to the second floor, alone with L for the first time. I unlocked the door to my apartment, and we went in.

It had been some time since I'd had anybody over, and the place seemed different with her in it. The cat mewed for her new attention. I had a lot of rocks and branches around my house, stuff from trips, and these seemed outlandish to me at that moment, too much, even eccentric. What she saw immediately was the one object she recognized—a prop from Rudolfo's piece. It was a gold and black shield that sprouted tufts of untwined hemp rope. We looked at it together, remembered Rudolfo and laughed about the performance. I remembered her warm back beneath my fingertips as I'd painted her.

We went into the living room, which had one big overstuffed chair and a convertible futon couch that was for some reason down, open like a bed before us and shouting with suggestion. She sat in the overstuffed chair. I sat near her, crosslegged on the futon, talking about anything as I tried to figure out how to kiss her and whether she would mind. She complained about her job—it's art slavery, she said, working all day and half the night. I took this as a cue. "Here," I said. I took up one of her feet, put it in my lap, pulled off her shoe and began to rub it. She looked at me with a flat smile that suggested I was cute but weird, not to mention obvious.

But she let me rub her foot. After a moment she said, "That feels good."

"Good," I echoed, stunned into stupidity by my incredible luck and my cagey desire. "I'll do the other one in a minute." Her long, high-arched foot was nice to stroke, the top cool and smooth, the bottom warm and soft and a little moist. I recalled the way she lay those feet before her as she came across the meadow that first day. I pressed her heel with the ball of my thumb and kept talking, saying whatever to engage her, to help her forget about getting her foot away from me. Words poured from my mouth.

But she pulled her foot away anyway and said, "I should get going."

"Okay," I said. But when we got up, we stood close for an instant and I kissed her, almost without thinking. For a thrilling second she kissed me back.

Then she put a hand on my chest and said, "Don't get ideas."

"It's too late," I said. "I already have them."

"Well, forget them."

It seemed best not to push my luck. I felt even then that I had to release L to win her. So she put on her shoe, and I got her coat, and we went back downstairs and out into the damp night to her blue car, which I already felt fond of. She parted from me at the curb and walked around the car to the driver's side. I could wait, I was thinking happily.

But before she got in, she stopped, looked at me seriously and said something I didn't expect at all, something that cut out the ground beneath my triumph. She could never see me, she said, while I was seeing S. "She's a friend of mine," she said.

That stopped me—I couldn't even say that I hadn't seen S for months. "Anyway, goodnight," she added. Then she got into her car, pulled the door shut by its damaged handle and drove off down Guerrero Street. I went back upstairs, cursing my luck and my tiny town.

The next day I thought about what "seeing" meant. Who was I seeing and who was I not seeing, and how could I stop seeing someone I wasn't seeing. Had L meant she would see me? And what would it mean if she did?

I knew how I'd stopped seeing someone in the past. I just stopped calling and—as I conceived it—let the maelstrom of urban cultural life sweep us apart. As a free-lancer, I didn't work anywhere, and so the maelstrom was particularly strong in my case. I had to make a serious effort to stay in touch, or people would disappear for years, borne off by the drift, then suddenly and sometimes horribly reappearing in the supermarket or the DMV. But I didn't want to stop calling S and lose her in the maelstrom. We gabbed, we gossiped, we were buddies. "Seeing" reminded me of the problem I'd had with "love," in the sixties, when I "loved" everyone.

Finally I simply called L and declared that I was not seeing S anymore.

"What does that mean?" she said, hitting the nail on the head. I wasn't going to call her anymore, I said.

"Don't be so stupid," she said, laughing. She added that S was my friend.

"So what am I supposed to do?" I said.

"Do I know what you're supposed to do?" she said. She was so impossible and fabulous.

"Would you like to play tennis or something?" I said.

"In the daytime?" she said.

"In the daytime," I agreed.

L was in a manic mood the first time we played. She came out of the lobby of her building, hopping around in her sweats. She exclaimed "Tennis!" and charged into the park, where a single fenced court lay on flat ground at the top of the hill, under the cypresses. I caught up with her on the court and told her she looked gorgeous, whereupon she curled her lip to look ugly on purpose. "Let's hit!" she cried, and began bashing balls at me.

For the hour we never slowed down enough to play. "Hitting" was for L a more intense matter than tennis, I understood. In tennis, you got to stand around, bounce the ball before you served, chat. As L played it, "hitting" was a game about running around a lot, hitting as hard as you could and continuing the ball in play. Once I recognized the pattern, I suggested we formalize it by calling it "ten times." The ball had to go over the net ten times before anything counted. Even then she wouldn't keep score, which was fine with me, it turned out—after a few strokes I could tell that if we ever slowed down enough to play tennis, she'd probably win. Her backhand especially had wonderful, hard precision. Down the line or crosscourt, she could put me away.

We played like this for an hour. She was a frenetic delight, shouting and jumping around on the pine-needled court. By the end we were both shouting and jumping around as we jogged back to my car and her door. "Thanks!" she shouted, heading for her door. "Wait!" I shouted. "Let's at least shower together or something."

"For sure," she said, mocking me, then called, "See you," and was gone.

There was that word again, I thought. "See you" was simply an idiom, a social stroke, the way "How are you?" was. Did she mean that she wanted to see me again? That I should keep trying? She might have, I thought, and that was enough.

Later that week I got home late at night and there, on my answering machine, was a message from L. She just wanted to say hello, she said. Then she added, in her teasing tone, "I guess you're out with your other girlfriend," and hung up. I played it over a couple of times, listening for nuances, then began leaping around the apartment, whooping and scaring the cat.

Then the campaign for L began in earnest. The rules were only that it would be athletic and in the daytime only. So we did play more tennis, or ten times, or whatever it was. We ran on Ocean Beach and went for crumpets at a place she knew in the Avenues. By then I was so crazy for her that I was wounded when she said hello to the waiter. And by then I knew her well enough to know that she didn't like that aspect of me. My need to possess her was obvious, and she wanted no part of being possessed. I recognized that, and left off. That was the key, actually.

And we began to kiss and fumble—in the lobby of her apartment and on the beach, where she laughed and ran away, mock screaming. She'd let me start, then she'd say no, and I'd stop. I'd act like I could take it or leave it. This was difficult for me, and she saw it for the ruse it was. Still, she became gentler in her refusals, even saying after stopping me in the car once, "You must think I'm the Ice Queen."

"The Dairy Queen, more like," I said, starting the car.

And then all at once, she seemed to decide. She came home with me, and I could tell it was time, and it took the wind out of me. We went to bed. After so much buildup, I was stunned into silence, serious in my lovemaking, passionate. Happy in the sheets, she said, "You were so quiet. For some reason, I thought you'd do a lot of yelling."

That next week we went to get our blood tested. It was my suggestion. We'd been safe, but it seemed like a good idea in the urban maelstrom. We went to a clinic in the Castro on a street called Prosper. I'd been there before, in 1986, during a bout of despair when I'd become convinced I had AIDS. I'd still be negative, I knew, but I wanted to prove it to her. L had her own fears, wondering about men in her past. In the clinic we went to separate booths to have our blood drawn. I could hear her, joking with the nurse to ease the anxiety of the needle and what it meant. When we were done, the guy at the exit desk gave us one ticket for our return visit, writing both our codes on it. We chose our initials and our ages, and he gave us a yellow card with those designations and a date two weeks away for our return appointment. Then we went to dinner at the Zuni Cafe, but halfway through I felt exhausted, and I noticed she looked tired as well. I dropped her off at her apartment, went home to my own and slept deeply that night. In the morning she woke me with a phone call. "You think we're going to die?" she said, instead of hello.

Two weeks later, when we went back, we went separately to the booths to get our results. When I came back out, negative as I'd assumed, she was still in there. I stood around on the linoleum, wondering what I was going to do if she got bad news. When she came out her face betrayed nothing. Then she whispered, "Negative." We drove to my house before we let ourselves express anything. It hadn't seemed right to celebrate in the Castro, but once inside we danced around in the sunny kitchen, shouting that we were going to live.

After that I was certain that we were seeing each other, though what else we were, I wasn't sure. In the old days, I might have let my sense of possession reside in sex, but that confidence had slipped away in the eighties, when sex had gotten easier. L especially didn't seem possessed simply because we'd been to bed. And to possess her was what I wanted. So I was beginning to wonder how I might accomplish this when one morning I found amidst my mail a thick envelope from the French Government Tourist Office.

10

THE MASTER OF THE
PLACE DE LA CONTRESCARPE

That week we walked in Paris, and I was still hopeful about possessing her, though I began noticing the dogs of France. These dogs were everywhere, but nowhere you'd expect. I'd never thought about French dogs much, maybe just poodles. Rin Tin Tin, Old Yeller, those were American dogs, friendly dogs with wide tongues, their coats glowing from the big outdoors. But there were all kinds of dogs everywhere in Paris, dogs who ate in restaurants and understood French. They were dignified characters. In America the dogs were still barking and begging, jumping up. Here even the street mutt lying next to his owner's vegetable stand might not have appeared ridiculous wearing a beret.

The master of the Place de la Contrescarpe, for instance, was a droopy, traffic-blackened brown hound, keeping watch beneath the sunny southern-facing wall of the square. Happy and interested in everything that day, I noticed this dog as we ate lunch on the Place, *salade niçoise* for L, *croque monsieur* for me.

The Place was the dog's turf. He lay beneath the placard of a pub called Le Morte Subite Que Vous Propose and with an arch expression made his lookout. He noticed a Yorkie enter the square at the opposite corner, on a stylish woman's leash, and watched the flippant intruder through the wheels of the traffic until the other dog had departed, then rose and nosed around the busy plaza, marked the spot with piss and as unobtrusively withdrew, settling and tucking his legs under him and resuming his watch beneath the placard.

Across the square at our little white table, I remarked to L at the dignity of this dog, its independence among people. "People are like cars to this dog," I said. "Just moving objects in the world of other dogs."

I was the lucky dog, in Paris with L. At lunch everything was of course delicious, and we were hopeful and happy with our cancelled obligations to one another. L seemed happy, anyway, and I hoped that her happiness might bloom into something like what I was feeling.

L didn't like dogs much. "There's no dogs allowed in the Luxembourg," she said, speaking of the park. "And that's a good thing, too."

"You don't like dogs for the same reason you don't like me," I said.

"Believe it," she said, laughing.

On the Rue Mouffetard she got an outfit. She tried several on, emerged from the dressing room each time, brightly transformed and modeling for stunned me as I sat in a chair and liked, unhelpfully, each new outfit.

I hadn't completely imagined what it would feel like, being in France, I thought as she changed again, the pomaded clerk handing her further clothes over the swinging door. France was so much more all-encompassing than I'd imagined. In California, France was only a place on the globe, a cluster of associations that might apply to me. But now I was in France, among France, immersed in France, which was vast and real. There was no way of approximating it if you weren't there. And no way of counting on it, I thought—it was too big, too rich simply to mean what I wanted it to mean.

L emerged in Balinese silk culottes and a matching blouse in burnt orange with a subtle gold, black and green pattern, she, too, suddenly seeming beyond my intentions. The blouse bared her midrift here and there as she moved. "Something for the South," she said, though she decided to wear the outfit out of the shop into the warm afternoon.

Then in this Indonesian brilliance on the narrow sidewalk of the Rue Vavin, sexy and resplendent L walked fast as usual, striding through the crowd of shoppers. I kept up as she crossed the street and plunged into the green dogless Luxembourg Gardens. There beneath the bright canopy of the stately, rectilinear trees, sunlight lay calmly on the grass as in a Seurat, and children shouted, their cries claiming the air.

11

THE BASTARD WITH

PRIORITY

Old rascal God cast a fit on the emperor's daughter, and the poor girl in her delusion took her treasure down to the sea and tossed it in, a disaster for the royal dowry. Later and far off, in the land of Israel, Akiba, famous by now, was having his own effect upon women. God's servant Akiba, big, bald and attractive, had gone forth into the world and had become a great rabbi with his own academy, not to mention something of a ladykiller. Once Akiba needed money for his school and approached a rich woman of the town for a loan, and in asking so charmed her that she declared she would take only God and the sea for collateral.

Time passed, as it does in stories, and the day arrived upon which the loan came due, and the rich woman, who is not named in the legend, prepared to receive the great rabbi. But the sun went down, and Akiba did not come. Crushed and furious, the woman rushed out of her house and ran to the shore of the dark ocean. "Sovereign of the Universe!" she shouted at God. "Thou knowest that to thee and to the sea I did entrust my wealth!" Obedient and timely, the waves tossed up a treasure chest at her feet. Or so say the Sages.

Illiterate at forty, Akiba began his reading of the Torah not with Genesis, but, as was traditional, with the Book of Leviticus, which detailed among other things the ordination of priests, the ritual of the scapegoat and the treatment of lepers and menstruating women. Necromancers must be stoned, ordains Leviticus. Both sexes must wash after intercourse. Each category in the book foliates with rules and regulations, the commandments of Yahweh to Moses regarding purifications of all kinds. So Akiba learned to read Hebrew, as did all students of the Torah, from this complex legal document. From there, he went on to Adam and Eve.

Akiba must have known by then the difficulty of learning anything beyond one's youth, must have felt that he had to part the steel curtains of habit and make time to learn. Acquiring a language at forty seems especially excruciating. But Akiba bulled into his chore, learning these symbols for language, a new tongue for him, in several years of study. She'd said, "Become a scholar," and so he had begun. But to continue as a scholar meant joining the academy, and joining the academy meant abandoning his wife with the children in that hard time. Still, he was not a man to leave off, once he had begun—this determination after all had won her in the first place. And it was more than simple ambition and Rachel's insistence that finally led him away from her. Reading the Torah, one might move from the particulars of one's own existence toward the absolute, the mind of God. In the end, say the rabbis, Rachel gave him her blessing when he left. She'd see him just once in the next twenty-five years.

. . .

Life in the Jewish academy was rigorous, a continuous intellectual tournament among young men for superiority in learning. To become a master was first to know the Torah so thoroughly that no one could challenge you on scripture, and only secondly to discover—and debate—God's will in it. Akiba of the Amme haarez, a grown man who had beaten scholars—literally—brooked a challenge from no one, even from the authorities, it appears. In the course of his studies, he was summoned before the chief rabbi and punished, says the record, more than forty-five times.

One day the teacher seemed to brag a little. This rabbi had spoken often of an uncle who was lame, and on this day the teacher, reminiscing of his uncle and the old days, said his uncle had blown the shofar at the temple in Jerusalem. In fact, claimed the rabbi, his uncle had blown the shofar on Sukkoth, the festival of the booths.

Not true, piped up Akiba. Silence fell over the students. Your uncle, he said, blew the horn only in the informal ceremony outside the Temple. The teacher was dumbfounded at his student's insolence. Imagine, he must have thought. Instructing me in my own story!

Akiba explained. "The law is," he said, "that only the whole in body can blow the shofar at the Temple. The teacher's lame uncle could not have done so." And hearing this the rabbi fell silent, for he had suddenly recalled.

This was the time of the Sages, and among the laws they formulated for the nation was this one: "If the bastard is learned in the Law, and the high priest is ignorant," they ruled, "the bastard has priority." So the student Akiba excelled at the academy, despite his rebellious bent. When he proved expert in arguing the Mishnah—the painstaking codification of Hebrew Oral Law—then he was that bastard with priority.

He had a great advantage, being an outsider. His colleagues, more invested in the society, were more fixed in their ideas, even after its demise. Akiba had no allegiance to ideas that no longer mattered, and the great task before them then was to remake the nation. In this work, he was a bull breaking down the fences, restless and ready to question that which the complacent orthodox might have left alone. Ultimately he would be known as a Sage of Sages, a founding father and a martyr. Finally, his name would be mentioned in the same breath with Hillel, whom he followed. Like Hillel, his guiding light as a scholar and a teacher was love. Once challenged to recite the whole Torah in a single sentence, Hillel said only, "Love thy neighbor as thyself."

Echoing Hillel, Akiba wrote that the fundamental principle of the law was love. It's not clear what he meant by this. He seems not to have been thinking of his old calling, of love between a man and a woman as it appears in the Song of Songs, but of his new one, of love as one's devotion to God, to the absolute. Love's expression, he wrote, was worship.

Twelve years passed, goes the story told of him by the rabbis, before Akiba returned home. He walked unrecognized through his old village. Nearing his own house, he overheard his wife speaking in the street. For whatever reason, he did not reveal himself to her, but stood quietly nearby and eavesdropped. A neighbor was asking Rachel, as always, about her husband. By now he was a famous rabbi, and still he hadn't returned.

The rabbis say that Rachel answered, "If my husband would double his learning, I would wait another twelve years." So Akiba turned away and walked back to his academy, like Odysseus returning to the sea.

In A.D. 90, Akiba was called to the Council of Jamnia, the body of scholars given the weighty task of deciding what the word of God would be, what would and would not be included in the new Bible. Certainly the Pentateuch was sacred. And so were the

Nevi'im, the prophetic works, but which of the Writings would be included? In particular, what would be done about the Song of Songs? So Akiba was present among the seventy-two elders who took up the matter of this erotic work, never officially sanctioned for inclusion in the canon. The rigorist Palestinian school of Shammai opposed the Songs; the Babylonian school of Hillel supported them. The debate would center on the insoluble issue of what the Song meant.

In neither source nor structure did the Song lend itself to its own defense. There is, as was noted, no mention of God in the book, and as a literary work it is chaotic, a profusion, an organic riot that has baffled scholars for centuries. "The Song of Songs is an enigma," begins its treatment in the compendium called *The Interpreter's Bible.* "There is no agreement among scholars as to its author or its interpretation." Contemporary commentators view the work as an anthology of ancient love poems, but no one can agree where one poem in the work ends and another begins, or how many love poems are included overall. Current scholarly estimates range from thirty-five down to five, with some scholars, Robert Graves among them, seeing no need to divide the work at all.

The language itself inflamed the debate. In part because the book is so ancient—even by Biblical standards—the Song of Songs has its own lexicon, bears more unique instances of words than any other book in the Bible. More than a hundred words remain mysterious, their meanings guessed at from cognates but never satisfactorily rendered out of their quirky and cryptic actuality.

The work's ancientness, too, is no doubt in part responsible for its complex structure. Material has been deleted, dropped in, added on. The book seems to end at least twice. The work of generations of scribes, it was subject to errors, interpolations, editing, scribal creativity. As in geological strata, its parts piled up, eroded and collided over the generations of collection and transmission. Almost every assumption about its meaning must be qualified by this ancientness, by the wear, as it were, on the words.

The organic structure of the Song bears a gathering of voices, no one rising above the rest, as authority or narrator. "It is the only book in the Bible," notes *The Interpreter's Bible*, "to have all its content put into the mouths of speakers." A royal procession—a king borne upon his palanquin, or couch, with a train of attendants—mysteriously enters and exits the work. From its first lines, the book is protean, its pronouns shifting in number and gender: "Let him kiss me with the kisses of his mouth, for your love is better than wine." Most translators have emended these lines to keep a consistent second-person address, though the shifts throughout the Song suggest a method, a washing in and out of identity, a repeated gesture from distant to intimate. Even the title of the book is both collective and particular, singular and plural.

There are certainly particular ancient voices within the work, and we may identify them as both female and male. "I will rise now and go about the city," a woman seems to sing. "I will seek him whom my soul loves." The Song celebrates a woman's desire as well as a man's, and their gifts for one another. And there seems not to be just one woman and one man, but all kinds of women and all kinds of men. The voices have a tonal range that seem to come from all strata of society. The speakers, as Norman Gottwald notes, might be rustics playing nobles or nobles playing rustics. Female and male appear as bride and groom, courtesan and king, shepherdess and shepherd. In this way, though perhaps by accident (this sense of range in the work, of a human spectrum presented, may simply have occurred as poems of various kinds were saved in its collection), the poem conforms to the literary genre of travesty.

To some this welter of voices suggests that the work is a play of sorts, the libretto for some lost opera. These commentators make much of marginal notations of two Greek manuscripts, copied about A.D. 450, more than a thousand years after the Songs were first written down. These notes identify speakers of the verses in the margins: a bride and bridegroom, choruses, a king. The Greeks saw drama in text easily by then, of course, and the poem's profusion gave them plenty to go on.

First and foremost a mystery, the Song of Songs has always provided fertile ground for interpretation. At almost every level of analysis, the Song of Songs is confused—fused together, undifferentiated. All this unaccountable flourishing befits a celebration of love and fertility, of course, the book suggesting a tangle of tendrils and fruit, its repetitions too random to be called refrains, its voices rising, calling, falling away, perhaps responsive, perhaps contradictory, perhaps simply nearby.

But no matter what else it was to the Academy, it was plenty to go on. For confusion only seems to frustrate interpretation. To the scholars, debate on the Songs was a free-for-all. Opponents used the obscurity to suggest their own meanings in it—where it bore none, it might bear all, patterns seeming to rise from it, as bidden.

Akiba became the champion of the Song. One might assume that it spoke, in its passion and praise for love, to Akiba's inner heart. Akiba the late convert and anarchic rigorist must have found the work's unboundedness—its wild energy—attractive. Surely this quality alone warranted its inclusion in the canon.

Apparently not. At least this was not his argument, which would have failed in any case. The challenge for those who would include the Song in the canon was to justify it to the Law. And whatever else it was, the Song of Songs was no Leviticus—though they gave a name to human love, they did not describe, for instance, the strictures for purifying union, nor detail who may marry whom, nor what the bride-price should be, nor what role parents or rabbis might have. In many ways, the Song of Songs is at the opposite pole from Leviticus. The poem seems to thwart authority and distinction at every turn, just as its imagery abandons the tight rooms and streets of the city for the garden or, more often, for the wild green places, oases in the desert.

Further, the Songs could not hold the day as a mere collection of love songs, especially as women's love songs together with men's love songs. This was profane and violated the Sages' assumptions about women. The Sages had ruled, for instance, that "the saving of a man's life takes priority over a woman's." Akiba's record as a judge suggests his priorities on issues concerning women. He lifted restrictions on use of cosmetics during menstruation, for instance, granting them, after a fashion, greater liberty. Though intercourse was forbidden during menstruation, Akiba felt that it was important for women to remain attractive to their husbands. He also ruled that a man might divorce his wife if he found himself attracted to a more beautiful woman. A man's liberty, to behold and possess beautiful women—this was of prime importance.

Judging from the debate on the Songs of Songs, we find a similar justification, which seems at first to honor the work, but which finally places it within a context that reduces its meaning. In the matter of the Song of Songs, Akiba's argument was brilliant, his ploy simple and devastating. He first announced to the assembled body of scholars that the Song of Songs was sacred. Anyone who sang the Song for the sake of entertainment, trilling their voices as though they were profane, he proposed, "would have no place in the next world." He called the Song the "Holy of

Holies"—equating it to the inner sanctum of the temple itself—
and said that there was nothing in the world to equal the day on
which it was given to Israel.

When this point was accepted by the council, everything else
followed rather easily. Declared sacred, the work quickly found
an appropriate meaning. The Songs, it was decided, would be
included in the canon with the special understanding that the
book was not literal, not a collection of secular love songs, but a
divine tract, and that the love celebrated in it was not between
individuals, but between the nation and the Lord. And so the
Song was saved as a kind of national anthem, not as a glorifica-
tion of desire and fertility and boundlessness, but as a justification for the state and its authorities, interpreters of and surrogates
for the Lord. So the love in the Song was made to reflect the love
of the Sages for their own power.

In the ensuing centuries, commentators would set to work,
fleshing out the meaning for the Song that the Lord had given to
them. In their hands, the poem became an allegorical procession
of abstract ideas instead of a profusion of sexual flowers. The
pomegranates weren't pomegranates, it turned out. They were
symbols, said the medieval interpretive text called the Targum,
for the descendants of Israel, as full of good deeds as is the fruit
of seeds. The animals of the field by whom oaths of love are
repeatedly sworn in the work, creatures sacred to the fertility
goddess Asherah, these were merely mistranslations. The original
word, which might have been taken for gazelles, said the commentators, was actually a common title for Yahweh.

And when, some centuries later, the Torah became the Old
Testament of the Christians, they, too, adopted this institutional
perspective on the Song of Songs, excluding any literal interpretation, and reading the work as the delineation of Christ's love for
his Church. "For my head is drenched with dew, my hair wet with
the night" reads the Song. Explains one Christian commentator:

"At that time the Church was as full of superstition as the grass is with the nightly dew." So, lacquered with institutional gloss, the Song survived the censors and the centuries.

A cynical, modern and romantic reader might be forgiven for thinking that Akiba's argument for the Song was strategic, not heartfelt; that in order to save the Song for the canon, he defended it with the one argument that he knew would persuade the Council. To many, it seems not quite credible that he believed this interpretation himself. After all, the work was beloved by the Amme haarez from time immemorial. And Akiba was of the Amme haarez himself, a wily outsider whose identification with the land of the pomegranate must have claimed his first and deepest loyalty. The Encyclopedia Judaica argues that Akiba's defense of the Songs showed his "independence of spirit." Otherwise, say the editors, "he could have never perceived an allegory expressive of the love between the Almighty and his beloved Israel in what is ostensibly a romantic dialogue."

Surely we can still see him wink, down through the centuries, having saved the Song for us. But the evidence seems otherwise. By then he had given over his power, and his mind to the absolute, as men like himself had defined it. He might qualify the Song for eternity, but only if it too served this absolute. We can't know this, of course. We can only rely on the record, which was kept to justify that same way of seeing.

One legend of the Sages describes Akiba's ultimate return to Rachel. By then he went nowhere alone, and so walked back to his village among a multitude of twenty-four thousand disciples. When Rachel tried to make her way through the crowd to greet him, they refused to let her pass, thinking her, as a woman, unclean. When Akiba saw this, he commanded his multitude, saying, "Make way for her, for my learning—and yours—are hers." The Sages intended this tribute to show his gratitude, to stand as repayment to Rachel for her sacrifice, though somehow it seems a little cold. He may thank her, though he may not come home. He has disappeared in service to his nation, his absolute, as has the Song of Songs, which once married them, perhaps. One imagines another ending, in which he returns alone. Were they ultimately reunited? This, not being important to the Sages, isn't stated.

And what of the Song itself? By the nineteenth century, the standard interpretation had begun to be eroded by the recognition of its obvious erotic character. At that point a new reading arose—or to be exact an obscure twelfth-century French reading was revived—and began to be favored, especially in America. This version, conducted as a gloss upon the text, is a melodrama, with all the trappings of a dime novel for the age of Dickens, the tale of a damsel in distress. Writing in 1857, Christian Ginsburg summarizes this view. The Song describes a humble maiden taken away from her beloved, an equally humble shepherd, into the court of King Solomon. The commentator fleshes out this reading with his own romantic detail: "Struck by the beauty of this damsel, the king conducted her into his tent." The King tempts her to transfer her affections by showing her the splendor and luxuries of royalty. She does not, of course, succumb to these royal blandishments, but remains faithful to her betrothed, desiring only "that he whom she had prized above all things should come and rescue her." He does, of course, and the Song stand, in the end, as "an example of virtue in a young woman."

In our own time, though the erotic content of the Song may now be acknowledged, it has come to seem merely bits, broken pieces of something. Scholars find them fragmentary, artifacts like shards of some ancient urn, inconclusive and incomplete, "a variegated collection of types of love poems," as Marcia Falk writes, "that did not all necessarily derive from a single author or serve the same function in their original society." The Song, which began on earth and was applied to heaven, has descended to be distributed among us, each to each. For now we, too, are in fragments. We, too, look into the Song of Songs, and what we are, we find.

12

Found Poems

....

When the invitation from the French Government Tourist Office arrived, it was like an echo of the decade: outwardly promising and secretly encumbered, apparently expensive and ostensibly free. Printed in script on thick, creamy paper, it requested the pleasure of my company at a luncheon for writers. It was to be the Year of the French Provinces, it said. An RSVP card was enclosed. I put the invitation and the card on the kitchen table and left them there as I ate lunch, imagining our names on the card, just to see how they'd look. Not quite right, I decided—not as good as our encoded initials had looked together on the clinic ticket. It wouldn't be quite true, I knew, though it might work. I couldn't resist. In France, maybe she would give me her French self, and I would feel, finally, that I had won her.

That afternoon I took the invitation into the bedroom and put it by the phone, then waited for her to get off work. At the time she was working out in the Avenues for a company that made audio tapes of various natural environments—the rain forest, the mountain brook, the desert at dawn and the like. When I figured she'd be home, I called her and told her about the invitation. I'd received them before, I said, and I knew what they meant. What? she said. It means if we want to, we can go to France together, I said. They were recruiting.

She didn't believe it. I'd done it before, I said, in the early eighties. It was a scam.

"Why don't you do it all the time," she asked, "if it's so easy?" I explained that sometimes there were strings attached.

"But I'm telling you, we could do it." I said. "If we went to this lunch and told them we were interested in doing an article or a book or something about France, they would arrange for us to go."

"No," she said.

"You want to go to this lunch anyway, just to see?" I said. She guessed so.

We talked in a playful way about what we'd do if it were true. You could be the translator, I said. No way, she said. She'd be a writer. She'd do her own story.

"Okay, we'll both be writers," I said. "That's better, actually." After I got off the phone, I wrote in our names, where I had imagined them on the RSVP card. Beneath the names, there was a blank on the card for "Company." "LJ Media," I wrote. It still didn't look quite right.

When the day arrived, I put on a blue suit—the first time I'd worn a tie in months—and went to the luncheon. It was held downtown, at Pierre, a glossy French restaurant, all brass rails and mirrors, in the Meridien Hotel. I went through the receiving line of French public relations people at the door, smiling, saying I was part of a local writing team, and when I met the director, I told him we were interested in doing some work on Provence, and that we'd write him a letter. When he nodded I knew that my work at the luncheon was essentially done.

In the crowded lobby I searched for L, couldn't find her, and so I stood around drinking the Kir Royale until she came in, gorgeous in a cream-colored suit and getting a lot of charming attention from the men in the line. She smiled back—with her teeth only—and looked around for me a little desperately. I had to laugh when she found me. "You didn't tell me about that!" she whispered. "I couldn't remember the name of our company."

At the table we found our place cards at opposite ends, and so I ate my delicate lunch, which was composed on the big white plate like a minimalist painting, and watched L eat hers, attended by a young French hotelier. At our table were other writers, including a well-known novelist who was almost always present at these functions, I recalled. Also in attendance were editors from most of the local magazines.

Someone at the head table clinked a knife against his crystal wine glass and silenced us. The director rose to speak, toasting to the heavens our lunch and our illustrious gathering, also our great countries, France and America, and the deep-rooted ties between them. "Dip-rutted dyes," he said. I looked at L, but she could no longer look at me and keep a straight face.

She had to leave early to go back to work, and I watched her go, then excused myself and left also. I found her outside, leaning against the pink granite wall of the building. When she saw me, she collapsed in laughter. She'd been playacting the whole time, she said, telling people she was a writer.

"Well, you do write," I said. She didn't know how easy it was simply to announce what you wanted to be and have people believe it.

"Well, it isn't true to me yet," she said.

"Don't worry," I said. "I know about this. Whatever we said we are is what we are." This sentence I was to recall.

I drove her back to work. She still couldn't believe that they were actually going to send us to France. She denied it over and over as we drove, and each time she did, she came closer to believing it. By the time we got to her workplace, she seemed to look at me differently. Before she got out of the car, she kissed me sweetly. "Team," I said. It already filled me with hope, this French trip. "You better decide that you really want to go," I called before pulling away from the curb. "Because we're really going."

As the summer went on, I tried to make it real for her. I showed her the letters I sent on LJ Media stationery. I mailed her a copy of the itinerary I'd proposed to the French Government Tourist Office. Still, she remained apart from it until, one day in July, I put the plane tickets in her hand. Then she only looked a little shocked. And in the last week before we left, it seemed to come home to her that we were going to be together for almost a month in France, and she kept away from me, hiding out among her women friends. I, of course, was feeling victorious and smug.

We took a shuttle bus to the airport when the day arrived, and were sent into the first-class lounge at the gate. I'd expected someone there to meet us, but the only other people in the leather couches were a couple with two kids watching the 'Niners in a preseason game on the big TV. I'd expected free drinks, but there were no free drinks.

It was to the be last of the free trips, and the end of the eighties. I'd invented myself in that decade. I'd come to the city in 1980, sick of my own intentions and enamored of almost anything foreign, which the city seemed to proffer at every turn. Before that, living in a small Midwestern town, a place with a water tower and cornfields a ten-minute walk away, I'd written my poems, expressing myself. Then suddenly in San Francisco, in the midst of a conglomeration of cultures and voices, I felt as if nothing I could say could be as distinctive, as gorgeously ungainly, as surprising, as exactly mysterious and as expressive as what I found all around me. On Church Street I found a note from a man to a woman, a threatening and pleading message. The couple had evidently had sex together, and now he didn't want anyone to know about it. Her friends would kill him if they found out, he thought. "Hay girl," he began, "that if you say I alone with you, then you wants to kill me, right? Why don't you do it now?" My poems had begun as small memorials, lyrical, melancholy and—I hoped—universal. But by then they had turned into experiments with abstract combinations of words and phrases attempting only some kind of suggestion and verbal excitement so as to invoke the "other" by refusing to be explicit about anything.

When I found this note, it seemed perfect. It was only semiliterate, and if I hadn't taught freshman English for a time, I never would have been able to decipher it at all. But it had power. It had otherness. When people who didn't often write did so, I realized, they wrote because something important—sometimes life itself—was at stake, and this note was infused with that urgency. "I'm not your kind of human," the note read, closing with the surprisingly cool and literate-seeming sentence, "I will try to forget the words." I titled the note and arranged it into lines, and it became the first of many such poems that I would find in that decade. I overheard a security guard talking about being beaten by his father back in Alabama and wrote down what he said verbatim. A friend's phrases, as she complained to me on the telephone about taxes and relationships, suddenly seemed numinous and profound. Only one editor ever liked any of these poems enough to publish them, and when I showed them to a class of poets at Stanford, they were dismissed out of hand, but at the time I felt they were my best work, work that honored and reflected the world—indeed that *was* the world—and compared to which most poetry was mumbling and presumption.

While I was producing these poems, I was becoming a free-lancer for a living, a writer of prose for newspapers. Arriving in the city, I'd looked through the newspaper for a section that might accommodate me and had found at first only the book review. But book reviewing for a living was not exactly a stunning proposal, I would learn, especially as it took me weeks to read a book carefully. I was assigned Norman Mailer's gigantic book on ancient Egypt, finally, and that was the killer. After that I gave it up in despair and began writing press releases for a small production company working South-of-Market that made videos for MTV. I spent all night on Alcatraz with the German heavy metal band called the Scorpions, freezing while they ad-libbed their script. This didn't seem like it, either. Finally I landed another assignment in the neighborhood. I wrote a Philippine Foods catalogue, working from the pictures only. Everything had to be delicious, of course, though I could neither taste the food nor read the labels.

Then I learned about travel writing at a writer's conference. There I met Murray, who'd arrived in San Francisco a couple of years before. He was to my newcomer's eyes a Titan, an amazing specimen, a levitation artist. I'd even seen his byline in the Pink, I said, referring to the Sunday entertainment section.

"I've got bigger problems than bylines," he said, then changed the subject, asking what I'd been doing lately. I was a book reviewer, I said.

Murray had been doing travel. He'd just done a piece entitled "The World's Most Perfect Deserted Island" and had gone to Curaçao and the Seychelles and somewhere else. I was astonished and jealous, having never traveled anywhere, except to California. "The best thing about being a book reviewer," said Murray, rubbing it in, "is getting free books. The best thing about being a travel writer is getting free trips." He'd been sent to these places, he explained, by countries eager for publicity.

Six months later I was standing on a cliff on the South Island of New Zealand. I looked out at the broad, slate gray expanse of water, still in disbelief over how easy it had been to get there. I asked a man nearby what ocean it was. He looked at me as if I were crazy, as if I'd asked in what century we lived, and exclaimed, "The Tasman, of course."

In those days it began to seem as though the world had reached some sort of critical mass, every bit colliding with every other bit. And one might surf on the chaos, finding poems everywhere. And travel writing, too, seemed right; it seemed that I had found the only place in the newspaper that might accommodate my new dedication to whatever happened.

But free trips turned out not to be, exactly. The best places wouldn't publish junket stories, first of all, and you never got away from the PR people, whose job was to make sure that you never actually saw anything except what they intended for you to see. Found poet that I was then, trying to ban intention from my work, I found this sort of thing was intolerable. Even on my first trip to New Zealand, I'd realized what had to be done.

I ran away. I'd proposed to hike into seacoast wilderness near Nelson, on the South Island, and had found myself saddled with an itinerary and a guide who was loading me down with press releases and booking appointments in town. So on the second day of the trip, I simply got up before dawn, packed my rucksack and walked into the bush, coming out a week later and making my own way to the airport, where I was met by the anxious agent. I thanked him briskly and went on through customs. By the way he looked as I left, I knew I was in trouble. What could they do? Only never again give me a free trip halfway around the world. I had a higher calling and so felt no guilt.

Though it was difficult and embarrassing to turn free trips into actual travel, I had to do it. Junkets didn't put you in the presence of the other. I realized this on a day in Malaysia, which I spent walking around a gigantic hole in the red earth beneath a broiling tropical sun as an extremely friendly and officious young woman entreated me to envision the convention center that would be placed in the hole the following year. The next morning I disappeared for two weeks, off to the outer islands as government agents searched the mainland for me.

Then one last trip convinced me that it wasn't worth it. I'd gone to Ireland, where their canny PR people had made it impossible to escape. They brought me over with a group of writers, picked us up in a van at the airport and then didn't let us out of their sight for the next week as we blitzed around the Emerald Isle, stopping at tourist attractions and souvenir shops and pubs where they'd buy us ale and Irish whiskey, then put us back, bleary, on the bus. What I saw of Ireland was a green blur beyond the hedgerows as we raced along country lanes to make the next stop on our loaded itinerary. We got off to kiss the Blarney stone, get a press release, have a beer, then got back on. On the road, as we raced along, the other travel writers, veterans all, topped each other with stories about eating bear's lips in Beijing or windsurfing in Tahiti. When I complained to an older writer that I couldn't get any writing out of the trip, he confessed that he didn't usually write anything. "They never check," he said.

"So you just do this for the sheer fun of it, I guess," I said. That's right, he said.

Finally one afternoon at a pub, I asked one of the Irish PR guys to let me off the bus the next day. I'd find a story and make my own way back to the airport, I proposed. They couldn't let me do that, he said. They feel that they'd failed as hosts. Instead, they simply tried to make the whole trip more fun for me. That night at a medieval theme park in a real castle, I was crowned king of the banquet, wrapped in an ermine cape and placed on an elevated throne. I sat on high, furious and depressed, refusing my supper. Afterward they told me that I'd looked like a real king up there.

In the end I had to stop finding poems, too. I'd gotten good at it. I could listen, I was alert to possibilites, and so had become adept, despite myself, at finding poems that said what I would have said, anyway. I had completed the loop and was expressing myself again. So the whole thing began to seem absurdly round-about. I might as well just stay home and start with the word "I," I thought, and when I did, I found that my own voice seemed a little foreign to me, as if, after so much practice, I could now "find" my own thoughts, now placed somehow at a distance from me.

Emerson called travel a fool's paradise, and by the end I had to think he was right. I'd held myself so faithfully to the flux, the rush, in the name of the other, but I hadn't reached it. What had I wanted, anyway? To find the world unmarked by my own names for it. And what had I done? I'd named it at every turn. So my life finally took on a curiously stultified quality, which arose from its frenetic change of scenes. No matter where I went, my apartment seemed empty and still when I returned, filled up though it might be with souvenirs, mostly rocks and branches. By the time I went to Israel, I knew that at home or among foreign multitudes I was alone. And at last it began to occur to me that if I truly wanted a trip to a foreign place, all I had to do was stay home for a while; to feel what it was that I had so busily dodged; to recollect in tranquility, as it were. There was the true other, lifelong and awesome, as if snow-capped.

13

THE SEAL

She'd been out surfing with her girlfriend, L told me in the morning on our last day in Paris. L had begun to tell me about her dream as soon as she woke, opening her eyes and her mouth at the same moment. With this same inner urgency she often began a phone conversation, just jumping in without saying hello. I seemed always to fall in love with women who had vivid dream lives. Still, I was happy to listen. I'd been lying there, awake already, thinking that Paris had been a draw. The South of France, romance's original home, still awaited us.

They'd been paddling out past the break, waiting in deep water for a big swell, she reported, when a harbor seal had surfaced near them. I'd wanted to appear in her dreams. I'd wanted her to wake and tell me that she'd dreamed about us. She hadn't yet. Still, I thought I was beginning to make an appearance in symbolic form.

"That's me," I said. "I'm that seal."

"Get out of here," she said. "It's my dream."

"I'm just offering an interpretation," I said.

"Well, don't," she said. "Not everything is about you, you know."

"I'm not talking about everything," I said. I felt sure about that harbor seal. It was me making my appearance in her life, a whiskery denizen, big-eyed and sleek, up from the deep, a man. It was true, though, that I was capable of finding myself in any dream she had. Once she dreamt of a woman hit by a car, and it made me a little sad when she told me, because I knew I was that car. And when sometime later she dreamed of a woman winning a car, I was secretly cheered.

So I didn't insist on being the seal. This was exactly my sense of being with L, of trying to locate myself in her life, in the things she said, even in her dreams. It was possible to do this, though I was never precisely confirmed. She was a mystery to me. Her dreams, for instance, were wild and long. Things kept changing. There were abrupt transitions. If I'd had them, I'd have thought of them as several dreams. They arose from some abundant world of creatures and colors, but whether I was included there, I could not know. Maybe in the South, she'd give me a place, pledge me her troth. As it was, I could only try to take heart in knowing that I'd be part of Paris in her memory, from now on, no matter what.

14

M

....

As the burgeoning decade of the eighties opened, I came to California for love. I drove down the western grade of the Sierras into the peach orchards of the valley in a state of ecstasy, the theme from *Chariots of Fire* blasting on the stereo, returning at last to the place of my birth. I had known early childhood there, then gone East for twenty-five years. So I remembered almost nothing of the actual San Francisco, just the clear light and the smell of eucalyptus. These and everything else I associated with San Francisco—its hills, the Pacific Ocean sparkling in its notches—I had placed in service to my feeling then, my love for M, who lived there. When I finally pierced the Coast Range at last to see it, the water, the bridges, the far cliffs, the Sutro Antenna, the Pyramid—it all seemed exactly arranged for our future life.

M was petite, curly-haired and looked a little like Carol Kane. She had come from Manhattan to live in San Francisco. She was a painter of gorgeous abstractions. We'd met under the most romantic of conditions, as artists and fugitive lovers at an artist colony in New Hampshire, in October. At the time I was an ascetic, a vegetarian, running fifty miles a week, writing poems every day. M's painting's were rich pieces in pastel, purple and red, with lacy rice paper sometimes collaged in. I went to her studio, saw her work and kissed her. Later she'd get me to eat meat as well, beginning with sashimi.

We were both fleeing marriages at the time, as were others at the artist colony, which we joked at the table was like a halfway house for the recently spouseless. M had had a green-card marriage in San Francisco. She had been living with the guy, a Japanese man, and had agreed to marry him, to help him out with his visa, but he'd immediately begun to take it too seriously. She should have known, she said, when, coming down the steps at City Hall, he turned to her and said, "Now I am husband!" After that Toshi had to go. When M had gotten her letter awarding her a residency at the artist colony, Toshi threatened to go back to Japan and divorce her if she went. She went. Toshi went back to Japan.

I had burst from the Midwest, fleeing not just my marriage, but everything there. That whole year previous I'd had a phrase in my head, which appeared like a caption beneath whatever I happened to be considering in that town—my house, my job, my marriage, even the little Main Street, held up a dozen times a day by Illinois Central Gulf freight trains. Whatever it was, it was Not What I Had in Mind. So the letter from the artist colony felt like fate. I called my chairman, took a leave for the fall term and left town three months early, driving around the Midwest for the summer, listening to Joni Mitchell's *Hejira* and crying over the songs, though not over my lost life.

Then I met M at the artist colony. I hadn't intended to get serious, but after several weeks of passion as the woods went russet, as it grew cold enough to build a fire in the studio hearth, I found myself in love with her. There was this family sense at the artist colony that having an affair seemed to violate, so M and I slept in separate rooms in the big farmhouse that served as a dorm, spoke as colleagues among others at the big tables in the dining room, walked a distance apart in public. And in private pressed ourselves into each other for hours. One morning we took a shower together in the communal farmhouse, trying desperately not to cry out under the blast we'd created to mask the sound, a torrent that filled the tub until it overflowed, and which we had afterward to mop up with our towels.

Almost everyone at the colony was very discrete, of course—so much so that we actually thought nobody knew. But these were artists we lived among, sensitive to intention and details, and later that morning a smarmy sculptor from Manhattan sidled up to me on the path to the studios and said he liked my style. Ashamed, I rushed into the forest, then found my way to M's studio.

"Everybody knows," I said.

"I know," she said. In that moment the thought first occurred to me that we might end up together. M said that an old fiction writer, a resident of many years, had already wished her luck with our affair, adding that she'd never seen a couple who'd met at the artist colony stay together for more than a year. "After that, reality sets in," she'd said.

But we ignored her warning and, by the time our residencies were over, couldn't part, and so went to New York City together, sleeping in the same bed for the first time at M's friend's place in Chelsea and walking around Manhattan every day all day for a couple of weeks until she had to return to San Francisco. I had the whole term off, and no home to go home to. So I went to California and M's high, hard bed in the loft.

We arrived at Folsom Street on Halloween, in the afternoon. There, among the armature-winding places and the auto body repair shops, it was Folsom's high leather period, and the street was crowded with throngs of silver cowboys and black leather cops with motorcycle boots and nipple rings. They looked fearsome to me, but M felt safe in the neighborhood, and said they were nice guys. During the day they were corporate lawyers and church organists. One man often set up his portable stereo beneath our window and played Mozart until dawn—*Eine kleine Nachtmusik,* like a happy nightbird's song. The loft she lived in was an enormous raw industrial space above the Rebizzo Brothers' Machine Shop. Downstairs, the brothers ran their machines and yelled. Often in those weeks before Christmas, they worked all night to fill orders, the long squeal of their metal lathe beneath us, cutting through the traffic sounds and the Mozart that came in from the street.

I was in love with M and with San Francisco. Life seemed vast and surprising, the limits I had placed on it before habitual, arbitrary, stupid. We split the rent, which was about two hundred dollars a month, for a place we might have played full-court basketball in. No walls interrupted its empty expanse, and far in the back, M had arranged her kitchen and bedroom spaces. One didn't have a place in San Francisco, I learned. One had a space. At night the windows at the front seemed a half-mile off, shining with the streetlights on Folsom Street, the big four-lane one-way artery downtown, which roared twice a day weekdays and lay sunny and silent on weekends, when we called it the Beach. Everything made me happy, and I wrote poems that simply recorded anything that happened: that one night we watched from the window as the police pulled a drunk from his car and arrested him, as his girlfriend screamed, over and over, "How am I supposed to get back to Vallejo?" Or that one Saturday morning when the winch in the machine shop woke us, we could hear the brothers already shouting about some bastards as the steel garage door went up, and M got up wearing only her purple socks, put on Bob Marley and the Wailers, and then we jumped around, dancing and singing about Babylon going down.

On New Year's Day I went back to Illinois to resume my teaching job. I rented a house on a rural route out of town. The yard was full of snow. My landlord was a Transcendental Meditator, gone to Fairfield, Iowa, for the term, and the house I rented was sky blue inside. It came with a wood-burning stove and an old dog named Otis, whom I agreed to take while his master was studying with the Maharishi. Otis barked at me.

I called M daily. She'd agreed to come out to Illinois, but now she wasn't so sure. She'd never been to the middle of the country, she said.

"Come on," I said. "We have a house. We have a wood-burning stove. We have a dog."

Finally M flew out. She arrived wearing gold boots in the Illinois winter, amazed at the cruel cold, at the distance between things. The freeway overpasses, she noted on the way home to our new house, were the tallest things around. Everyone seems tiny here, she said. At home the wood-burning stove smoked up the house, the sky blue walls and the bare branches drove her crazy, and Otis the dog was bad. He barked at her the whole time she was there. He wouldn't let her into our own back yard. He stood at the kitchen door and growled, barring her way.

One afternoon we took Otis out to the snowy woods for a walk. We let him out of the car and he ran away, instantly and as fast as he could. We followed his tracks and called his stupid name into the bare limbs until the early night fell. Finally we left him to freeze to death out there and hiked back to the car. I started the engine, already rehearsing what I would say to his transcendental owner, when a Jeep drove out of the woods and pulled up next to us. "This your dog?" yelled the driver. Otis sat in the back of the jeep, grinning idiotically.

"No," said M, "but we have to take him anyway."

Soon she broke out in hives. Big, red welts, head to foot, all over her cute body. She had to go back to San Francisco, she said. She was allergic to the Midwest. She stayed though, until spring, when the thaw turned the backyard into a cacophonous frog-filled marsh, when Otis was finally licking our faces to wake us in the morning. Then M went home to San Francisco. I'd come out as soon as the term was over, I said, and drove her to the airport, where we kissed like mad at the gate, and then she was gone.

I stayed in the sky blue house, pining and writing letters. I finished my classes, and when I had sold most of my possessions at a huge yard sale, and stuffed the rest into my car, I left, driving out of that town, never to return. I drove west, first dictating on a portable tape recorder my letter of resignation from my teaching job, then working out anxious, eager plans for my life in San Francisco with M. In the San Joaquin Valley I stopped at Davis to call her, to let her know that I was only an hour away. By then she'd already started thinking about it. "Maybe this wasn't such a good idea," she said.

Of course, I didn't listen. I couldn't. I was too far gone. I talked her into it and moved in. Eventually I got a lump sum from what I'd paid into my retirement fund and we lived on it—I was a retiree, I joked, at age thirty. Sushi chefs knew us by name. M wanted a cat, so we went to the ASPCA, where she picked out a beautiful tortoise shell cat and named it after a character from Isaac Bashevis Singer. I froze that summer, coming down immediately with a cold so virulent that I feared it was pneumonia. "What are you thinking?" said M. "Only the tourists wear short sleeves."

In one corner of the big loft, I put up an office, dropping bamboo blinds from the ceiling to make a den. There I practiced touch-typing, which I thought I would need for the temp jobs I intended to get. She tried to paint, as across the loft I pulled an old hat down over my eyes and typed the narration of my trip westward, which I had taped by talking into the microphone in the car. I had a million plans, and I shouted them out to M. She was trying to concentrate and wouldn't answer.

"Sometimes," she said over dinner, "you're too intense."

Soon she wanted a wall, and so I built one—a Sheetrock screen really, the studs six feet apart, its whole bulk pinned to the ceiling beams only twice. It wasn't quite up to code, but behind it she could work in private. She did a drawing of me, as a black nude figure with a saw.

And one night I lay looking up at the raw ceiling, at the inadequate insulation and the beams threaded with cable, and began to feel—against every effort I used to hold it off—regret. I remembered my wife, more sweetly than I had thought of her in years, maybe ever. I remembered mowing the lawn around my sweet Midwestern house with its rosebushes. I remembered that sleepy town with its wild honeysuckle between the yards. I remembered my students as grateful, my salary as huge. What had I done? I thought, as M slept beside me. What had I done?

Things were bad between us by the end of that year. I was too intense, she'd said, and I was. I'd awoken from my romantic dream of California to find myself in mid-air, like the coyote in the cartoon. We'd had to find jobs. M and I had gone to temp agencies together, and she'd gotten hired. Despite my practice, I still couldn't touch-type.

And M had never realized how much she'd loved her solitude. She felt squashed, she said. She had no space at work and no space at home. I was losing her, I knew, and I was accordingly jealous, nervous about my possession of her. What did she do all day? I'd ask when she got home. Who did she see?

"I feel squashed," she said again, and dreamed of garment bags.

Alert for the signs, I knew she had a boyfriend even before I read her journal, drawn fatally to it during my long day at home with my jealousy and the metal lathe squealing downstairs. What I saw in it, her agonies about having a man in her home and an affair at work, cured me forever from reading anybody's journal. With M, I pretended I had not read it, and went secretly insane with jealousy, even following her around the city in my car and finding out where her boyfriend lived.

One evening, M merely mentioned that a friend of a friend was giving up his place in the Mission District, and I went over. As soon as I saw it, I felt my need for simple comfortable domesticity, pent up and denied for months in the loft. The building dated from the twenties and had been built modern after the quake. The place was small but had a big bell-shaped bay-windowed room at each end of a hall. An ironing board folded out of the wall in the kitchen; all the doors had cut glass knobs; there was an ice box beneath the draining board. The former tenants had squandered their labor on the apartment, even sanding the floors. The walls were painted in pale colors, exquisitely trimmed: the kitchen the whitest pink, the bedroom the coolest gray. They'd left behind the bed and the bookcases, even a little kitchen table and chairs. The windows overlooked a little courtyard and a billowing avocado tree, its shiny dark leaves rising above the roof into the southern sky. I wrote a check for the deposit on the spot. This was more than good luck, I thought. This was a higher calling. I was supposed to be alone, the place had said to me, and that was the way I put it to M, who didn't know what to say at first, then said that part of her wanted me to leave. She suggested I take the cat.

Moving in was easy, as I had little stuff, having filtered it through two drastic moves. I filled the bookcases—most of what I'd stuffed into my car were books—and put everything else on the floor. I had two towels, one set of sheets, a carved wooden bodhisattva my uncle had given me at my wedding—Avalokiteshvara the Merciful, whom I figured I was going to need. I bought a set of gray dishes in the Castro and picked up two bad overstuffed chairs at a yard sale.

Despite my having moved out, despite her other boyfriend, my romance with M went on for three or four years, as my apartment began to fill up with things. By then the bodhisattva stood among a collection of various kinds of granite and abalone shell; and even the little niche where the telephone had stood in the old days had a plastic dinosaur, hawk feathers, a dreidel, a postcard of a Renaissance angel, a piece of green silk.

In the end, M and I took a trip together to try and work things out. We drove up the Feather River Canyon into the mountains to Quincy and hiked from there up to a glacial lake at the top of a peak, where we stripped and swam in the clear, freezing water. I wore a diving mask, and I can recall swimming deep beneath her as she stroked across the bright broken surface, her nipples puckered against the cold. She lay atop a pillar of shadow, exalted there like some new kind of creature. I held my breath as long as I could.

Then that night in the motel I lost it. I told her I could make her happy and she said she didn't want me to make her anything. I threw a sneaker at the wall after that, and called her names I'd never called her. She ran out of the room into the dark, across the highway without shoes on into some dumb field. She didn't have to take this, she yelled, as I went after her, mad and sorry.

And when we got back, that was that. I would learn to be alone, I thought, and was for years, until L in her blue jeans came striding down that yellow meadow, calling my name.

15

TGV

....

That morning we had to catch the train. We made our own breakfast of white peaches and bread and coffee, and then we cleared
out of Phillipe's apartment. He'd be returning home himself that
afternoon, coming back to this spare place he had made in his
image of himself. L went down to the avenue to buy flowers, and
I washed the dishes and the kitchen window, the biggest in the
apartment. By then I felt fond of Phillipe, grateful to this guy
who'd only excited my jealousy at first. Now that we'd lived in
the apartment for five nights, Phillipe seemed familiar, a friendly
spirit invoked by his posters of the festooned canals and his huge
French business cards on the nightstand. Plus I was full of hope
about the South. Oh Provence, I thought as I cleaned the window.
Work your magic.

When she got back with yellow tulips that seemed an extrava-
gance in that place, we proceeded to depart. By then they'd spread
out around Phillipe's place, having found their way to where
they'd been used. I went from room to room picking them up,

pleased to see how L and I had diffused and intermingled. But finally there weren't many things; and very soon the place was spare and clean—even cleaner than we had found it.

When we had gathered our things, we packed them. We had a suitcase each and a garment bag for L, and each of us had an overstuffed canvas briefcase with a shoulder strap. Even traveling that light, I had taken too much as usual. My tweed jacket lay at the bottom of my bag, having made its way down there already like a geological stratum, excess baggage, the weight of error. In cold San Francisco it had been impossible to imagine not needing it. It would stay in the bag, too, as the South would be even warmer. Someday I'd learn to imagine the world accurately.

I went around making sure we hadn't left anything, beginning already to miss the little apartment as I went through it, confirming the absence of evidence of our having been there. The place was blank, clear as an empty stage, and it seemed odd to me, in the last instant I surveyed those rooms, that so little could take on such subtle and changing meanings. I bid farewell to the white chair, which sat vacant by the window, irresistibly suggesting that it was waiting for someone else to come and occupy it— which it was not. Then we went out, locking the door behind us—never to open it again, I thought—and hiding the key under the red runner on a certain stair, where Phillipe had told L to put it.

After that I had no leisure to think, as by then we were late and had to rush to catch the train. Suddenly seized with anxiety, we lugged our baggage hurriedly down the block, then into the Métro, where we fidgeted beneath the overarching billboards— multiples of a man and woman and the word "Chanel"—before the rubber-wheeled train pulled up. We stood for this short ride, having to change anyway at the Concorde station, and moved toward the door before it opened. By then we had just fifteen minutes, and rushed, breathless, through the tunnel, trying to find the word "Nation" among the list of strange names on the sign for *"Correspondances."* The second subway crawled through its stops: Tuileries, Palais-Royal, Louvre, Chatelet, Hôtel de Ville, St. Paul, Bastille. Finally we reached the Gare de Lyon. Then we had only three minutes before we would miss our train to the South.

So we ran. I loped ahead with the two big bags, shouldering my way up the escalator and shouting *"pardon"* in a semblance of French. At the quay there was a complex mechanical schedule board, where L found the track number and took off; I followed. Finally we reached the train, the TGV, orange and huge. We reached the door of the first car and scrambled aboard, up steep steps into a baggage compartment, where we panted and I pounded my pockets, terrified for a moment that I'd dropped the tickets during our dash. The train pulled out.

I found the tickets. "Let me see them," L said. She looked at the numbers and added, "This isn't our car." Out the window a raw Paris was already fleeting past—railyards, brick factories, ugly apartment buildings, graffiti that might have been imported from Queens. "Ours is number twelve," said L.

"What's this one?" I said.

"This is two," she said.

"We can just walk through," I said.

But we couldn't, it turned out. We hauled the luggage through about a dozen hissing pneumatic doors and through cars packed with passengers and resembling airplane cabins. Finally we found a door that would not open, which bore a sign informing us in French that the door would not open. We couldn't get to our assigned seats.

"What do we do now?" I said. By then we stood in another baggage area, a gray anteroom with a stainless steel rack and rubber floor. A dark-eyed young French guy in a Sorbonne sweat-shirt sat on one of the piles of luggage, rearranging it to make a bed for himself, and in the corner next to the stairwell, an older Frenchman wearing a black watch cap and smoking a pungent cigarette sat in a small seat that unfolded from the wall. The train was already speeding south, its roar blasting the uninsulated compartment.

L didn't seem fazed. She asked Monsieur Sorbonne something in French, as I waited around for the translation, helpless. "He says the door will be locked for the whole trip," she told me. "Part of the train is detached at Valence and goes somewhere else."

"What do we do?" I said. I hadn't seen one empty seat in the cars we'd come through, let alone two together. L spoke to the French guy again, who seemed only too happy to chat with her from his comfy position on the luggage pile. I was completely dependent on L and her French, and I wasn't used to it. Before we'd taken this trip I'd been afraid of being completely out of control in France, and although I'd thought it might be good for me, now I didn't care about that.

"That's the only seat," L said finally, pointing to another folded orange seat attached to the wall above the little stairwell to the door. Across the car, the old Frenchman looked impassively up at us, holding his cigarette in a way no American would, his hand cupping its heat. His face looked carved and polished. A farmer, I thought.

"You take that one," I said. "I'll go look for real seats." She sat in the little seat, got her Walkman out and put the earphones on. I threw the suitcases and garment bag on a rack above the one holding the reclining Sorbonne guy and went back through the train. In the cars proper, it was a different world. Each car was silent and sunny, and the complacent passengers had puzzles or books or bread spread on their laps. One woman was reading a story aloud to her little girl. Nothing, I thought. I walked through three cars before I found a single vacant seat next to a window. I went back to tell L about it.

"You take it," she said. "I'm fine here."

So I went back, anxious, into the calm car and, unsatisfied, took the real seat. Next to me sat a woman with a dog in her lap, a tiny black poodle who'd roused himself and sniffed in my direction, then had actually growled as I'd eased past and sat down in the window seat. I got the Proust out as the idiot dog settled down.

Exquisite Proust as a boy was being sent to bed in the midst of a dinner party. Miserable, he schemes to get his mother to come up and kiss him goodnight, in an agony of thousands of words wrought into ornate and amazing sentences. He stands weeping at the top of the stairs, smelling even in the varnish on the bannister his desperation for her kiss. Was he kidding? I rested between the paragraphs, reminded of L down there in the swaying, roaring, pungent baggage compartment with those two French men.

Outside, France raced past. We were already out of the city. What would be best? I wondered. It would be best to remain in my seat here, reading my Proust, for at least a couple of hours. Maybe she'd begin to miss me by then. Sitting apart would encourage her to think of me as capable. It would enhance our understanding, the understanding that had given us five wonderful days in Paris, that had left L free to be with me without worrying about what it meant.

"The fingerbowls," wrote Proust, "seemed to me to be concealing pleasures that were baleful and of a mortal sadness because Mamma was tasting of them while I was far away." I couldn't take any more after that, but just looked out the window, trying to distract myself from wondering about life in the baleful baggage car.

The train was so big and so smooth that it reversed things and made the land seem to be rushing by while it stood still. Out there the foreground was fluid, blurred, rising and falling as the level track sliced through rolling fields. A bridge flicked overhead, its shadow at that speed just a blink of shade. In the middle distance trees lining a road fluttered, too fast to count, and beyond them the country wheeled by, revolving as if on a vast platter, its center somewhere beyond the horizon.

Then a forest plunged past, the trees near the track so quick that they seemed insubstantial. I discovered that I could look through them and focus for an instant on something distant and relatively still. I saw for a flash a tall, old tree behind the others, a single solid pale trunk that made phantasms of everything else, the way huge columns turn passing people into shadows. For that tree, the years that had passed until that moment were as nothing as well. It had stood there, maybe, in winter during the war, troops huddling near it, as those dire trains headed north, the rumble of their wheels vibrating through the frozen earth up to the tips of its stiff, bare branches.

I didn't want to spend two hours without her, I thought. I didn't care how it would appear. I had to admit it. I was in it. So damn the rest. What was I going to do, waste my life being apart from someone I was in love with? So I got up again and went back to the baggage compartment.

L, still in her earphones, smiled when I came in. I sat down in the stairwell. She'd been writing in her journal, but from where I sat beneath her I couldn't see what she'd written.

"What is it?" I said. She lifted one of the padded earphones, and I asked again. It was Les Negresses Verte, she said, a group she'd bought in Paris. Their name suggested the African women in their robes whom we'd seen in the Métro. It made me uneasy. She went back to listening. The roar was loud in the compartment and we couldn't have talked easily, even if she'd wanted to.

I settled and looked through my shoulder bag just to make sure

I still had everything. I'm subject to fear of loss, especially when I travel in a foreign country, when I have to carry on my person all that is my home and country. This is a place I won't see again, I think—if I drop something here, it is lost forever. The confusion about seats seemed like particularly fertile ground for losing things, so I checked the bag, opening its zippers and pockets, each of which was significant. As I did, I repeated to myself my sentences—my way of holding the location of these things in mind. My passport is in the gray wallet with the Velcro closure. It was. My notebook is in the side pocket. It was. The extra money—in dollars, with American presidents and English words on them—is in the envelope tucked into the green Michelin guide. It was. I wouldn't have minded checking my suitcase, to make sure of the tickets home, which would stay hidden throughout the trip, like a tiny passageway back to America deep at the bottom of the bag under the ludicrous tweed. But I couldn't do that with the Sorbonne guy asleep on the luggage rack and so only repeated the talismanic sentence to myself in consolation.

L, amid her music, had watched me look at the cash. She didn't seem afflicted by this same anxiety. L with her complex and inviolate dreams could seem at home wherever she was. Finally she lifted an earphone and asked what I'd been doing.

"Just checking," I said.

"Why don't you just get traveler's checks, if you're so worried about it?" she said.

It was a dispute we'd had before, and I gave my standard answer. "They're like a bet on disaster," I said.

"You'd rather worry about it," she said as she'd said before. Then she returned to black green female land.

She had the luxurious habit of possessing things without having to hold them in mind. I could fake that attitude at home in America, where things tended to stay put, but even there I was occasionally jolted with possession anxiety. Maybe it wasn't such a bad thing to feel, though. In the past, people's lives had depended on such vigilance. Maybe my anxiety was an inheritance from those riskier times, analogous to that physical jolt that shook me sometimes just before I finally fell asleep, which I'd heard was a legacy of the time our species had spent in trees, when that reflex kept you on your branch.

Among L's things at her feet was the box for her tape of Les Negresses Verte. When I looked at the little box for their picture, I found only several proud white male faces. These were men she was listening to, and neither black nor green. Naturally, I thought. Who else would think to call themselves that?

Out the window French fields poured past in blurred, blond bands. The sound in the compartment was like a sustained clang with a rumble beneath it, and the place shuddered with the speed. If our train passed an oncoming one, the compartment sounded with a pop like a rifle shot, which made me jump. After an hour, the farmer's wife brought him his lunch—a thick chunk of ham in a roll. With her came yet another dog, a mottled border collie who nuzzled the old man and sat beside him, then watched and licked its lips as the sandwich passed overhead.

I tried to adapt. This wasn't so bad, I thought, though it wasn't the way we had planned to make the trip south. There could be a specialness about being in the baggage car, as if we were stowaways, taking what came and getting by on just enough. The old farmer gave the dog a chunk of bread, and the dog, receiving its morsel at last, set upon it with appetite and gratitude. Out the little window, the land seemed to be growing brighter. The country was gathering itself into green hills and pale ridges, which rose and came closer, enclosing the train.

Suddenly L started singing. She had closed her eyes, and she sang along to her Walkman. She sang in French that I couldn't understand, and her voice rose strangely in the racket of the car. It was especially thrilling that she didn't know she could be heard.

Once, after M, after a bad spring in 1986, I'd wanted only to live and not to require anything to mean anything, ever again. Now, though, I wanted her, I wanted us, to have meaning. Why was it I had to learn the important things over and over? Why, especially when I couldn't forget trivialities? I tried just to listen to her sing and not want anything, but I could not. She gave me that ache of looking at the sea. So I gazed out the little window in the door, attempting to watch the onrushing land. The hills around us had given way, and we rose above a broad green valley, where there was a river and vineyards. She took off her earphones. "The Rhône," she announced. "We're in the South."

16

THE CRYSTAL BRANCH

A sound mind tolerates a mystery. This had been the lesson of 1986. To see portents, hear clarions, read meanings everywhere in the calm, complex world that so easily bears such weight, this is poetry, lunacy, love. I remembered this, on my way south with L, but could no longer credit it with belief.

Lovers crystallize, said Stendhal, writing in his abstracted memoir *De l'Amour*. Stendhal produced the term "crystallization" by analogy with a phenomenon occasionally witnessed in Salzburg. A tree branch might fall into an abandoned salt mine and after a time emerge encrusted with crystals. Then what was the living wood became "a galaxy of scintillating diamonds." So, too, the lover "draws from everything that happens new proofs of the perfection of the loved one." Evidence is everywhere. You break your arm, for instance. *Pas de problème.* "Wouldn't it be wonderful," the crystallizing lover contends, "to be looked after by the woman you love. . . . A broken arm would be heaven!" We seek, in other words, and we find, reducing the world to what we hope or fear. And though Stendhal describes it as adoration, one might simply call it madness, a process of delusion that must, as he would learn to his sorrow, finally betray the love it seeks to confirm.

This hard image of the crystal branch, which might be taken as an emblem for the Enlightenment as a whole, is a bitter inversion of the living branch, still connected to the tree, bearing its leaf and fruit, nourished by the soil and nourishing in its turn. That he thinks of salt expresses Stendhal's own bitterness. Rationale encrusts his emotions, as his pseudo-scientific diction and his abstraction encrust this youthful memoir. Always in *De l'Amour* it's a friend who has the problem. La Bedoyere, rejected by his lady, fires a bullet into his temple—this from Stendhal, who drew pistols in the margins of his manuscripts. In later life, he would be forced to become whatever he was.

....

As, in 1986, I was. Believing that I was not in love, that I did not want to be in love, that I had gotten beyond being in love, I'd begun to believe I was dying. I had symptoms to prove it, which I compiled as spring went to cold summer that year. I listed them on a piece of paper that I kept with me so that each recurrence might—as with the tolling of a bell—confirm my diagnosis: night sweats, extreme nervousness, hot and cold flashes, inability to eat, obsessive thoughts, lassitude, a ringing in my ears, bouts of fear. And whatever it was, it would be fatal.

One day, struggling against it, I decided that a jog in the country would be good for me. I drove up into the Marin Headlands, into Tennessee Valley. From the parking lot I jogged down the trail that descends into this deep valley with the sea at its mouth, then decided to climb one of the steep side trails, heading north up the ridge. I'd run over toward Green Gulch, I thought, toward the Zen Center. Just the thought of it was enough to calm me a little. That afternoon the fog was starting to come in off the ocean, a towering summer fog into which I climbed as I ascended the ridge. Soon I was in the thick of the clouds that the northwest wind whipped inland—clouds that tumbled across the brush, opening intermittently to show the sky overhead.

It had been warm and sunny when I'd gotten out of the car, and I'd begun running without a shirt. Now, climbing the hill and soaked with sweat, I felt naked, cold, slick and suddenly full of dread, as if fate were pulling me up this hill to witness something. The fog grew denser as I reached the crest. Then overhead I heard a hoarse cry, like a bark of laughter, and saw a flash of a raven, its black wings outstretched, hovering against the strong wind above the ridge, for an instant distinct and vivid, black as a cutout against the sky, then gone. A Japanese demon. Freezing and wet, I followed the red road as it faded and intensified, feeling the ache in my legs and the dreamy sense of reiteration, of running and running and going nowhere.

I heard the caw again, and again there he was, still for an instant and then lost in the fog. I stepped up the pace. The road turned and started downhill. Suddenly the fog opened and before me was the Abbot's House, a low deserted hut, dark wood and glass, perched on the brow of the ridge with the fog breaking around it. The farmer Wheelwright had built it to give his dying wife a view of the ocean. I came to the gate, barbed wire with tufts of cow hairs on the barbs. It was locked, the house beyond it silent, empty. Shivering, I turned back and ran down the hill to my car, which was by this time completely obscured by fog. Everything, every bit of the hour had seemed personal and symbolic, fateful and mortal. By then I had stopped finding poems. They were finding me.

• • •

It had begun as an inauspicious spring. My neighborhood in the city seemed to be shimmering with lost souls, rippling with panic about AIDS. The Challenger with its grade school teacher aboard had exploded at the start of the year—the commander, in his flat, straight, flyer's voice saying "Uh oh," just before the explosion. "Uh oh"—that about summed it up. Then the reactor at Chernobyl melted down. The birthrate among birds in Northern California was half of normal that spring. I read this in the paper, unsurprised.

In a panic about my finances, I had put aside my poetry to go after some good money, a big mistake. I had taken a job in Marin County as a kind of court reporter on a huge probate case. One of the parties in the suit employed me to produce a daily summary of the trial. The case concerned the disposition of a huge and accidental accumulation of money that a doctor's widow from a suburb in Marin had bequeathed to the needy of the county. In the time it had taken to settle her estate, the money had burgeoned tenfold. Left in oil land in the energy crisis, it suddenly amounted to nearly a half billion dollars. No one of right mind would have left such a fortune to the needy of Marin County, the second richest per capita in the United States. Worse, this Vesuvius of bucks continued to spew interest income at a rate that almost defied spending—a problem that could have only arisen in the eighties. The foundation charged in the will with the disposition of the cash intended to alter its terms to share this wealth with the area's poorer counties. The citizens of Marin had reacted with outrage, with greed disguised as concern for the sanctity of probate. A banner on a Marin storefront confronted me in my dire mood. WILLS ARE SACRED, it read.

The trial took place in a blue spaceship designed by Frank Lloyd Wright, a truly bizarre building, seat of the Marin County government. The skies above it were filled with the white-tipped, fingery black wings of carrion birds, turkey buzzards. Inside, the courtroom was full of lawyers representing the needy. They, too, had their needs. They quibbled and nastily impeached each other's witnesses and earned their huge fees, running up ten million dollars in legal costs in this case that went on for months even though it was probably decided beforehand by the mere selection of Marin County as its venue.

The lawyers doodled in their foolscap notebooks. The more senior the lawyer, I noticed, the bigger the doodle. The clerks, on the other hand, did miniatures in the margins of their notebooks. The chief lawyer for the foundation, who looked like a Labrador retriever to me, was doing full-page pictures—slashing, expressionist images in two colors of ink. He was losing his case, and his drawings had his rage in them. At the breaks the attorneys gathered in the hall and speculated about how long the trial would last. The consensus was that it would go all summer, at least.

They were delighted by the prospect. To me, miserable, beyond being in love, choked by a tie, electrified by caffeine, this was a terrible sentence. My sense of dread and despair grew stronger as I sat there, day after day. At five I crawled home, my clutch nearly gone and barely hauling me up the Waldo Grade. For dinner I stuffed down a cheese sandwich, drank my third espresso of the day and went to the computer, where I composed my summary until nearly midnight. This text I turned in the next morning for editing by the lawyers, after which it was reproduced and sent out to the execs. By the second week, I was beyond exhaustion, and everything had become imbued with Fateful Meaning; theories and symbols and the need for sleep stormed around me all day and most of the night.

If I could have lain my head against another shoulder at night, things might not have come to the pass that they did. You can go crazy, I would find out, from not being touched. But having finally gotten over M, I denied myself any other that spring, convinced of my failure at romance and believing that thinking about it would help. Then I had taken the job, foolishly deciding to try to right myself. Even hurtling headlong has its aerodynamical efficiency.

Suddenly, during my morning commute, all my turmoil gathered itself into physical symptoms: My ears stared ringing—roaring, actually. My face looked swollen in the rearview mirror. That day I began to entertain the notion that the case would actually kill me. The judge and lawyers looked bestial, like demonic Disney characters in a fable about greed: the Labrador attorney truly doglike, and the others, rodents and rabbits on the stand, badgers and foxes at their tables, a wizened old wolf behind the bench. The testimony crawled along. My hands seemed far off, miles away, taking my notes.

I raced home beneath the usual vultures—not just pondering them, but really oppressed by their symbolic insistence. At home I couldn't eat or rest—I just went to the computer and began composing my summary. By ten o'clock, when I'd written a couple of thousand words, the screen froze. The computer didn't scramble my work or blank the screen or anything—it just froze, the cursor stuck in midsentence. The keyboard was dead. I pounded the return key, the escape key. No escape, no return. I couldn't make anything happen. It was all out of reach. Nothing would respond and nothing, of course, could be saved. Worse yet, I'd neglected to backup my hours of work. I pulled the back off the computer and blew on the circuit boards, hoping the thing, like a car, was just overheated. Next I spent a frantic hour calling my friends who were programmers, hoping they had a solution. They didn't. They all said the same thing: that I had to turn off the computer, kill the text and start over. By this time it was after midnight. The ringing in my ears sounded like a DC-10. Of course, none of the symbolism of this was lost upon me. Here was the promise of love and the lesser promise of work. Here was my

life, in green letters on the monitor, and no way to get at it—
nothing to do but kill it, admit I'd wandered into a dead end. It
was all painfully apparent—I'd have left it out of a poem.

In the end I extinguished the text. Then I had to work until
nearly four A.M. to finish, and when I finally lay down to sleep, I'd
reached that stage where even sleep isn't possible. The sheets
seemed to be wired with some low-level electric current, and I lay
there, my mind racing, going over and over the text of my notes,
until it grew light outside and, horrified at the prospect, I had to
get up and go to work.

I walked into the weird azure courthouse in a state of mortal
dread. What had seemed tiresome was now intolerable. The cast
of characters in the courtroom now seemed like the walking dead.
All day long the judge kept interrupting the trial by producing
ripping sounds in his throat. All day I fought to stay awake, but
by that night could only lie down and listen to the roar. And in
this state, what had happened seemed obvious. I had contracted
AIDS.

Never mind that I had none of the symptoms, that I hadn't
engaged in unsafe practices, that I was gaining, not losing weight.
For one thing, in 1986, who knew? Maybe you could get AIDS
from kissing, people thought. Maybe there were unknown symptoms. For sure something was wrong, and this very lack of definition forced me to consider my worst fear, then—drawn down by
the irresistible gravity of hypochondria—to believe it. Obsession
requires vagueness, so that one's projections may emerge in the
dimness, the way monsters emerge in the clutter of a child's darkened room. And this was my irresistible obsession, held faithfully
for that dark season: that the disease was rushing through my
system, that these would be the last months of my life.

In the morning I called a therapist I'd gone to in the past, and
he prescribed sleeping pills, even phoning in the prescription so I

could get them right away. They were called Halcion, a dreamy-sounding name, as in halycon days, the word (I happened to know) deriving from the Greek for "Kingfisher," most auspicious of birds. They rendered me into a fitful sleep, but taking them in my state, it turned out, was throwing gasoline on a fire.

I finished out that week at the trial—which ended the month I had contracted for—and turned the Foundation down when they asked me to do another month. I found another writer to take my job. He accompanied me to court so that I could fill him in, but I didn't mention the animals or anything—he'd find out soon enough for himself. He seemed to be in bad shape as well, gaunt and broke and obsessed with a novel he'd started but couldn't finish without rent money.

I took my pills, stayed home and wrote a will worthy of Emme-line Grangerford, giving my car away to M. This is it, I thought. I've been condemned. And for the next three or four months I lived in a state of conscious mortality, looking at the world with eyes of farewell and seeing everywhere the signs of my imminent departure. I saw the shape my life had taken and remembered everyone I'd always thought I'd see again.

I visited my local HMO, called HealthAmerica, where they found nothing wrong with me. The doctor only smiled knowingly when I said I was a free-lance writer. He gave me a hearing test after I told them my ears were ringing, found nothing, and refused to let me see an ears, nose and throat doctor, claiming my ailment wasn't serious enough to warrant a specialist. I had nervously and theoretically asked about AIDS—some men had lost their health insurance, I knew, when they were found to have been infected. He simply told me not to worry about it. I continued to, constantly, anyway.

And when the money from the court case ran out, I did a story on Oakland, looking at it as if it were a foreign country. On a Sunday morning I went out MacArthur to the Love Center, a gospel church. The church shook with singing, with sweet gospel harmonies, but they were not for me. I was far off with my notebook, leaden and distant. The minister aimed at awakening us to repentance and tried in part to scare us into it. "You may sing pretty but that won't save you," he shouted. "You can have good looks, and all the wealth in the world, but that won't save you. Nothing on earth will save you," he shouted, "only the blood! ("Praise Jesus!" yelled someone.) The blood! ("I love you, Lord!" shouted someone else.) The blood of our Savior Jesus Christ will save you!" Clouds of song rose in the intervals of his harangue. The people stood, some crying and holding out their arms as if they could feel the spiritual heat from the pulpit. "Thank you, Lord," one woman exclaimed, again and again. "Thank you, Jesus."

When I stood up, the woman next to me shouted, "Praise God, he's going forward!" but I wasn't. I turned up the aisle and left, getting blessed as I did by the people in their bright suits and silks, and feeling alien, insulated, low. At home I wrote the article, which seemed hollow. The fact-checkers worked me for a week fixing misspellings and wrong names. I hadn't paid attention, having spent it all on my interior roaring and my impending doom.

Finally I went swimming at the pool at Strawberry Canyon and really flung myself into it. I would forget I was sick, I would drive this illness off by sheer will. I swam vigorous laps; I did flips off the board and threw myself off the high dive. That night an excruciating earache blossomed in one of my dull ears. I was in pain, but felt vindicated. At last an undeniable symptom! An opportunistic infection! By nine I was waiting for the nurse to unlock the door to HealthAmerica. I got new drugs: antihistamines, aspirin with codeine, antibiotics. By some grace, I decided to take these instead of the sleeping pills and to finally face facts and go for an HIV test.

Some days later I walked up into the Castro to find the public health clinic where the city was conducting its blood-testing program. The day was sunny in the Castro, and everyone looked fine. There were a few of us in the waiting room that day, mostly men, of various ages. One by one we went to booths in the back of the clinic to get blood tests. There I found a man in a lab coat sitting at a desk. He drew a syringe-full of blood from my arm, then sealed it, labeled it and tore off a card that he gave to me. It had my identification number on it. He told me to come back in two weeks to get my results. I left, walking out into the sunny Castro, holding that card.

In those last days of my life, forgiving everyone didn't seem like a bad idea. I didn't want to blame anyone. The disease seemed like a huge natural force, like a wave or a storm, transforming everyone but intending nothing personal by it and in its scale making me feel the largeness and complexity of life itself, and giving me the sense that whatever came next, beyond death, would probably be as large, as complex, as inconceivable. This prospect sometimes seemed almost exciting, as if I could greet dying with the mixed emotions of a passenger on an oceangoing ship, waving farewell, then turning seaward toward a new and liquid future.

An odd thing happened after that, in those days intervening between my blood test and learning its results. I lived. The ringing in my ears diminished, as did my dread. I started sleeping and stopped taking pills. On the day I was assigned, I clutched the card with my number on it and walked the ten blocks to the clinic. When I got there I was directed back to the table, to the same guy who had taken my blood, Steve was his name. Steve had a list of numbers on the desk in front of him, and across from each number was a word. Most of these words were the same: "Negative." Once or twice on the list appeared another word: "Positive." To be positive meant you'd been infected. Steve scanned the list for my number. "Yours is negative," he said.

Suddenly I felt the long aching in my neck and shoulders. I said, "I thought I was a goner."

"Not yet," said Steve. He suggested I use condoms, limit my partners and even think about a monogamous relationship. Then I got up and left, suddenly noticing the other people around me— men and women sitting quietly in that place, waiting to take tests or find out results or whatever, maybe to find "Positive" by their number. I went out into the bright Castro, noticing that the side street next to the clinic was named Prosper.

I had a strange feeling when I got home. The apartment was homey—sunshine fell through it, onto the leaves of the house-plants and the grain of the wood of the floor and the furniture. I felt like my own guest there. By then it was midsummer. I spent time with friends, bought clothes in neutral colors, asked for no special fate. I was still doomed in the long run, of course, though I didn't feel it every minute. I began to write what I thought of as my own work, in prose. I felt the need to be in love again, though I didn't—felt I shouldn't—try to make anything happen. I wanted to meet someone, but felt that she'd be along, if she was coming along. And finally things ceased to seem symbolic. They were blessedly themselves, as I was.

Let it be enough, I'd pledged then, simply to be alive in the big presence of things. But on that huge orange train heading south with L, I recalled this pledge and dismissed it. That thought had lost its force somehow, had become as weightless as a mote in a sunbeam, now that I was in love again and wanted that meaning, now that she had come along, if indeed she had. That was the only point that mattered. That L and I were ourselves—and accord-ingly vast, mysterious, unnameable—merely got in my way.

17

THE FEATHER BED

In the tiny hilltop town of Seguret, I walked as L slept, finally. Here, in the home of a family she'd known since childhood, she'd fallen, exhausted, into the feather bed they'd prepared for us in the little dormer room at the top of their house. So I walked the switchback streets, climbing above the orange tile roofs toward the sharp peak of white limestone that rose over the town. Vineyards striped the valley and the nearby slopes. On an upper street I neared a church as the bells began to peal, sounding at first like *"Parlé, Parlé,"* and then, as the sound doubled back on itself, like "Neptune, Neptune." A crowd emerged from the church doors and waited, chattering and excited, until the bride and groom came out—she radiant, he chagrined. They posed for cameras, then rushed down the steps, wincing and pelted with rice thrown by gleeful, wicked children. The couple got into a shiny car and were gone. I hadn't seen a wedding in a long time, and it was strange to me. The crowd seemed to expell the two from the town, as if love were an affront to the community, a rent in the order. It had been for me. All that time, I'd kept kept love back, mistaking my resistance—since it had been constant—for the absence of feeling. But now I'd let go and let myself fall, returning to some original condition.

After that I walked back to the house, a wonderful place, a villa, its walls covered with flowering vines. I went quietly inside, where it was silent except for the women's voices from the kitchen. I slipped upstairs to look in at L. She'd held up through a week of jet lag, keeping both Californian and French hours and sleeping little, but by the time we'd reached the South, the effects were beginning to tell.

At the train station in Orange, we'd been met by Sophie, a woman in her sixties and the mother of the family. She'd been delighted to see L and formal with me, which, however she'd intended it, I'd taken for disapproval. L and I weren't married, I thought, though we would sleep together under her roof. Perhaps this offended her. Or perhaps she was just formal in her French way, and I'd only felt that she'd looked askance at me out of my own insecurity about what L and I were, to each other and to everyone else. Whatever we said we are is what we are, I recalled. What had we said?

Her husband had been a pilot, and the family had retired from Paris to this town above the Rhône. In the car L had made small talk with Sophie—who spoke no English and drove fast across the valley floor, hardly slowing for the winding road up the mountain into town. She'd sounded the horn and barreled through the narrow curves. At home, we'd met her daughter Thérèse, who was blonde and vivacious and wore bright pink shorts and a matching top. Thérèse had been L's babysitter back in Paris in the seventies. The four of us had swum that afternoon, and afterward Thérèse and L had lain in the sun by the pool and gossiped in French, making each other giggle. Thérèse told sexy stories, L had reported. She'd told her the new slang word for penis. But L had tired quickly after her swim, and about three had simply collapsed. She'd taken off her bathing suit, lain in the billowing bed and fallen asleep in a minute. An hour later, when I looked in after my walk, she was still deeply asleep, motionless, breathing heavily, buried in the bed.

I crept out, and went back downstairs to face the language barrier. I found mother and daughter in the kitchen, the elder cooking meat in a pan. Two tiny fluffy white animals, a poodle and a cockapoo, squealed at the woman's feet as she sautéed. I made a pillow of my hands to indicate that L was still sleeping. Both women gestured openly for me to sit at the table, which I did. I listened to them speak to the dogs in that tone reserved for darlings. They adored these dogs, to whom we had been gravely introduced on our arrival. The dogs were named Oncle and—no kidding—Chagrin d'Amour, whom they called Shamu. *"Qu'est-ce que tu veux?"* said Sophie each time one of them yelped. Keska Tuvo, I thought. What do you want? It was a stroke, not a question, the way she said it. The dogs were ecstatic to hear it over and over. Nobody said anything else for a long time, and finally I had to say something, even though I knew neither of them had much English.

"That smells good," I said genially. "What is it?"

Thérèse and her mother exchanged words in French. Then Thérèse said, "Liver for the dogs."

In America, I might have made a joke, but here I didn't have the capacity. The ensuing silence began to feel alarming. I was tired, I thought. I needed the comfort of the English language. I hated not being able to speak, to put myself at ease, to control the situation. Finally Thérèse offered me some grapes, and asked me some questions, beginning with "Where are you come from?" San Francisco, I said. No, I had not known L long.

The sound of an airplane, of all things, rescued me. The women looked at each other when they heard it. "Come and see," said

Thérèse. I followed her out of the kitchen and across the big dining room to a veranda. At the railing she pointed up. We looked west from a height of a couple hundred feet, across the valley toward the Rhône. Coming our way in the sky was a small plane. As it drew near it banked north, showing its pale belly, then leveled out and flew by, tipping its wings in salute, as Thérèse and her mother waved and shouted.

Then she turned to me. "My father," she said. "Would you like to go up?"

"Upstairs?" I said.

"No. In the sky!" she said.

She meant that very minute, too. Thérèse was a woman of action, and the two of us seemed whisked instantly into her car, which she drove faster than her mother had down the hill, out of the town, then across the valley, where she floored it. We raced along a narrow country lane for a couple of miles, until we reached a small airport, and there we pulled into the long drive. Suddenly the plane was descending to our right, landing in the field beside the road. "Perfect," said Thérèse, honking the horn several times and speeding up to keep up with the plane. We parked next to the small hangar and walked out onto the runway as the pilot taxied in. He pulled up, cut the engines, pushed his window open and waved as the props stopped. Thérèse shouted to him in French, and he motioned for us to get aboard.

In the tiny cockpit, Thérèse got into the back seat, leaving me the front. The pilot was old, thin, reminiscent of Jacques Cousteau, I thought. He shook my hand firmly with his bony hand, his azure gaze and greeting suggesting something stronger than his physical body. We exchanged names. His was Louis. *"Enchanté,"* he said. Then he started the plane again, went through a checklist with Thérèse. As if I could help, or even make anything of anything, I concentrated on the instrument panel, the pressure gauges and the indicator with a front view of the plane drawn on it. The old man spoke into his hand mike a minute, and then we were gathering speed, rattling over the gravelly runway. Finally the little plane seemed to leap from the ground. The big window filled with clear sky, and I was pushed back into my seat.

We plunged upward for a time and then leveled off a little, and Thérèse's father shouted at me over the roaring engines. "Have you been flying like this before?" I finally understood. "No," I shouted back.

Then he yelled something in French to Thérèse, at which she laughed.

"What did he say?" I shouted.

"He hopes you don't vomit," she said.

"Very often," shouted the old man, grinning at me.

The fields and orchards dropped farther away beneath us, until they seemed abstract, and I had no further sense of the empty space between us and the ground. Beneath us the valley was map-like. Thérèse's father pointed out his brother's house, a country chateau that stood among the vineyards, next to a huge tubular greenhouse. And below us in a newly plowed field, a faint diagonal line of darker earth lay like a shadow over the ground. "The road of the Romans," said Thérèse's father, producing those r's in his throat.

Showing this ancient track to me, he banked the plane steeply and pivoted around the site on the wing so that I got a good view. "You don't mind this?" he shouted. I didn't mind, I said. I was not quite there, actually; everything had a cinematic quality.

He took his hand off the stick that steered the plane, leaving just his fingertip in contact. "I can control her with one finger," he said proudly.

Finally we leveled off and flew east toward the ridge on which their town stood. To the south rose wind-carved curtains and combs of white rock, cropping from another ridge. *"Les Dentelles,"* said Thérèse, when she saw me looking at them. I took the name to mean "teeth." We bore in on the little town, until I could make out the house, then the veranda, on which finally I could see a figure standing. I hoped it was L, but as Louis banked the plane, performing the same maneuver we had seen from below, I saw that it was Thérèse's mother, waving languidly again from the railing. L must still be asleep, submerged into the featherbed in the attic room, my dreaming darling. Thérèse tapped me on the back and said L's name as a question. Again I made a pillow of my hands.

She slept on, all day. We came back from the airport with Louis, who seemed frail out of his plane. I passed the hour before dinner in the courtyard, trying to make friends with the dogs. Oncle, the poodle, would chase pebbles like a maniac, but was standoffish otherwise. The cockapoo was friendlier but mostly just stared at me with that open-mouthed permanent smile of dogs. She had a perfect pink tongue, I noticed. Neither dog would fawn. They had known a lifetime of French adoration, and at this point almost nothing would move them to doglike obsequiousness. On account of this, they seemed attuned and human, an effect enhanced by their haircuts, poofs and bangs that seemed designed to make them look like unflappable French people.

L awoke just in time for dinner, coming downstairs drowsy. Sophie served and Louis carved and it was a good dinner, though I can't remember what we ate. L complimented the cook, and I thought that I should be paying attention to the food, too, since we were in the South of France and it was delicious. I should probably write it all down in my journal later, to make it one of those memorable meals. But I hadn't seen L for hours, and she was all I was interested in. And later I could recall only that she had liked the food.

L and I separated into male and female parts of that household for the evening. She went off to Thérèse's pink bedroom to talk, and Louis asked me to watch an American film with him, something he'd been waiting to see. A subtitled Rambo movie, it turned out to be, the one called *First Blood*. In the movie—the first of the Rambo series—Rambo is the rebel, the outcast, a Vietnam vet bent on avenging an insult. He singlehandedly destroys a small American town in which the police have brutalized him. In the climax he stands off the whole U.S. Army as he holes up in the hills, armed, literally, to the teeth. "Rambo" sounded French, I realized, as in the poet.

First Blood was the best Rambo movie, Louis said, and was the most popular of the series in France. Not in America, I told him. There, the second movie—in which Rambo, no longer an outcast but a sort of supercop, takes revenge on Vietnam—was the one that made the character famous and its investors rich. "Of course," said Louis in the French manner. On the screen Rambo blew up a gas station, stole a bazooka and ran off into the night.

At the end of the movie, Richard Crenna's character, a Green Beret commander, pleads with Rambo, "You have no chance. This mission is over!" Stallone barks back "Nothing is over!" but breaks down anyway, wailing about the abandonment of the Vietnam veteran and croaking into the commander's decorated jacket. The old man, Louis, wept along with the character, as if he, too, had known such disgrace. Then as the credits rolled, we turned off the set, and Louis shook my hand with both of his, acknowledging that we'd been through something together.

I climbed the stairs again to the top of the house, quietly entered the dark bedroom and found L asleep again in the feather bed. I turned on the table lamp to undress, but it didn't wake her. She was deep in the quilt. In this house we'd been treated like a married couple, which meant I hadn't been with her. She'd been carried off, into the world of company, of women, of her own deep sleep, in any case far off. I got out my notebook and, sitting in the small chair beneath the lamp, wrote down some of my feelings. I remembered how the house, the town, the countryside had looked from the plane, toylike, darling, beautiful, manageable. Like France itself, green on the globe that sat on the low table in my bedroom back in San Francisco. I felt somehow above the scene as I wrote, as if looking down on the two of us in that room and contemplating the semblance of the married couple we might be, as if in miniature. As I'd passed over the house in the little plane, I'd tried to wish her awake, so that she would come out and see me passing in the sky and wave as the old man's wife had waved. This and seeing Louis weep at the end of the movie had affected me, as had Rambo, alone, hunted, lugging his stupid arsenal around in the woods. Being a man was like being a weathervane, something solitary, as vulnerable as it was prominent, a mere indicator of great forces.

L's chestnut hair flowed over the pillows. The bed where she lay looked like a bridal bower from some girl's storybook. Nothing is over, I hoped, as I put down the notebook, turned off the light and got in, strange amid the extravagant covers and cool in that well of her warmth.

18

The Fountain

....

In the summer of 1950, the year as it happens of my birth, Jacques Cousteau announced that he would attempt to plumb the Fontaine-de-Vaucluse, an underwater cavern in the hills above Avignon. He was already a veteran of some five hundred dives, but afterward he would describe this one as the worst experience of his career. The River Sorgue emerges from underground at the Fontaine, breaking from the cavern at the base of a towering bluff. Probably the Sorgue extends beneath much of the Vaucluse as a subterranean river system. All we see, though, is its dark mouth, opening seven hundred feet beneath the limestone plateau. The cavern seems to descend straight into the earth, and in summer appears as a still pool about seventy-five feet across.

The scale of the place feels Utahan, more than French, and the stone as well, pale and striated over the bluff that breaks here, makes the gathering of low buildings at the base of the canyon seem cellular and miniscule. This sense of scale must have been enhanced for the Romans, who first wrote about the place. They approached it from the sea, coming up the Grand Rhône through the Camargue delta. They found the convergence of rivers where Avignon would be, then proceeded across the floodplain of the Sorgue into the foothills, finally entering the canyon for which the region itself, the Vaucluse, would be named. From there they looked up at this impossible cliff with the cavern at its base. So the Fountain of the Sorgue has always seemed symbolic, springing from that vast stone, concentrated, original, as if it were the source of all waters, and so Cousteau's attempt to fathom it was a natural-enough impulse for a diver, though it proved disastrous.

Cousteau and his companion attempted their descent in summer, of course, when the pool is quiet. They had to clamber down the rocks for fifty feet or so to the still waterline. There beneath the overhanging cliffs, they entered the pool tied by lifelines to a crew at the surface. Submerging, they simply let the weight at their belts draw them down, away from the light at the surface. They carried small lamps, which proved inadequate in the looming dark.

They proceeded down for a hundred feet but found no floor, and continued to sink, more slowly now, and in silence but for their mechanical breathing. When they had descended to two hundred feet, finding nothing but emptiness and pressure, dark water and sheer rock, they began having funny sensations, giddiness, imaginings. Bubbles of nitrogen were bursting in their blood veins, starving their brains of oxygen. Nitrogen narcosis, the bends, was setting in.

At first the bends don't hurt. They're mostly mental initially, and so it is then that they are most dangerous. One may simply begin to assume that one is somewhere else besides submerged in a foreign element. Deep in the Fontaine, Cousteau and his partner had no external clues, no insistence from the world to check the suggestions their tricked minds made, and they began to wander.

Then one of them, by some grace, recognized that something was not right.

He alerted his companion and they started up. Only then did the pain begin. As their ascent released the pressure of the heavy water above them, the gas fizzed in their bloodstreams like bubbles in soda. The roar in their heads gathered and they climbed for the light. Neither ever reached the surface. They blacked out underwater, and had to be hauled out on the lines, carried down the canyon to ambulances, taken to the hospital and revived for hours in a pressurized tank.

By the fourteenth century, the Fountain of the Sorgue had already been famous for ages. As a child, Francesco Petrarca—the poet Petrarch, on whom Cousteau had nothing, as far as rapture—had witnessed it in flood in 1314. That spring, the river erupted from the cavern, as it had done for thousands of years and continues to do. It boomed forth in a milky green torrent, filling the canyon and splashing the roots of cliff-bound fig trees that in the dry season dangle ten stories above on the rock.

Francesco, ten years old at the time, was taken to see this phenomenon by his father. His mother had resisted their trip. The boy was his mother's darling, a rare thing in that time when half the children perished before the age of five. If a child lived to be six, he or she was dressed and addressed as an adult. Before that it was best to assume that the child would die. Even Mary and Jesus were portrayed cooly then—the Christ child sometimes lying naked on the ground, the Madonna, calm, remote, large-eyed, standing off. But Francesco's mother adored him. Later, as the most famous poet of his age, he would acknowledge this. "She was a mother to me in love, as well as in blood," he would write of her.

And so, loving him, she feared for her child, and when his

father suggested that the boy join an expedition to witness the flood of the Sorgue, she refused. The man had to argue and bargain before his wife would consent. These were her terms: that Francesco would share a mount with a strong manservant who would hold the child tightly in his arms whenever they were near the water. In this manner he was allowed to witness the flood, gripped before the pale continuous explosion. It must have been an awesome and terrifying sight for the boy, all the more so, no doubt, for his mother's precautions.

Even by then the fear of flood, the threat of being overwhelmed, had been a leitmotiv in the young poet's life. Two years before, the family had been caught in a storm at sea off Genoa. Escaping the political chaos of their native Italy by boat, they had nearly drowned before they reached Marseilles. And as an infant Francesco had once been washed off a horse at a flooded ford. Small wonder that Francesco's mother feared for her child on this trip to the Fontaine. Or that Petrarch himself would distrust water all his life, referring to the danger of drowning over and over as a prime image for the vicissitudes and chaos of life. At age forty-four he wrote to his brother Gherardo, who had spurned the world's allurements and taken up a life in a monastery. He congratulated his brother for casting off his desires and compared him to an old sailor. "The novice at sea is frightened by the first rustle of wind," he writes, but "the old helmsman who has often brought into port his strained and battered vessel looks contemptuously down at the raging sea."

Odd then, perhaps, that as a grown man himself turning from the world and most particularly from his love for a woman, he would abandon the city and make his home at Fontaine-de-Vaucluse, on the narrow floodplain within the canyon of the Sorgue, where in spring the torrent would threaten his house and overwhelm his gardens.

•   •   •

Petrarch's father had been banished from Florence, where the ruling families' murderous competition had inspired the torments of Dante's *Inferno,* and had come to Avignon, his family in train. Avignon was then a kind of California, the land of the orange tree, a frontier where the tragic identities of the past might be jettisoned. At that time, the town's old reputation for sensuality had recently been enriched by a new arrival, the pope.

The pope had come to Avignon after the papacy had been ripped loose from Rome, where it had taken root for a thousand years. The struggle that dislodged the seat of the church had begun in 1304—the year of Francesco's birth—when the king of France, Philip the Fair, challenged the church's tax-exempt status and, in the resulting dispute, summoned the Holy Father to the French throne like a common claimant. The pope, Boniface VIII, refused, of course, declaring for his part that it was "necessary to salvation that every human creature be subject to the Roman pontiff." In answer, Philip rallied France and ordered an armed delegation to bring the pontiff by force. In the assault the old pope, Boniface VIII, was struck in the face with a steel gauntlet and killed, and afterward Philip the Fair achieved in a rigged election what he could not win by arms. The new pope turned out—no surprise—to be French, and as Clement V, he chose to live in Avignon, claiming that he feared revenge in Rome. The Italians, on the other hand, alleged that he kept a paramour in Provence.

It was a ready association. The poets of Provence, the trouba-dours, lusty youth in tights with lutes, had for more than a cen-tury made Avignon famous for adultery with style, for love at first sight and for the slender, blond, pale, precious and impossible mistresses whom they idealized in song, pledging their miserable troths. Such were their luxurious concerns, even before the pope arrived. Afterward, the earthiness of Avignon combined with the riches of the church to make the place into the sensual center of the world. The deracinated papacy proved vigorous, discovering new sources of income, and suddenly everything was for sale, from relics to positions to pardons. The pope threw up a palace, opulent but ungainly, with much tower space devoted to treasuries that were entered by lifting the heavy stones of the floor above. The money that was made was freely spent. The move had severed the church's old business ties, of course, and these had to be refurbished in Avignon. So the hopeful flocked into the walled city from all over Europe, and the town boomed with opportunists, its streets suddenly crowded, feverish, fashionable. Through the city's white gates came ambitious courtiers and clerics especially, bishops and diplomats and ambassadors, and attendant upon them, merchants, artisans, cooks, servants, whores and astrologers, several dozen banks and hundreds of poets. Such uproar resounded within the city walls, it seemed to Petrarch that the ground could not "contain the crowds, nor the sky the clamor." Pigs ran wild in the streets, eating raw sewage and sometimes sullying the finery of dandies.

It was no place for children. Ser Petrarca ensconced his family at Carpentras, a neighboring village, where his son Francesco grew up a dreamy youth, hearing Provençal songs and reading Latin poetry. Raised for the law, he proved too delicate for it. He was sent to Montpellier to study, but spent his book money on forbidden works of literature. When his father found these on one of his visits, he tossed them into the fire as the boy wept and plead. His father relented and spared two books from the flames: Cicero, for his son's rhetoric, and Virgil, for his fun. With the latter he needed little help—later in life Petrarch recalled his school days mostly for student riots, for singing and drinking, for dancing girls, for climbing back over the stockade at night after curfew—literally after the town's fires had been covered. And though he mastered his classical studies with great brilliance, by the last year of law school, he still felt himself above lawyering. "If I had been willing to practice," he wrote later, "my principles would have been ascribed to incompetence."

As it was, he was delivered from the legal profession by the death of his father. His beloved mother, too, had died while he was at school, and so he was left an orphan with an income. He moved into Avignon himself and took up the life of a troubadour, taking great pains, as he wrote later, "to be looked at, for people to point and say, 'There he goes.' " He and his brother dressed for hours each day, in perfumed, purple robes and tight shoes. They had their hair cut and curled to hang like hedges over their foreheads, which occasionally bore the welts from hot curling irons. Once abroad, they dodged the pigs and spoke in Latinisms, reversing their word order. They caged invitations to dine at feasts, where they sang their poems in praise of women and desire.

And "how eagerly," he wrote later, "we sought out a love." In this endeavor, the troubadours had dictated exactly the method and the model. Long before he met her, Francesco knew how she must look and act, and how he would feel and behave when he found her. She would be fair in complexion and passive, even icy, in demeanor. She would be beyond him. The courtly lady might be married or rich, but she would certainly be out of reach and dangerous—so that his desire for her would be as cruel as it was powerful. Francesco was well versed in all this by then and was waiting for the moment when the world might resemble his ideal.

Thus prepossessed, he searched for her all winter. Then when spring came, he found himself on the street outside St. Clare's church on Good Friday. On that day of all days, as the moment of the Cruxificion approached, the medieval church demanded that a Christian's mind fix on heaven and dismiss the earth as the mere venue of suffering, death, and redemption. It was sinful, even blasphemous, to fall in love on such a day and for that reason, irresistible. The troubadours had always located their loves where they might meet the most resistance. "Wherever a jealous husband . . . is reported to keep his prize well guarded," wrote Petrarch later, "a noble prey is scented out by our distinguished youths." To fall in love on Good Friday was to set the stakes as high as they might be set, and to take God Himself as one's rival. For Petrarch, it was, among other things, a stroke of literary genius, the first step toward his lasting fame.

It was April 6, 1327 and he was twenty-three, as he stood in the street outside the church. He saw an entourage approaching, the family and servants of Hugues de Sade, ancestor of the infamous marquis and a rich man of the town. Among that gathering, demure and as if radiant, walked the Lord's young wife, Laura, fair and chill, lovely and right. Francesco instantly felt "cruel desire" in his heart and fell in love. She was thirteen.

If life then was brief and fragile in a way we may barely imagine, so, too, its pleasures must have been rich beyond our measure. We wonder at the outright joy, of Chaucer's celebration of spring, until we see that merely surviving the winter then was a great deliverance, a miracle. What was good about life shone with an unbearable radiance, since it seemed sure to disappear at any moment. Something like this he must have felt when he saw her and, since he was young, imagined that he might bear it in any case. So he sealed his fate.

19

FLYING BUTTRESSES

....

Three days later, we had taken on a different appearance. We had become LJ Media. It was late morning on a workday in Avignon, the people on the avenue moving briskly in the dappled light beneath the plane trees, and we were writers on assignment, or at least the semblance of such. The crowd flowed around us as we stood with our bags, consulting the map, L in the gorgeous orange Indonesian silk outfit I'd bought her in Paris just for this. Thérèse and her mother, on their way to shop in Italy, had dropped us at the gates of the avenue, which was the Rue de la Republique, a central artery through the Old City. The straight street ran gently upslope from the medieval gates toward the towers of the Palace of the Popes, which enclosed the highest ground in the city, a rocky bluff above the river. At the foot of the avenue, one was supposed to feel lowly, I thought, as one meekly entered the town, seeking a pardon perhaps. The old city was still pretty splendid, crenellated ramparts enclosing the dense streets and all the old buildings cut from the same pale, goldish sandstone.

That morning we had a lunch appointment with a director at the Tourist Bureau. It was the first time in the trip that we'd been called upon to be the writing team, the business that we'd claimed to be. And we were being businesslike about it, though I was a little nervous. I hadn't exactly faced the question of whether I was in fact a writer on that trip, since my motivation from the beginning was obviously not literary. I'd taken this trip as a lover, and I wondered if that precluded me somehow from being a writer. I hoped not, but I feared so. I would take notes, which is what I always did, in the hope that merely writing would be sufficient to make me a writer. But I was supposed to be writing about something—France, in particular—and I hadn't exactly been doing that. All my notes starred L. My notebook was a valentine, a record of beautiful moments featuring the two of us in France. So far, France had just been a backdrop, I had to admit. I didn't feel guilty about that yet, though I thought I might.

L, on the other hand, was into it. She was was irresistibly self-possessed, her walk that morning a businesslike stride. She had taken up the identity without a bit of irony and had shepherded us along the avenue, notebook and pen at ready in the outside flap of her shoulder bag. Watching her, I tried to act decently, too, though her earnestness in particular made me forget myself. I had said I was going on a story, though, and I would be on a story, a professional. The term itself steadied me.

Four blocks up the avenue, we found the Tourist Bureau, in a prominent modern building next to a white medieval church. L exclaimed at the old edifice, which had flying buttresses and a Gothic bell tower in which the black lip of the big bell showed. The sleek, functional shell next door made the flying buttresses seem a little overdone, even dubious, a way of achieving soaring dimensions inside the church with medieval materials, before such a space was really possible. By contrast, the Tourist Bureau was glassy and rectilinear, its structure neatly internalized. We went in through the big glass door, and L spoke to the receptionist in bright tones, taking out her notebook as we waited. I got out my notebook, too. "L jazzed," I wrote, being a writer. "Office nice."

The director turned out to be a gracious, friendly, big-eyed woman, chic in her beige suit. She introduced herself to L and me with a careful equivalence and suggested we go on to lunch, though it was a little early. I had expected an itinerary, and suggestions as to what we might write about, but she gave us none. We simply went to lunch. She walked us out of the building and down several curving narrow streets of the old city, and finally into an enclosed courtyard where the tables stood in pools of shade under white umbrellas. L and the director chatted in French while I smiled and remained mute, not comprehending much. We drank a light white wine and ordered seafood.

The director herself was very graceful in her manner, I noticed. She liked American novels. I kept thinking that she'd get around to business, though we didn't. Throughout the meal she let slip no hint—for which I watched—that she thought L and I had arrived together as anything except a team of working writers. Though we kept our notebooks at ready, we didn't write in them as she spoke, in French to L and in my own tongue to me, about Phillip Roth and Ann Beattie and John Irving. This was the grace of the French, and it was beginning to worry me a little. For she would never touch us with obligation, I knew by then, and that very fact made me feel obligated nonetheless, as I sat there, sensing that here, truly, was not a PR person to have to escape from. I had depended upon having to escape before, on being importuned enough to have to go off on my own. But here I didn't have the luxury of defining myself by refusing. When I asked finally if she could recommend a guide to show us the old city, she said. "Of course." But that was it, for business. It had been an incredibly pleasant lunch, and I felt anxious when it was over, when she

parted from us, still light as air, as a friend might, leaving us free
again to be whatever we were, writers or whatever. That should
have been more of a relief than it was.

That afternoon on the windy ramparts around the palace, we
looked down on the town. The guide, Nadine, was Provençal, a
petit, dark woman in a flowered skirt. Beyond us lay Avignon,
orange tile roofs at every angle to one another, spires amidst
them, and in the distance, high rises. I liked being up on the wall,
though actually it wasn't the highest point in town, I noticed. The
towers of the palace still stood above us. I walked behind on the
parapet while L asked Nadine questions in French and wrote
down Nadine's French answers. I was trying to be professional,
trying not even to look at L, and recalling what I usually did on
trips, which was to walk around and speculate to myself, occasionally writing my speculations down. For instance, as we
climbed to the parapet it had occurred to me that, as gravity
conferred a strategic advantage to the high ground, so goodness
had come to be associated with altitude—God and the king on
high, heroes and art and women on pedestals. I didn't write this
down. I'd always done this kind of thinking on my own before,
and it didn't seem to have the same weight in company.

L was getting all the good information in French from our
guide. I listened to Nadine speak in her Provençal accent, a little
twangier even to my ear than the Parisian talk. In this tide of
French around me, I was beginning to pick up certain currents. As
we came to the edge of the plaza atop the hill, Nadine announced
in English, "This wall is called the Wall of Shame." Then she went
back to explaining in French. At that point the wall gave on the
Chapel of the Black Penitents, I understood her to say. "To give
on" was an odd expression, as if merely overlooking might be a
sort of gift. And just how did "overlooking" come to mean "missing?" Missing would be more like underlooking.

"Now," said the guide, pointing to the orange tile roof below us, "it is the prison of the town." We stood at the elegant parapet wall, but looking over it I couldn't see much of the prison, as another wall, of newer mortar and irregular stones, had been built just beyond the first, and blocked the view. I wanted to see for myself, so I boosted myself up the old wall, and stepped over onto the new one. It was the kind of thing I did on trips. "Be careful up there," said L. The view from that point was exhilarating. Below was the prison, all right, a long, elliptical building with a central court, all four stories marked by narrow, barred windows.

"I can see it," I called down to the women. This was more like it.

The central courtyard of the prison was covered with netting, though the prison had the same romantic quality as most of the other buildings in the Old City. I jumped back down to L and Nadine, who stopped in the midst of her stream of French, turned to me and said in English, as if in explanation, "Lovers."

Lovers of the men in the prison, I understood after an astonished pause. "They stood on the wall and called out." The wall, it turned out, was the place where the lovers brought messages to their sweethearts inside. Nadine went on. When a lover stood up here, she showed herself to the whole town.

"She confessed that her lover was in the prison," said Nadine. "So it was called the Wall of Shame." I had been up on the Wall of Shame. The second wall had been built recently, explained Nadine, to prevent the lovers from tossing down guns.

I didn't believe in just noticing the picturesque; this was a legacy of my found poetry phase. I would see whatever I saw for my own reasons, which weren't always—ever, actually—completely clear to me. In the little park at the crown of the hill, some of the big trees had looping trunks that needed to be propped up with poles, and swans swam in an artificial lake beneath a small waterfall and a grotto, made of cement sculpted to look natural, and in a little playground with a teetertotter and a merry-go-round, a child yelled for his mother over and over. He must have been yelling *"Maman!"* I thought, remembering little Marcel at the top of the stairs. At the north side of the park was a vertical drop of about a hundred feet, down to the water of the Rhône, which was thick and dark and looked squeezed by its banks.

Beneath us there lay the famous ruined bridge of Avignon. The bridge took three arched steps, then plunged away, then took another step, then plunged for good. It had not been destroyed in a battle, as I'd supposed, but, as Nadine explained, by a flood. Then we followed Nadine down the hill, down a steep walk along the palace. I wished L wouldn't walk in front of me when I was trying to act professional. I could smell her perfume.

There'd probably always been some human fort on that bluff above the river, I thought. Men had seen it and known it as a place that might help them with their lives by protecting them from other men. A place that made one powerful, just by being up there. By the Middle Ages, the powerful men in that place were popes, God's anointed. With windmills on the bluff, they drew their water from the river, and the palace would have been well stocked with everything else they needed. In case of siege they could shut the city gates and, with their stores of food and their attendants and their families inside, pretty much get on as normal. I liked that thought and wrote something down about it.

The palace wasn't just one palace, I noticed, but at least two. Its northern half stood as a fortress. It was thick and had square towers. This part was put up by the first pope in Avignon, said Nadine. With the place secured, the next pope evidently felt freer to be artistic, to make his Gothic statement. We could see this influence as we entered a broad plaza below, the new addition looking new yet, with high arches above crisp steps and slender twin towers that seemed to hover on the stone face of the walls, their points barbed with gargoyles. But this more flowery statement failed as well to dominate the whole edifice. The Great Chapel, a soaring block that overall had the proportions of a refrigerator, anchored the palace on the south. On its face, two tall pointed windows stood inside recessed arches, looking like arrows, blunt, reiterated indications to heaven. We climbed the palace steps beneath a crenellated guard tower, its overhang like the others graduated in delicate upside-down steps to the wall above the door. The tower itself had holes in the shape of crosses cut into it. They were thin crosses, the crosspiece of each just wide enough to accommodate a pair of eyes, the vertical part tall for shooting arrows through.

Inside, Nadine led us into a guard room and immediately across it and out again into a dusty inner courtyard pitted with diggings. From there we proceeded across, into an opposite door to the treasury, which now served as a museum for palace artifacts. I liked a pair of battered doors in particular, each several inches thick, bound in iron and studded with boltheads the size of dice. Someone sometime had pierced a hole through one door with a heavy, pointed object, after many tries. Nearby were chunks of carved limestone from the Middle Ages, one a stylized *Téte de Chien,* a dog with big ears and curled bangs. *"Chagrin d'Amour,"* I said to L, as Nadine looked on, puzzled. The stone dog had a guilty expression, as if he had been confused by his master's command that he pose for the sculpture and had considered it some kind of punishment.

L found a display of tiles that she liked. The private parts of the palace had been sumptuously tiled in the Middle Ages, and the display showed some blue and orange tiles from the pope's steam room. Checks and fleurs had been drawn upon them freehand, so that they might have seemed expressionistic, had they been painted after the age of machines. In another alcove we found a series of paintings of the famous ruined bridge, one a colored eighteenth century engraving with pictures of children dancing on it. Above them rose the rock and the palace. The artist had drawn in a picturesque aspect of the castle not actually visible from the bridge, I noticed, having just seen it. Beneath the picture of the dancing children, the verses of the old song were printed as a caption: *"Sur le pont d'Avignon tout le monde y danse, danse."* *"Tout le monde,"* I liked, for "everyone."

Then L led the way up a staircase overlooking the courtyard. The palace was huge, and in the older part some dark recesses had simply been roped off to the public. Before one, a silver-haired man in jeans aimed an elaborate video camera into utter blackness before moving on. "The keep," I thought, remembering that castles had keeps, but not remembering what they were, exactly. As I watched, a young woman, one of the guides, emerged from the dark adjusting her uniform, stepping over the cordon with an odd composed expression on her face. A moment later another guide, a young man, came loping as if casually out of the keep, studiously not looking at me as I looked at him.

In the banquet hall above, beneath the ribbed and vaulted ceiling, the wall held tapestries, one of Alexander the Great triumphantly entering Babylon on horseback, the crowd at his feet in awe. One blue-eyed blond woman, breasty and holding a lyre, looked particularly thunderstruck, gazing up at his majesty. That month in France I'd read every day in the *Herald Tribune* about Saddam Hussein's ongoing occupation of Kuwait, and so this picture of Western triumph in Babylon seemed ironic to me. But the historical tapestry was a recent addition. In the time of the popes, all of the art in this part of the palace had been religious, of course. In a chapel off the hall, we found pale original frescoes of miracles and martyrs, images of the sick suddenly well, the blind seeing, St. Peter crucified upside down, St. Paul prostrate on the road to Damascus, lying beneath the cold gaze of three soldiers clad in chain-mail. These were the chambers where the popes had received the public. We proceeded through rooms that the ordinary people would never have seen, rooms of increasing intimacy, from the conclave room to the private audience room, where a tapestry depicted Jesus healing the *paralytiques,* and finally into the pope's bedroom itself.

Here, the art changed. Suddenly the walls bore frescoes of woodland scenes, of a forest of splendid boughs and bowers in which birds sang. A tromp l'oeil scarlet curtain encircled the room at shoulder height, hanging by painted brass rings on a painted brass rail, and lending the room the effect of a royal enclosure amid a wild and abundant wood. The walls of another bedchamber elaborated this motif of nature's bounty. Sturgeon crowded a marble pool. A hunting dog pointed out hidden game. A servant seemed to be stalking birds with a net at night. And all around them rose masses of foliage, curly and heavy with fruit. This was the world that the popes had reserved for themselves.

At last I followed L and Nadine out again into the air, beneath a hazy sky and the tolling of bells. Then we said good-bye to Nadine and walked back to the main boulevard, the Rue de la Republic, which that afternoon was crowded with shoppers going to the department stores. The sidewalk was lined with glossy advertising in clean, illuminated cases. The ads, for clothing mostly, had no effect upon me, since I didn't recognize the products and couldn't readily read the captions. By the time I had finished translating them, it was too late for them to set off the intended impulse.

We laughed to see what was American on the street. Popular at that moment in France were clothes and accessories emblazoned with American-sounding slogans and worn the way one might wear a Chinese character as a brooch, for effect and without regard for its meaning. Here the desired effect was of American confidence and with-it-ness. One schoolgirl's rucksack read "The Most Exciting Way of Life!" A boy's jean jacket recommended "The Best Experience of All," and a woman's yellow T-shirt announced: "Means So Much More!" Despite myself, I felt homesick reading them.

Eventually we turned back to the town square, which was commanded by the thick pillars of the Hotel De Ville, the neoclassical city hall. I assumed, looking at the blackened letters on its pediment, that it was an enormous, fortified hotel. This L found funny. She suggested I try to check in. We found a café near an elaborate two-tiered carousel and sat down to finish our notes. L went right to it, but I got distracted by an annoying mime, who hung about the central plaza, sneaking up behind pedestrians and mimicking their walks. He sometimes startled them as they suddenly discovered that they were the subject of his mockery and art. The crowd at the café tables roared to see his victims jump. Try that in Chicago, I thought. MAN HELD IN SAVAGE BEATING OF MIME. Seeing the mime made me uneasy. Just moments before, I had walked through that plaza quite unaware, and hadn't noticed him then. Had I heard the crowd laugh as I'd come in?

We had fruit and coffee, and read each other our notes. "Office nice" she thought funny. I'd tried to write about everything, though my real subject always seemed to surface. Her notes were full of detail. They came from the ground up, spontaneous in a way that mine were not. As I listened to her read, I noticed that a lot of bad oil paintings, for sale on easels, lined the square near the café tables. Clowns and castles, and a lot of sunflowers. For some reason, possibly my sense of the superiority of L's notes, these paintings seemed particularly annoying at that moment, as did the paintings of characters from the town's summer theater festival, who waved from trompe l'oeil windows on the façades of some of the building. These weren't worthy of Avignon, I thought. After all, this had been a splendid place in the olden days, one of the glories of the fourteenth century. Petrarch him-self had probably walked through this very square. A gust of wind blew some of the paintings down, and I was pleased. L stopped reading when they slammed onto the pavement, and I told her my thought.

She said, "How would you make it different?"

"I don't know," I said. I had been complaining, not proposing a plan for civic betterment. "Actors in period costume, maybe, like they do at Williamsburg."

She knew I wasn't serious. "Or just cordoned off—that'd be even better," she said, kidding me back.

"Nah," I said, though in truth I was a little taken with this cordoning-off idea.

20

PEEKABOO

....

I assume that trees, for instance, are patient, and that waves are eager. I'd have to be patient as a tree, anyway, anchored in the soil and still but for the inching of my own growth. And as a wave I'd possess eagerness, my sense of destination stronger every instant. As a stone I'd have gravity and anger, as the sky, wisdom and cheer. Never mind that, as it is, I possess none of these, purely. Afterward, after L, I could see this, though by then I had no faith that I could do anything about it.

I see the world as some ideal version of myself, though in bits, each purer than I am and yearning to be whole. For what would a wave be eager for, except for the shore where I stand? And who would the trees be waiting for, except for me, witness to such patience? I people the universe with feelings, a god for every leaf, though in this my self stands in for the god, infantile, as if still supposing the world disappears for peekaboo.

Seeing things otherwise, swept clean of human reactions, is nearly impossible, requiring constant effort and leaving me un-

sure if, so revealed, life is richer or poorer. Richer by far, larger
and more mysterious than I can imagine, my own interpretations
by comparison minuscule, merely personal, bound by language,
not applicable—this is what I want to believe now. But this is
desire talking.

Rocks and trees, I suppose I could live without knowing. More
to the point, though, if I can't know the world, what can I know
of this woman who, besides being as strange in herself as the
earth, stands as I do at the center of a sphere, reading the world
for what she needs, for how she feels, and only by some grace
imagining it otherwise?

Still in love and pouring forth poems about it, the young Francesco Petrarcha lived for six years in Avignon in the relative splendor of the palace of his patron, Giovanni Colonna, nephew of the
very man who, in the year of Petrarch's birth, smote the elderly
Pope Boniface VIII with his steel gauntlet, precipitating the removal of the papal court to Provence. Giovanni had also studied
law in Bologna, had admired the poet Francesco there, and, when
the two returned to Avignon, summoned him to the palace, gave
him a place to live and provided him with a clerical income to
write his poems. In this manner, enclosed within the city's walls
with his Laura, Petrarch began his great and lifelong work in her
name. This was expected of him; as a poet attached to a great
house in Provence, one wrote love poems in troubadour fashion.
Three attributes would make Petrarch excel at this task. First, he
was wily and ambitious, wise to the ways of authority. Secondly,
he had been closely trained in classical Roman literature and in
the traditions of Rome so that these country airs, love poems,
might be deepened and enriched thereby. Finally, he seems actually to have suffered, to have been obsessed with her, to have been
in love with Laura. When the Sienese painter Simone Martini
visited the palace, Petrarch commissioned Laura's portrait in

miniature, says his biographer Ernest Wilkins, so that he might carry her image with him always.

Laura never shared his obsession. Judging from the evidence of the poems, his love for her went unconsummated. For one thing, he presented his love poems not to her, but to his patron and assembled attendants in the palace. He and Laura saw little of each other. Throughout the sonnets, he writes of his eyes and of hers, of what he may see and may not see. As the perfect disdainful maiden, she won't see him, and further, keeps her face veiled, so that, as the poet wrote, "I see not anywhere what most I love." In his poems she appears as a perfect star over the proceedings of his life, a glimmer compared to the one we see most clearly, Petrarch himself. As his biographer Morris Bishop writes, "the poems are not so much celebrations of his beloved's merits as they are analyses of his own feelings in certain situations, usually the sequel of some rebuff." They are Petrarch's dialogue with himself, the way he held himself in love.

Bishop concludes that the affair with Laura didn't come to any fruition in the flesh because it was impractical in a small town in which everyone talked. A cardinal's palace was no place for a tryst, besides, and the whole adventure was dangerous, as her husband might have legally killed them both. Further, writes Bishop, a scandal would have ruined Petrarch's literary career. But these are suppositions, practical objections that many lovers in their passion never paused to consider. A larger consideration for Petrarch may have been that for him fulfilment in the flesh was unpoetic. For poetry, this unrequited love affair was perfect, a trajectory of desire cast out infinitely, an earthly love ungrounded. Unconsummated, they could be as the lovers on the Grecian urn would be, always within reach, so long as they never touched.

And perhaps he never touched her because she did not exist.

But for a single piece of evidence, Laura might be a fiction. So exactly does she fill Petrarch's poetic needs that many critics have argued that she was merely the distillation of a literary trope, plucked from the troubadours and applied with the cool artistry of the Latin poets. Her very name is too right to be real, some contend, having such rich literary possibilities as a triple pun—on gold (*l'auro*), on the gentle breeze (*l'aura*) and on the laurel itself, of which the crown of poetry is made—that it would seem an astonishing coincidence had there been a real woman of that name. And Bishop points out that April 6th, the Good Friday upon which Petrarch claimed to have first glimpsed her, was in fact a Monday in 1327.

Her description in the poems does not serve much to confirm her reality, for if she was real, she happened also to be the flaxen-haired lady of the troubadour tradition. And when she physically appears in the poems, she is enveloped in classical allusion and literary circumstance. In one poem he comes upon her bathing, nude in the sunshine in a pool amid a wooded glen. She splashes water into his eyes with the heel of her hand, seeming real enough, detailed, though the scene itself is familiar from Ovid's tale of Acteon and Diana, and at the end Petrarch claims to have been transformed into a stag at the sight of her nakedness. Elsewhere, she turns him into a stone, into a tree anchored in the earth.

Some historical details conform. In 1333 he journeyed north, to Paris and beyond, and in a later prose work called *Secretum,* he confessed that his purpose in traveling was to thwart his obsession with her. In this of course he failed, for travel only feeds obsession, providing ample evidence everywhere in the wide strangeness of foreign surroundings. As he confessed in Sonnet XVI, "I roam, seeking your true form in others." All in all, a reader can only infer Laura's actual life, far off in time and un-touched by these poems, which in any case might have been in-comprehensible to her. Though Petrarch decided to write them in his vernacular language, Italian, rather than in formal Latin—so that his Italian audience at the Colonna estate might readily understand them—Laura, it has been presumed, spoke only Provençal. But this, too, like other realistic assumptions about her, may be too much. She is real and she is not. She appears as if within some pure, pale light that drowns the details.

Petrarch came to hate Avignon. "I am living in the Babylon of the West," he said in the end. He called the time of the popes there "the Babylonian Captivity," making Rome by analogy Jerusalem and himself a Jeremiah. In 1348 Petrarch composed a letter, addressee unknown, on the evils of adultery. Jeremiah's indictment of Babylon—"They are become as amorous horses, stallions, each one neighing after his neighbor's wife"—Petrarch finds only too true for Avignon, where things are even worse. "Even the lust of horses has sometimes shown more restraint," than the citizens of Avignon, he notes, citing an unlikely account of a stallion blindfolded and put to stud to his own mother. When the blindfold was removed and the horse recognized what he had done to his dam, the story went, he turned on his master and bit him to death. In Avignon, Petrarch found that "nothing is more vile, more base, more abject, than one driven by nature's impulses with no restraint of reason." This was written in 1348, the year of the Black Plague, and of Laura's death by it.

The date of Laura's death in the plague is the single historical detail that tends to confirm the whole legend. For there was a Laura, the wife of Hugues de Sade, who in 1348 lay dying of this swift and terrible disease, which had come upriver from Marseilles to Avignon in March. By April the plague was killing four hundred people a day. In the end, it would kill half the town. On the third of April, Laura wrote out her will. She died soon after; the disease usually proved fatal within three days. Petrarch later wrote that his beloved Laura had died on April 6th, 1348, another Good Friday, twenty-one years to the day from the moment he had first laid his eyes upon her. Petrarch himself was spared.

One might assume that it was at this time that Petrarch, grief-struck, left town and went to live in the country at the source of the Sorgue, to write his poems for Laura. In fact, he'd fled Avignon ten years earlier, escaping its intrigues—Petrarch was accused of necromancy, for reading Virgil—and its contagions, its narrow streets where you had "to mingle your breath with that of a thousand others." But the healthful aspects of the country were perhaps just auxiliary benefits. In letters he wrote that he had abandoned the city in despair for his love. "My only hope," he wrote, "lay in flight." To convey his vulnerability to her, he invoked his old fear of the engulfing sea. "As the benighted steersman fears the lurking reefs," he wrote, "I recoil in terror from her face, from her words that fire the mind, from her golden-clouded head, her necklaced throat, her quivering shoulders, her eyes delighting in my death."

In the wilderness of the canyon, he planted a garden in the narrow meadow by the river, and lost it in several springs to the torrent, despite his construction of upstream jetties and earthworks. His house in Vaucluse was well fortified, though he still had to defend against brigands. The river protected the house's front, the ridge its back. A tunnel, cut through the sheer limestone as an aqueduct originally, was his entry, and in it he placed a thick, studded door that might be barred. Once Petrarch was inside, the Vaucluse—the closed valley—was his alone, which was the way he liked it, unmarked by others.

If he had sought to avoid her appearance by living in the wilderness, he failed. Everywhere he looked in her absence, he found her. There in his solitude, he cast her image upon the face of the bluff, saw her in the trees, heard her in the river. *"Più deserto lido,"* he wrote, *"tanto più bella il mio pensier l'adombra"* ("The wilder the shore, the more beautifully my thoughts may render her"). And while she lived and died below, within the pale, crenellated walls of Avignon, he created his own beloved image of her above, which he enshrined in the poems. When he heard about the plague, he began part two of his work, those verses composed for La Madonna Laura after her death.

Petrarch had been an exile since birth, not just in territory but in time. Whether in Avignon or in Vaucluse, he recognized that he lived in the boondocks of Transalpine Gaul, so named by Caesar. More profoundly, Petrarch himself was a sort of remote Roman province, as well. Though history would view him as one of the sources of a new age, he lived feeling that he had been born too late, that he was witnessing the paltry conclusion of history. From his house at the source of the Sorgue, he wrote often to cry out against fresh barbaries, invoking the ancients. He would carry out his literary life in emulation of the great Latin writers and would manage, through a great feat of favor-seeking and political juggling, to have himself crowned in classical fashion with a laurel by the senate in Rome, albeit in a Rome where cattle grazed on the site of the Forum. He would leave for posterity all kinds of classical literary works—orations, invectives, epitaphs, triumphs, ecologues—and would document his life to an astonishing degree for a citizen of the early Middle Ages, compiling his *Epistolae,* his letters, which he would collect, edit, revise and publish. He wrote prose tracts as well, copied and translated the great works of the past and of course composed a corpus of poetry in all the classical styles, ranging from his epic entitled *L'Africa,* about the exploits of Scipio Africanus, to the lyric poems for Laura, which late in his life he would finally finish revising and publish as the single work known as the *Canzoniere,* a collection finally of three hundred seventeen sonnets, twenty-nine canzoni, nine sextines, seven ballades and four madrigals.

The *Canzoniere* are beautiful, various and delicate, like petals crystallized with frost. This comes as a grace. Far more often, literary work from the Middle Ages is interesting only as arti-fact—doggerel celebrating King Robert, for instance. The rav-ages of history are a kind of lottery, in which works with certain physical and economic characteristics, literary quality not being one of them, have better odds of survival. It helped, though it was not necessary, for a work to have been popular—the more copies made, the greater the chance that one copy might survive. A num-ber of cheap copies, though, might be not much more permanent than a single one. High quality manuscripts on expensive vellum, owned by people with property who didn't have to move around a lot and who had the wherewithal to care for their books, didn't get lost as often. Such works weren't fed to the fires, even in the worst winter. And it was best of all for a work's survival if the king or the pope himself kept and honored it, as the institutions attendant upon them might employ generations of scribes, re-copying old manuscripts when they began to crumble. It follows that what we see of literature from that time is, with little excep-tion, authorized. Petrarch would see to this for his own work.

His younger contemporary Chaucer may have composed his well-known "Retraction" with the resultant advantage to the survival of his works in mind. At the end of his life, Chaucer appended this apology to the *Canterbury Tales,* as if adding one last tiny dour pilgrim to that lively parade. In the end Chaucer begs God for mercy and retracts his bawdy and earthly works— "many a song and many a lecherous lay"—recommending his saints' lives and other work more pleasing to the church. Cer-tainly he may have actually felt repentant, of course, though he did in fact leave his work intact. The Wife of Bath and the Miller still speak to us, though Chaucer claimed to retract them. That they do may be because he did.

An inveterate reviser, Petrarch was more thorough, incor-porating his apology into everything. He covered over Laura with it. Had he died as a young man, at thirty-three say, he might have left behind a more potent, realistic evocation of her, in poems eager and immediate, full of desire and hope, grief and despair. But such youthful and earthly verses most probably would not have survived the censors and the ages. As it was, though some eighty early poems appear in the final volume of the *Canzoniere,* they appear in their later manifestations, their originals reworked. Of his youthful poems Petrarch writes disparagingly in his old age—at forty-three—calling them "silly songs, full of false and indecent praise of loose women and shamefully revealing our lusts." So the ultimate version of this volume written in Laura's name shows in all its parts the hand of an old man who claims to have turned away from the passion of his youth. In the end he completed in isolation the work he finally titled *Rerum Vulgarium Fragmenta (Fragments of Vulgar Things)*—that is, lyric poems in the vernacular. The suggestion in this title of modest self-denigration is as unmistakable as it is false, for the work is finally exalted and complete. The first step of his falling in love—on Good Friday—he crowned with his rejection of it. This rejection of Laura, one might add, had as little to do with her actual being as had his earlier devotion.

Though Petrarch was a formidable stylist, a master of exacting, interlaced forms like the sestina, he was not, in much of his matter, original. He was the great codifier of what had come before. Petrarch's principle invention was that he both articulated and denied this new, romantic conception, invented by the troubadours in the century before his birth—that for a man, the highest good in life was achieving the love of a woman. He subordinated this new idea to the credo of the church. He framed his poems about Laura between a late sonnet condemning the youthful folly of his love and a final hymn of praise to the Virgin Mary, who replaces Laura as his beloved. So he honored, as Chaucer would, the scholastic, patristic doctrine of God's eternity, before which all of life and love was but a brief dream and woman the snare of the devil.

In the end, Petrarch even claimed to be thankful for Laura's death. He thanked Jesus for permitting him to taste "such deceptive sweetness, mixed with pain," and hoped to end his days "meditating on my own perils." To his brother—who had taken refuge in the monastery after the death of his own beloved lady—he writes, invoking God: "And in Thy great mercy Thou didst ordain that our loves should not overwhelm us, for Thou didst remove the objects from this world," these objects being the living women they had loved. "Their death was, I hope," he adds, "useful to them." In the end, he attempted to make Laura into an emblem for his sin and the earth itself, that he might abandon these by abandoning her.

Thus he won his success. The church had an interest in making earthly life seem worthless, so that it might offer in its place the solid appearance of eternity, as if on a far shore, and gain thereby earthly power for itself. Petrarch's repudiation of human love served this interest. After his death Cardinal Pietro Bembo would authorize for the church the Petrarchan doctrine of love—that is, its renunciation—as the great archetype for literature. Many of Petrarch's lyrics, copied in his own hand, are still preserved in the Vatican library.

He became a poet for the ages. His work survived for centuries and, in Italy and across Europe, was copied, honored and emulated, especially his poems for Laura. In England, Wyatt, Surrey, Shakespeare and the Elizabethans especially would be influenced by his example. The type of Laura—her looks, her demeanor—would proliferate, would become desirable in life as in art, as poets across the ages imprinted her image on the wilderness, as Petrarch had.

·　　·　　·

As one of the last acts of his life, Petrarch gave his tiny crabbed copy of St. *Augustine's Confessions* to a young monk, an Augustinian. By then Petrarch had carried the book with him for forty years, and his willingness to give it away was a sure sign that his life was coming to a close. Still, he gave away his Augustine, though he did so with reluctance. It had preserved him, Petrarch felt, through his most terrifying moment, a storm at sea. Whether he still kept his miniature of Laura, he does not say.

By the medieval church's creed, Petrarch had to renounce not just Laura and his love for her, but his writing as well, as vanity. He pays lip service to this. In the letter to his brother indicting the excesses of their youth, he writes, "There is no help in literature." But the letter itself, before and after this remark, is studded with literary references, to Plato and Aristotle, Horace and Seneca, Cicero and Homer. "Let me allege some secular testimonies," he pleads, "which even the Apostle Paul did not blush to use."

Similarly, he cannot banish the real Laura from his work. She is there, in some ways suggested all the more irresistibly by his negation of her. Try as he might to surrender himself, in his youth to love and in later life to chilly Heaven, Petrarch finally fails. He touches two worlds and inhabits neither. For he is a weak, vain man, and in the end his failure breathes life into his poetry. It lets the real Laura live forever, if not fully revealed, by inference at least, as if behind her veil.

A late, apocryphal note reports that Laura once visited Fontaine-de-Vaucluse when he was there in his exile. She came with a group of high-born folk from Avignon to see the river erupting in its flood. Wandering the canyon, Petrarch happened to meet them, and there exchanged words with Laura, says the legend, for the first and only time. She'd heard about his years of literary devotion to her, but she greeted him with words of rebuke. "Sir," she is supposed to have said—I imagine her words rising over the roar of the flood—"I am not the woman you take me for." After that she left, and he went on nonetheless, for the rest of his life imagining the woman he took her for everywhere, her lines in the limbs of trees, her voice in the sound of water.

21

Pêches Blanches

....

By the time we'd arrived in Aix-en-Provence, I'd begun to fear for my composure. The intensity of my feeling and the demand that I stand off, that I not act like I was in love, was beginning to wear on me. At times I wanted to shout, though just what I would have shouted, I had no idea.

We were still supposed to be observing, although I was in the midst of such strong feelings that noticing anything wasn't easy. My thoughts were always so full of a possible us, a possible trip, a possible France, that it would have been a relief to see anything purely. But the pressure just lent to whatever I tried to notice a vicious symbolic effect: whatever it was, it inevitably reflected back, commenting on us, on my fate, up or down. What I wanted most—some hint, some evidence that, as a strategy, this casual-ness was working—clung to everything. Still, I was with her, I thought as we walked through the railroad station on our arrival. What more did I want? I couldn't say, exactly. Just more.

We were watching life go by twice a day, by then—once at
large and once on paper. We'd seek something out, try to observe
it, then find a café and make notes—rehearsing to ourselves what
we'd seen. Then we would often read the notes to each other,
reliving these things yet again. This exercise, of course, only enhanced the weighty quality everything had by then. Every pebble
posed my problem.

In this context, the bland, firm, descriptive sentences in the
Michelin guide seemed like salvation. Here, if anywhere, were
unpoisoned details. "Around old Aix a new town has developed,
which is both a spa and an industrial complex." So walking into
Aix, I forced myself to notice that the place did look several centuries newer than Avignon. In Avignon the railroad station sat
beyond the walls of the old city; here the town seemed to radiate
in avenues away from the station, like Paris or D.C.

On Aix's main avenue, the Cours Mirabeau, young people—
seemingly students, many of them Americans—crowded the sidewalk. I could hear refreshing snatches of English at the pay
phones along the boulevard. One guy shouted into the line, "I'm
fine!"

Separate groups of young men and young women lounged at
the cafés amid the patched trunks of the plane trees. These trees
shed their bark in sheets, and several layers of old bark clung to
the trunks, gray where it was oldest, green beneath, and yellow
where the new bark had just been exposed to the light of day. Try
as I might to make nothing of that, it gave me a queasy feeling.

Crossing the avenue, we found, on a circular island midstream
in the traffic, the ancient thermal fountain that had brought the
Romans to Aix in the first place. I tried to look calmly and mean-
inglessly at the spring, but it only made me want her. Long capped
in stone, the hot water had nourished a coat of steam-fed moss,
thick, so verdant it seemed to have gold in it. "Its water," said the
Michelin guide, "gushes out at 34°C=93°F." A bath, I was think-

ing. With L. I was aching all over from travel, and I could feel the weariness of those Roman legions, having tramped for days down their long, straight roads to Aix for hot water. The hotel that the French Government Tourist Board had reserved for us that night had three stars, according to the Michelin. At that moment, I wasn't observing but imagining a Roman delight, a vast, tiled tub, a steaming bath.

We walked on through the narrow streets of the Quartier Mazarine, where I noticed that some of the parked cars had had their side mirrors sheered off from near collisions in the close passages of that old neighborhood, the old way not exactly accommodating the features of the new. The Quarter had been modernized, said the Michelin, meaning that in the seventeenth century inconceivably ancient buildings had been razed and replaced with merely old ones, a baroque village, the golden sandstone of the new buildings darker than stone of Avignon. Every house was elegant with carved doorways and wrought iron balconies. At the first intersection, we found another fountain, this one with four leaping dolphins. "J. C. Rambot," said the guidebook, "1667." My whole nation was younger than this "modern" French fountain, by a century. What chance did I have?

Bounding the old quarter was another avenue, beyond which new buildings stood. Over them rose hills that I seemed to remember from Cézanne, but where we were going it was for sure the late twentieth century already. There across the avenue crouched our hotel, glassy and barely finished. It had three flags out front and a patch of perfect new sod in a triangular space amid the small descending plaza before the door. Its façade attempted to echo the old quarter, its cement composite dyed almost the shade of the weathered stone, its iron window railings small and useless, as the windows were sealed for climate control, seeming to hope for approval from the real ones across the avenue.

The hotel's electric doors slid open for us, and inside the lobby the marble floor had islands of carpet in it, on which clustered low purple couches. It was a place of stainless elevator doors, soprano arias from hidden speakers, bellboys in uniform with their trundles, the whole place bathed in pale blue light, reflected off the pool beyond the bank of windows.

She balked at the door, eyeing the gleaming place with suspicion. "It's kind of too much," she said.

"Of course," I said, trying to sound seasoned. "It's always too much."

We went to the long mahogany desk, where the young and impeccable clerk said "Good day" as we walked up. I gave him our names and was relieved when he found them on his computer screen.

"How many rooms?" he asked.

"Uh, one," I said, noticing that L was not nodding.

"And what method will you choose to pay for it?" he said.

I was stopped by this, partially because I was still flurrying from his first question. I had assumed the place would be free, and I knew that I could never afford it. I looked at the black felt board behind the clerk, listing room prices, but I could make nothing of the list of big numbers, except for one, "*Animaux 50.*" There was a whole world out there, I felt, but I had no hold on it, not with L at my elbow.

"Credit card," I said.

Finally the mild and merciless clerk gave us our key and nodded to a bellhop, who whisked us and our bags into the steel elevator. In there, the aria had proceeded to a chorus of hallelujahs. The upper hall was pink and ubiquitous, that effect enhanced by the rotary shoe polisher next to the elevator and by the posters, spaced evenly between the doors, picturing Florence and the Côte d'Azur. The bellhop popped the lock with a magnetized plastic tab and showed us our room, which was large and built-in, modular looking and smooth, in mahogany and purple. The pink tiled bathroom had a low white tub. I overtipped the guy, just to get him out of there.

"You put this on your credit card?" said L, as soon as he was gone. "Did you see how much it was?"

"No," I said. "How much was it?"

"It was a thousand francs a night, I think," she said.

"How much is that?" I asked.

"Two hundred dollars."

"Oh," I said, as calmly as I could. We couldn't stay there more than one night on my credit card. I was still hoping it wouldn't come to paying, though. "Don't worry about it," I said. "They'll cover it."

"They said they would cover it?"

"I assumed they would."

"Maybe we could move into the old city," she said, looking around. After a moment she added, "I don't even like this place." I opened the curtains, to brighten the place up, and to get a view of the old town.

"It could be anywhere," L was saying as I drew the blinds.

Outside, we faced the broad, deserted inner courtyard of the hotel, an acre bounded by empty tiled balconies over the blue keyhole-shaped pool. When L turned around and saw it, she groaned aloud. "It could be Saudi Arabia," she said. "It isn't even finished yet."

Beyond the pool the windows of the upper stories had X's taped on them, and the balconies were stacked with construction debris.

"At least we can swim," I said.

"Maybe we should just get out of here," she said.

I agreed. Without reservations, it would be difficult to find another place, but we'd try. We'd bolt, as I had before on these PR trips. But as soon as I decided that, I regretted it. Leaving the three-star place didn't feel like bolting, exactly. The place was plush. There was a tub, and we didn't have to look out the window. I felt pinned, in that French way that seemed to involve exactly no pressure from any direction. Still, if L didn't like the place, we'd go.

So we went back out, walking again. We found a couple of small hotels in the Quartier Mazarine—one off a church square with another fountain called the Cardinale that we loved immediately, L for the spray of flowers in the lobby and I for the ancient, warped, waxed wooden floor. But it was like another life we weren't allowed to be living. We couldn't get anything without a reservation, as I'd thought. When we came out of the Cardinale, I suggested we go to the market to get peaches. I knew L would like fruit, and I was taking care of her in order to avoid my sense of impending explosion.

L loved fruit. At home she bought mangoes every day when she could and fed them to me sometimes. I ate them warily, deciding they were okay, though their undertaste of evergreen, which she actually liked, repelled me. She'd tried to get me to eat papayas with her also, but these I couldn't even pretend to like. Star fruit she loved for their shape, their greenness, their crispiness; also guanabas, which she found only rarely, and Japanese persimmons, which she ate like apples in the car on the way home.

In France she sought out *pêches blanches*—white peaches—finding them in fruit stalls like one on the Rue Mouffetard in Paris, where each peach was displayed, separate and perfumy, in its own green tissue nest. You waited to be handed the fruit in these places. The grocer asked when you intended to eat the peach, and chose one ripening with you toward that moment.

Fruit was fruit, I thought, a kind of food. But L took these peaches seriously, and in France I went along to please her, concentrating as she did on the eating of the peach. By Avignon I'd begun to enjoy the routine. And just then I needed peaches to make her forget about the business of our hotel. It would be our first peach of Aix, I said. It was a beautiful town. It would have beautiful peaches. We set off toward the marketplace, and L became intent. She seemed to have an instinct for the direction of the fruit stands, and led me into the square, where it happened to be market day.

Dozens of bright, striped parasols made a single canopy over tables heaped with grapes and lemons, oranges and peppers and string beans and smooth, yellow-skinned potatoes. Atop a pile of cantaloupe, one had been cut into a crown, to show its aureole. A cart of leeks presented their calm white stems and their wild flourish of leaves. L pushed ahead, exclaiming.

I read the chalkboard labels over the fruit. Nectarines were *brugnons*, I noticed, a word with a sound in the middle I couldn't easily make, even mentally. I liked the way pineapples rhymed with bananas in French. *Ananas* was a more tropical and appealing name than pineapples, which had to have been coined by analogy by someone from the north.

I followed L as she sought out the stacks of light wooden boxes—those slats thin as bark—that held the more delicate fruits. *Pêche* I was wondering about by then—if it derived from the root for sin, as in peccadillo, as in Adam and Eve's. The peach as forbidden fruit in Eden made more sense to me than the apple, with its comical crunching and its hillbilly quality.

She found the stand, its *pêche blanche* box tipped up and displayed at eye level. *"Pour maintenant,"* she said to the fruitseller, and he selected two edible peaches for her. We went immediately—as if contracted to do so by her request—to the outskirts of the square and found a sunny bench near the door of the town's cathedral.

L liked to smell the peach first. *Pêche blanche* was more floral than other peaches, she'd said. It had qualities of blossom. She liked also to touch it to her cheek, to feel it there like a kiss, and to test the fuzz, which shouldn't be too long. When she was ready, she simply bit into it, leaning away from the juice, which ran over her lips.

This peach was, as I was hoping, perfect. She praised it, praised the wisdom of the grocer and the inner color of the peach, white and rose-tinted toward its quick, where it was scarlet-black and comby. I watched her eat. Earlier in the trip I'd been using my Swiss Army knife to cut my peach into sections before I ate it, parting the fruit's freckled skin with the sharp blade. But then I just bit into it, as she had, as if wading into its wet sweetness. We made a mess, getting the juice all over our chins and laughing about it, but otherwise saying no more.

I wasn't there yet. I was aping her, to please her, though I could feel, somewhere beneath my vigilance, the reality of the peach, its nectar. I couldn't feel but could conceive that the peach and the two of us and the town and everything else had been created for this moment, and for this moment only. That would be how it would be, I thought, but couldn't reach it.

Then we were left with the intricate pits at the cathedral door in Aix, and decided to go into the dark church to see its master-piece, a fifteenth-century painting of the burning bush. We watched with a small group of tourists as a guide, a young woman, spoke in English and opened the panels of the big wooden triptych. She secured the hinged wings to hooks with bungee cord and stood back, as if from the heat of the flaming subject of the painting. The fire seemed wholly external to the bush, like a halo hovering around its foilage of small, rounded leaves. In its center were the Virgin and Child, and above it a long perspective of castlelike thrones, on which sat the elders. Miles into the painting the sun rose, crowned with hosts of angels. Cé-zanne, baptized in that church, had viewed the painting as a child, said the guide. By then it had already been four hundred years since King René the Good had employed Nicholas Froment to paint it, in Aix's Golden Age. For a nice moment I thought only about the painting. In the form of this work, the good King's generosity and wisdom had remained there on the wall for centuries, perhaps fully felt by no one until the boy Cézanne was stirred by it, taught in that moment that masterpieces might be made by human hands like his own.

When we emerged from the church, I remembered the crowd outside the church in Seguret, waiting there with handfuls of rice. Here, though, was only the market. We walked along its edge, near the sausage stands. Here at the periphery, trucks had pulled up, swung up their glass doors and put out baskets of cheeses, trays of lamb chops, pâté in tubs, big naked chickens with their horny black and yellow feet still on, also the elongated, skinned bodies of rabbits, a few choice organs left inside. We came out past iced tables of gleaming bluefish and crusty stacks of anchovies and salted cod, and through a stand selling fifteen kinds of olives, fresh spices, ropes of garlic, tangles of thin hot peppers. Then we walked around town a little and visited Cézanne's little studio up the hill, where the paint on his dried palettes was still bright. But by then I couldn't look anymore. The details could no longer even tempt me to distraction. The moment was over, and it was all suddenly too much. My anxiety rose as we proceeded back toward Saudi Arabia, as L called the hotel.

"You're right," I said, as we again approached the sliding glass doors. "We've got to get out of here."

"But where'll we go?" asked L.

"Let's go to the sea," I said, not thinking exactly why. It was the beach, even the thought of which seemed to release the pressure a little. The ocean had all my life posed some possibility to me, some promise in the broad water and the edge of land. "Let's take the train south to the coast. We'll go off on our own, to the beach," I said. "We'll bolt."

"But what about LJ Media?" she asked.

"Forget about it," I said. That irritated her a little, I could tell.

Still, there was that one night, with that bathtub. L wanted to bathe alone, but let me stay to shave her legs. Cradling her pink heel with one hand, I soaped her leg to a lather, then drew my own razor over it, taking the hair off with the lightest touch I could muster, until her skin felt completely smooth. I had to be exquisitely alert, but this was no problem, as I had been that way for days and days.

After her bath she dried her hair, sitting on the bed in a big pink towel. She drew her hands over her legs. I'd done a good job, she said. Later, as we lay in the sheets of Saudi, she let me touch her—just her legs, to feel how smooth they were from heel to thigh. After that she rolled over decisively and went to sleep. I lay awake, wild with just that taste. Off on our own by the ocean, I fervently hoped, this hint would come to something.

22

B EST W ESTERN

....

The next morning L was curled up acres away in the big firm bed. And we didn't linger. She got up with resolve and we swiftly repacked and were out of there. We bore our bags downstairs and checked out. At the desk I paid and acted as if nothing bothered me, though my dignity and patience were wasted on the new clerk, a young woman who'd never seen me before. So, too, as we passed through the hissing glass door onto the bright streets of Aix and made our way back to the railroad station, my sense of purpose seemed to dissipate in the morning air. After all, we didn't know where we were going, so it seemed silly to go firmly and directly nowhere. Even so, I had my misgivings to keep me from ambling and so strode pointlessly ahead.

She didn't seem to mind the openendedness of our current state, but walked along admiring Aix and stopping for fruit. I was beginning to tire, and the need to extemporize felt like an added burden. L had slept, passing through the exhaustion of her jet lag in Seguret, the day I flew in the plane. But I had pressed on then, intent on the definition of the trip, trying to take hold of it, to define it and us, until it seemed to be nearly in hand. But now she and the trip had shed those definitions. And now I had no resources to reinstitute them. L in her white T-shirt and jeans still seemed beyond me.

The railroad station with its rigid arrivals and departures, ordinarily so dedicated, only made me feel more aimless. I wanted to go south, to the sea, that was all I knew, and it turned out there was no train south for an hour. So we found a bench amid hedges and sat there. I couldn't think of anything to say—the first time I could recall being so deprived on the trip. I was glad to be out of that hotel, I said, though I didn't really mean it—it had been a three-star hotel, with a keyhole-shaped swimming pool.

L said little. Her mood was opaque that morning. She sat there in the sun, in an easy way I could not even call patient, and ate dried apricots. She who wanted to be everything and everywhere when she was at home—who wanted to dance, to walk across Africa, to be a bird—seemed content to be nowhere now. She had an unusual face, I thought for the first time. It was dominated by her big eyes. She had a long nose, now touched with sunburn. Her thick hair had been lightly streaked by the sun, and her shoulders and arms had grown lean and strong from hauling her luggage. She looked composed and focused, extraordinarily *there*, like sea cliffs on an offshore island.

I took refuge in thinking about the sea. I remembered a line of James Wright's: "Where is the sea, that once solved the whole loneliness of the Midwest?" I knew what he meant. There was that firm edge, the sense that even vast things might singularly conclude and offer a vantage on the ocean. The edge of the Mediterranean, especially, seemed promising, sea of Odysseus, shore of home.

Finally the train pulled in. It was electric and so fell silent as it slid to a halt, rather eerily exposing the rustle of footsteps and possession gathering around it, and, when we got on, felt not so different from the bench on which we'd spent an hour, the car like some long gazebo, quiet and still, as if permanently placed there in the sun. A hummingbird flew through the silent car, in one window and out the other.

Finally the train jolted to a start and bore us out of town, over arched trestles I did remember from Cézanne's paintings and out of that green bowl of a valley that wore Aix on its broad upper slope. For a moment, the pale crag of Mount St. Victoire appeared in the east, then the track curved away. On a long curve I could see the engine of the train, and most of the cars between it and ours, and it seemed odd to be moving in something so long, dragged by an engine so far ahead. It was like fulfilling some prosaic prophecy. We rose into drier, paler country, which looked Arabic to me, the limestone bedrock breaking more and more prominently from the ground, and leaping up more often as white walls next to the train. Then we seemed to descend into the stone itself and, with an almost palpable click, plunged into the dark of a long tunnel. When we emerged, we seemed to have pierced some last ridge before the sea, for after that the land gave way in a series of steps, the track sweeping across them to retain its mild gradient. I couldn't see the ocean for a long time, but I could feel it there, washing over the last step. Beyond that the white stone plunged again and went on, beneath the sea.

L read her book, and I pretended to read Proust. By then I had moved on to *Swann in Love,* which I had hoped would be inspirational, though it had proven the opposite. There was no telling what Swann saw in Odette. I couldn't even get a fix on her, on her feeling for Swann, or even on her physical appearance, amid Proust's clouds of prose describing Swann's feelings. Plus Swann's need for Odette and for the world to offer up some proof of her love pained me with recognition. Even solid objects betrayed him. If things went well with Odette, then her lamp, her orangeade, her armchair soothed him with their presence. If not, these same objects tormented him. There was no world, just need. I couldn't stand Swann and I couldn't stand Odette. I glanced up at L, who rode on, still opaque, borne contentedly southward to wherever, insistent by her very being that sheer physical presence was evidence enough. She was there with me—what more could I want? I thought again, and again could think of no answer. I could feel a little knot of anger beneath my solar plexus, as if I'd swallowed an acorn. I looked out the window and waited for my first glimpse of the sea.

It came—a wink of bright water—above Cassis, one of two adjacent towns on the coast. The next stop, La Ciotat, had more hotels listed in the guide. I was thinking of amenities at this point, and as the train pulled into Cassis, I argued for going on to La Ciotat.

"Cassis is supposed to be wonderful," L said. "Wild and beautiful."

It appeared empty to me. "Look," I said, as the train came to a halt, "there's nothing here." Beyond the small train station rose what seemed like nothing—an expanse of scrubby hills, no taxis, no signs for hotels in evidence. "We'll probably have to walk," I said.

She'd heard from friends in Paris that it was great, she said.

There'd been brushfires in the area, I said. I'd read about them in the *Herald Tribune*. L hesitated, hearing this, and in a moment the train pulled out again, and we were on our way to La Ciotat, by default as much as anything. I had filibustered her.

For twenty minutes as the train ran along the coast, I was sure I had been right. But as La Ciotat came into view, my heart misgave me. The town's main buildings stood at the western end of a small bay, where container cranes rose around a big rock on the point. The cranes looked like gigantic skeletal horses poised at the shore. I'd seen the same kind in Oakland. La Ciotat was an industrial port, a working harbor. Suddenly the wild landscape around Cassis seemed romantic, natural, picturesque. It had looked empty, but now that nothing seemed preferable to this something.

"At least there's taxis," I said as we pulled into the station. There were, in fact, several taxis, though the one we chose seemed to take a long time, and several minor streets, to descend to water's edge, and I had the bad feeling of being taken for a big fare by the driver, who kept up a patter with L as he profited on my ignorance of the terrain, until we at last reached the main highway, which ran parallel to the beach around the bay into town.

"He says we won't find much without a reservation," said dubious, irritated L. "He only knows one place."

"I guess we'll have to go there then," I said.

L groaned out loud when she saw the place, which was familiar. It was a low motel out on the highway, like a Best Western.

In its little lobby we were in America again, a sea-warped America in varnished pine, out of the fifties except for the rock video, which played to the deserted chairs like a simple light source. Janet Jackson and her dance troupe worked out in military uniforms, on a stage made to look like an oil refinery. Behind the glass-topped, ruffled counter with its credit card emblems, a woman in jeans told us in English that they had just one room left. "Can we look at it?" I asked, hoping it would be better than the lobby.

It wasn't. We followed the desk clerk up to the one room, a tiny blistered pastel box with a white tableau of a bamboo grove stenciled onto the wallpaper opposite the bed, which was clad in nubbly white chenille. The bathroom was moldy; the shower a spigot at the end of a flexible steel tube and a drain in the floor. The clerk threw open dingy shutters to reveal a little balcony,

where a single person might stand and enjoy the view of the highway. A slice of the sea blinked beyond the road like something
denied.

"How much is it?" I asked, hoping it would be cheap, anyway.
No such luck. The room was about a hundred dollars a night. L
seemed frozen in horror as I considered things. She'd been right.
We should have gone to Cassis, that was obvious now. There was
probably some nice French country inn up there, surrounded by
trellises of bougainvillea and filled with the smell of pastry. Still
I wasn't going to give in. I was sick of placating her, and we
couldn't go back there now anyway. It was late in the day already,
and the idea of retracing our steps filled me with exhaustion, as if
to return to an earlier choice was somehow to swim upstream.

"We'll take it," I said, amid a mighty silence from L. The clerk
left us in the room. I sat on the bed, which was squeaky and
flabby. She sat in a white wicker chair beneath the fake bamboo.

"At least we have something," I said. "We can look around. It's
only one night."

"It's disgusting," she said. She didn't even try to be cheerful. I
struggled, but was sinking. Left on our own, this is what we had
come to. Nubbly, mildewed, ersatz, American Tropicana.

"Well, it isn't Paris," I said, hoping she would modulate if I
joined her in criticizing the place.

"Paris wasn't even Paris," she said.

"What do you mean?" I said.

"I hate this place," she said, dodging the question. Her further
dismissal was too much already. It made me mad.

"Maybe this whole trip wasn't such a good idea," I said.

She turned angry as well. "That's exactly what I was thinking,"
she said, her voice rising.

I stood up. "You've been impossible!" I shouted. "I've gone
around on tiptoe! I've tried everything! And you're not happy
being here with me."

"If you know what I'm feeling," she said, "why don't you just have a conversation with yourself, and save us the trouble?"

I couldn't consider what she meant by that. "Why did you ever agree to go to France with me, then?" I asked.

This time she got up and faced me, really mad. "I wish I knew!" she shouted. "I wanted to see France again, and you wanted to get into my pants. I guess that was the bargain."

I couldn't say anything to this. I tried for a second to attribute it to our immediate, tawdry circumstances, but it was too big for that. Was that really how it seemed to her? Could she see the trip as just a trade-off, travel for sex?

"That's not true!" I said. It was all I could think of to say. "We were happy in Paris."

"I hated you in Paris!" she said. "It wasn't even Paris!"

"Fine!" I yelled, defeated by this. "Just fine. That's the way you want it—that's the way it was!"

It was fine with her, too, she said. Then she turned away and we fell silent a moment. My throat was burning. I felt like I was a long way from home.

"Look," I said again, although she wouldn't. "I'm going to take this place because this is where we are." I couldn't do anything about her, I was thinking, but I could at least try to deal with the situation. "Great," she said, still not looking at me. "Just great."

We were at an impasse. The whole trip seemed suddenly clear to me, as if at a stroke she'd dropped a veil that I'd hung before it. There, amid my growing exhaustion and the cheap hotel room, the daylight failing and the traffic ripping by outside, I felt like we'd really come to something—the truth. It never had worked and it never would work. I had been deluded, obsessed and deluded.

After a while of feeling this, full bore, I had to get out of there. I was going to walk to town, I said. Maybe I could find something else, for tomorrow. I had to get something to eat anyway. She didn't say anything, but when I got up, she got up, too, and followed me out.

On the way out I put the room on my overloaded credit card. Outside the daylight was draining out of the sky, and it was suddenly clear we were in a beach town in September. There was that sense of sudden absence, of the dying echo of summer. The ice-cream stores and T-shirt shops were deserted, some already barricaded for the season. We walked along the highway as the occasional car blasted past us, and the day glowered to a close. Everything was wrecked, I was thinking. It was over. She had hated me in Paris, and I had been walking around like a happy idiot.

By the time we climbed up the hill into the little town, it was night. We found the garish shopping strip that was the main street of town. We had come to the Atlantic City of France. The crowds on the street looked native, urban, intent, displayed, the women dressed to kill, passing in wafts of perfume, the men sullenly claiming their possession by draping an arm over them or clutching their hand. These were working people, from Marseilles, probably, whose vacations only took them an hour down the coast, not quite to the Côte d'Azur, but in that direction at least, and they seemed determined to be having as good a time as anyone at St. Tropez or Cannes.

Everything was on sale, marked down for the end of the season. Shopkeepers barked at the oblivious crowds. I had the feeling of being able to see into everyone's face, to see disappointment or fear held back but made more dominant in their features for that. Finally we turned off the strip and climbed a sidestreet, hoping to find an inn, but found nothing, only the sense that we'd made our way to the back of the façade. Here were alleys, loading docks, an undistinguished church, a dog with its ribs showing.

The sight of this dog just stopped me. I was at a loss. What had

I been thinking? That I might ride into her heart on her sweet associations with France, and now this, this starved mutt, for an association, these images for memories of our trip to France together. What a farce.

Why did there have to be all this struggle, anyway? Why all this performance? Couldn't two people just feel right together? Couldn't a relationship just begin to blossom, unconsciously, and without all this work? I'd always despised the idea of working on a relationship, as if it were some kind of mine, requiring the removal of tons of dirt for every ounce of radiance. Why was she so difficult? Why didn't she like me? I could do no more, I thought. I didn't care what happened. For the first time on the trip—maybe ever with her—I didn't care what kind of impression I made.

She turned back toward the strip and I followed her. She found a little grocery and bought grapes and yogurt, having to get also a whole pack of plastic spoons. Then we walked back toward the Best Western, on the seaward side of the highway this time, and found a place on the sand, where we huddled behind the rocks of the breakwater to get out of the rising wind. She gave me yogurt, grapes, my own spoon. We ate.

After a while, my feelings of hurt and sadness gave way to simple strangeness, as I found myself on the shore of this strange ocean, in a far-off industrial port, eating yogurt in the dark with a woman I didn't know. How weird it was. What had this been about? What was happening to me? I was suddenly very hungry. I realized I hadn't eaten anything except this fruit and yogurt all day.

When we returned to our hotel room, she retreated to the bathroom for a long time, running the rudimentary shower, the door firmly shut between us, as I lay in bed and watched incomprehensible French TV, a simple cop show I could not figure out no matter what. I just stared at the screen, actually, and remembered what she said—"If you know what I'm feeling, why don't you just have a conversation with yourself?" I had been having a conversation with myself all over France. Maybe even all of my life. Finally I shut off the television, turned off the light and pretended to go to sleep. She came out and strictly took her side of the flabby bed. Its old springs amplified her movements, so that even after she settled, as the rare car swooshed past outside, I could feel her twitch.

She lay awake a long time, and I knew it, and knew that she knew that I was awake as well. If she was staying over there, I thought fiercely, I was staying over here. I held myself clenched for an hour or so, until I was exhausted, then repeating the day's refrain—I could do no more—to myself a last time, I turned over, strenuously, just to shake the springs and let her know for sure that I was there, and threw my face into the stale pillow.

23

Into the Sea

....

THE MEDITERRANEAN,
SEPTEMBER 1990

Somewhere, over a megaphone, a man counted out complex French numbers: *"Trente-deux, dix-sept, trente-deux, dix-huit . . ."* It was morning in the Bamboo Room. I lay there, considering us with absolute clarity—for the first time, I thought—and listening to those numbers. Men need women more than women need men, I was thinking. The hurt I'd felt the night before about what L had said—it was a trade-off—had proceeded into wonder at my own need, and the blindness it had inflicted upon me. I wanted to go to France and you wanted to get into my pants. It even rhymed. Of course that was how it had looked. I had been too busy being in love to notice. Now it explained everything. Of course she couldn't get near me, if it looked like that. If it looked like that, I couldn't get near her either. Maybe we should get separate rooms. Maybe we should have gone on separate trips. I remembered my attempt at the Opéra to comfort her by telling her that she didn't have to feel any obligation to me in France.

Whatever made me think that I could cancel the meaning of anything, just by saying so?

The numbers echoed up from the street, in pairs. They were minutes and seconds, I realized after a while, which made me recall that on that morning we were entering the third and final week of our trip. How ironic my plans to propose had become. This was, like all the others, a junket. It hadn't ever been real, and now that it was, it was the Best Western.

"Don't you want to see what that *is?*" said L, meaning the numbers.

It hadn't occurred to me to wonder what they were, since they were in French. It was some French thing, numbers, early in the morning over a megaphone. But now that she mentioned it, it gave me somewhere to start again, and I got up in my underwear, drew the sunbleached drapes and opened the window onto our tiny balcony. The numbers came from the direction of the highway, its four lanes sunny and deserted in the morning. Across the road, on the strip of beach, a small crowd clapped feebly at intervals. Swimmers were coming up out of the water, leaping onto bicycles and speeding off. It was a triathalon.

I told L, and she got up, and we stood there awhile, watching in our underwear. The swimmers arrived at the shore one by one, some high-stepping, some staggering from the sea. They picked out their bicycles from racks and rode off into the sun, down a broad sidewalk and beneath an underpass, then rising again, up the hill that flanked the east end of the bay. It was idiocy, American idiocy yet, but it cheered me up.

"It looks like the evolution of man," said L, and we both laughed.

"Look at this place," I said, bearing the good mood as we turned from the window. "And we thought Saudi Arabia was bad." She laughed again, and delivered me a little from the previous night's awfulness, though I wasn't going to relinquish the shift in my feeling on account of it. Otherness clung to everything, especially L.

We got dressed and went down to café tables, which had been set up outside in the cement plaza of the hotel, and we sat there under a parasol, waiting for coffee, as the numbers were called at wider and wider intervals, one each for each of the last, slowest swimmers to come ashore. From the table we could no longer see them, though I imagined their spent faces, among them the comical local favorite, making a show of his incompetence on a bet and grinning despite his exhaustion. The thought of riding a bicycle, rolling on dry land after all that swimming, would be momentarily refreshing.

"How long do they go?" asked L.

"I don't know," I said. "Maybe it's the Trans-France Triathalon and they're riding to Paris." She poured hot milk into her coffee. I went on, as if on the same subject.

"I know what you're thinking," I said. "You're just trying to be sure that we're still going to be whatever we're going to be."

"I never said that," she said. "You said that."

"I'm just trying to say that I know how you feel," I said.

"Gee," she said, refusing to be lured out. In her tone, I thought I heard her quoting herself from the night before, letting me know that I was claiming to be able to read her mind again.

"I *have* been having conversations with myself," I said. "Constantly." After that, I had to say it straight out. "Do you really think this is just a trade-off?" I said.

She was alert to my aim, to my hope to hear her deny it. The understanding was poised there between us. She sighed.

"I'd like to go for a swim after breakfast," she said. I took this as good enough. I didn't really want to press it. I guessed we were just going to let it go for now, neither denied nor affirmed.

"I know," I said. "Let's go down the beach a ways, swim up, grab two bikes and ride off."

"Great," she said, somewhat fiercely. I suddenly recalled meeting her for the first time, and it awakened in me a surge of feelings—admiration, desire, fear, sadness.

Blessedly, after that, we just ate and talked. She told me about being a "surfer chick" in high school. She'd go down to Santa Cruz with her first boyfriend. She had streaked blond hair then, and she'd lie on the beach at Fourteenth Street or atop the cliffs above Steamer Lane while he waited for waves outside the break. Boring, she said, it was boring after a while, dudes and tubes and all that. He was the first one to try to French-kiss her, she said, but his tongue was huge and gross, a banana slug. Really, I said, feeling my thick tongue there in my mouth.

She was bristling with otherness, now. She was impulsive and innocent in a way I had not noticed, and there was something a little crushing about it. She was different than I'd thought. Still she *was* there, and she wasn't going to ruin the trip by holding us to what we'd said the night before. Oh, just be glad, I thought, but couldn't be.

I told her a story of my own, of learning to scuba dive with an old girlfriend. We'd taken lessons in the pool at a local college. She'd been tentative, concentrating on her technique as I did barrel rolls in the deep end. In the end, we were terrible as buddies. On our ocean dive—which was a sort of final exam—we had to walk backward into the surf on a beach south of Monterey, then swim down the steep sand slope of the beach into the kelp forest. I'd reached the grove first and plunged in, excited to swim into the dimness beneath the thick yellow canopy. Later she told me that all she'd seen were my fins, disappearing over a big rock. When she'd caught me, underwater, she was furious, and accused me wordlessly, grimacing through her mask and making the sign of a tiny man walking fast across her left palm. I made gestures of apology there, under fifty feet of water, but after that we just swam around, got our certifications and drove home, still mad.

L laughed at the story. "She was scared," she said. "That's terrible."

"I know," I said.

And after these stories we swam together in the ocean, which we hadn't done before. We put on bathing suits—Speedoes—and sandals and bore our towels and notebooks and bottled water across the boulevard and down stone stairs to the beach, where the sea wall was honeycombed with stands for food and sundries, one with a red-and-yellow PRESSE sign. The sand was white and fine grained, powdery almost, Mediterranean sand pummeled to bits by Homer's ocean, the wine dark sea itself, which lapped the shore like a lake, compared to the formidable Pacific. It was turning into a hot day, and the water was already an inviting blue. Already on the sand were sunbathers, in clusters. Some of the women, I noticed, had their breasts exposed.

We set up our own encampment, smoothing the sand and laying out the towels. She didn't like her bathing suit, she said. It was for laps, and she'd never liked the color, which was light blue. It looks fine, I said. She wasn't convinced. I got up to go buy a *Herald Tribune,* and when I came back, she had her T-shirt and sandals on and said she was going to shop for another suit. Stay with the stuff, she said, and don't go in the water without me. I watched her go, striding down the concrete boardwalk.

I read my paper on the towels and pretended I wasn't waiting for her. Saddam's invasion of Kuwait was all over the paper, of course, the secretary of state requesting more ground forces from the NATO allies. I turned to the sports page. Nineteen-year-old Pete Sempras had beaten Andre Agassi in straights sets in the U.S. Open. The match had "unfolded like an unrequited love affair," read the lead, and ended in an upset.

Soon the sun was higher—or rather, the old earth kept turning.

Children chirped at the waterline. The gurgle, murmur and wash of little waves reminded me of Michigan. An old man lay especially prostrate nearby, the sagging wad of his penis like a baby asleep in the pouch of his tiny, striped bathing suit. A few swimmers had ventured into the water, which seemed, from their reactions to it, to be cold. I watched a bare-breasted woman walk gingerly into the sea. She hopped the little breakers when they threatened to wash over her hips.

There was something disconcerting about seeing breasts in public, something that connected to my feelings about L that morning. Out in the sunshine, breasts began to look as idiosyncratic as any other body part. Almost none were the breasts I'd seen in magazines. Every woman's breasts seemed to express just that woman. Even the pairs, I noticed, often only just matched. I didn't want to see this, really. Maybe I wanted to believe in breasts as emblems. It seemed, too, in the light of day, that whatever it was that had hidden breasts from view was the source of my feeling of sexiness about breasts, not the breasts themselves.

Finally L came back in a new bathing suit. It was neon green and black, a shiny fabric, the colors in a geometric pattern. It was terrible, nearly grotesque. And she seemed to know it. "I'm not a moose or anything, am I?" she said.

"You're not a moose," I said.

The water was frigid and shallow for a long way out. There was that long, torturous decision to take the plunge. I couldn't stand the ocean's freezing tongue licking up inch by inch, and I dove at last into a small wave, the cold lighting up my skull with a pain like ice cream at the back of the throat. L just walked in slowly, until her feet left the sand and she began to swim, keeping her hair dry and paddling around, exclaiming, "Oh my God!"

We swam way out. The bite of the cold proceeded into a feeling of heat with sting and numbness at its edges. I dove again and could see vaguely underwater, though the sea looked empty. I swam down to the flat and featureless sand and found a small shell, like a straight-razor blade, and brought it to the surface, thinking to present it to L. By then she was backstroking sedately into deeper water, her face disappearing behind the little swells. Suddenly out there a fat face appeared near hers, and the two were talking in breathless French as they treaded water. I listened for and heard the word *"froid."* I dove again and swam out toward them, finding only blueness and a layer of much colder water, which shocked me and sent me to the surface.

She was still talking to the fat French man, whose head reminded me of Mao's in the Yangtse. I was treading water and waiting for their conversation to stop when the sudden thought hit me that I wasn't in love with her anymore. I had seen things—the breasts and L in her strange bathing suit—without their special quality, and it made me sad. Breasts were breasts and L was L. The specialness had somehow dispersed, and I missed it. At that moment I had no faith that its diffusion into the rest of life could ever mean as much.

L finally stopped talking and swam over. "He says it's cold because the Rhône flows into the sea near here, with water from the Alps."

"Oh," I said, feeling no different from the fat man, really. She swam by, and as she did her purple velour snood washed from the knot of hair at the back of her head and floated near her in the water off her shoulder.

"Look," I said, pointing to it.

She reacted with fright, not recognizing the snood, thinking that it was something dangerous from the sea. She swam off with a flurry of strokes and kicking.

"It's your hair thing," I said. She laughed when she figured it out and retrieved it, finally. "I thought it was going to sting me," she said.

"It was purple so it had to be vicious," I said.

The floating snood, there in the empty ocean, sharpened into a pang the feeling that had been building in me that morning, of the strangeness of people and the power of our assumptions about things. I treaded the cold seawater, just one more head bobbing in the freezing sea.

I had to swim to shore after that. I was hoping that doing something strenuous might ease my odd feelings, and I put my head down and stroked thirty times before I looked up to find myself off course and seemingly no closer to the beach. I breast-stroked after that, concentrating, and finally the sand rose to me and I could step down and push off the bottom. I remembered a theory I'd read, that human bipedality had started when swimming primates had learned how to walk in the water. I felt myself take on weight as I began to emerge, first shedding the cold water from my shoulders, then from my own vestigial nipples puckered and blue, then from my numbed penis, the old idiot, and at last from my thighs, as I stirred the water to froth with my knees. On dry land again, I climbed the beach to the towels and fell heavily on them, shocked. The trip hadn't worked out. L hadn't worked out. I was in a foreign country with a strange woman.

After a while, the strange woman swam out of the ocean to join me. She who had gone delicately into the ocean strode loosely from it, seeming strong. She was hungry, she shouted when she got near enough. "Let's get some *merguez.*"

Eating in my condition was odd, like participating in a biological ritual. I ate lamb sausage on a toasted baguette—*merguez*—and got potatoes as well, out of sheer habit. L looked healthy. She'd wet just the ends of her hair during her swim, and these curled around her neck and shoulders, and she smelled of salt and suntan oil. I could feel, as I looked at her, my old need to leap, to be in love again, to put my faith back in those assumptions. I would not, though.

"It's almost checkout," she said, when she'd finished the *merguez.* "I've decided where I want to go." Not waiting for a response from me, she said, "Arles."

"I guess," I said, "I'll go, too." She didn't agree or object.

So we went. I could only let the trip happen to me at that point. If it happened to be Arles, fine. So to Arles, then, where van Gogh pestered the locals and supposedly attempted to impress the woman he loved with the gift of his ear. Maybe he'd decided that he hadn't been listening, and by then had to take everything literally.

24

THE WELL

I stayed in bed. In the charming hotel L had of course found in Arles—a place that shared a medieval wall with the cloister in the old town—I cloistered myself. Our window overlooked a little courtyard, which was almost entirely shaded by the elephantine leaves of a single, enormous and unidentifiable tree. It pained me even to look at it. In the morning L opened the thick wooden shutters—bound with iron and painted white, layer upon layer, for centuries—and then closed them again, after I insisted. I had to rest, I told her. I was afraid that I was coming down with something. Truth be told, I was boycotting life—or being boycotted by it—hiding from the ongoing recognitions that loomed up tangibly everywhere, even as the mystery tree outside the window. Still, sunlight leaked in through the cracks, as I lay feigning a fever, and L, long-legged in her shorts, prepared to go out into the brightness to see the festival. I was hoping she'd stay and comfort me, but she, with her unnerving ability to converse out there, gave me a perfunctory kiss and left.

So I lay there, listening to the morning go by. In the tree in the courtyard, some bird sang for a while, giving up its call again and again, a song I hadn't heard in America, though it had that same stark pause between repetitions. "Shut up!" I yelled in one of those pauses, though he only went on, more vigorously than before. Life was easy for trees and stupid singing birds.

We'd arrived in Arles just in time for the Rice Festival, finding ourselves among parade spectators as we'd walked from the station. Surrounded by sheaves, the Rice Queen herself had welcomed me, waving languidly from atop a haywagon pulled by a big green John Deere tractor, as a formation of riders, Provençal cowboys from the fertile Camargue, followed on small white horses. From that southern delta, these local farm people had come to town, in paisleys and ginghams and cowboy hats and as of old, to celebrate the rice harvest. L and I watched from the curb, charmed and shocked respectively, as truckloads of singing children passed, then princesses beaming and waving, waving, waving back to their shouting boyfriends, then amateur marching bands, their dispersed formations dismantling their music, then Gypsies on a flatbed pounding guitars and singing loud in unison. Everything was festooned with bolts of grain, as if in honor of Ceres herself, goddess of the earth's fruitfulness. L especially loved the horses and the children. I was horrified.

Riz sounded nothing like it looked. All three of its simple letters betrayed me. Under my breath, I tried to at least get that click in my throat, hoping to shake my alien sensibility, to participate. But it was no good. I'd looked at L's large blue eyes and had found them large and blue. She wasn't being unfriendly, but she was who she was, a phenomenon, and acted that way. We were two phenomena. Coming up out of the cold sea, I'd been shocked by the singularity of things, and since then had been out of it. I could feel my disassociation distinctly, like a hole where a tooth should have been. Underneath, it was jet lag and travel fever, that mute, wide-open-to-everything feeling that I'd often felt—had even sought out—on the road. But with my loss of L, whom I'd never had, this condition had sharpened into something relentless about my life, about life in general for that matter. So the rites of the Rice Festival seemed through my ironic eyes strange and bitter and remote, as seen from the moon or through the wrong end of the telescope.

And so that next morning as I lay in bed alone, I hoped that the world might come back into its old, thoughtless, nearby range. So far, it hadn't. A couple came into the stone courtyard beneath my shuttered window and spoke to each other in German. I could understand nothing of what they said, of course, except that the man was holding forth, in an explanatory tone, which, after the bird call, was easy to hear as the same kind of song. I could almost see him nodding as he spoke, making gestures, as she, a little impatiently, unfolded her arms to flick her hair from her neck. Between his elaborate calls, she answered with a word or two: long signature, brief acknowledgement, long signature, brief acknowledgement. I heaved myself into sadness about it, then tried to buck up. What else was there? I thought angrily. You either were or you weren't. Either you called out or you fell silent. The rest was manners.

Thinking of rice and domination, I recalled a brief visit I'd made to Japan when, on a layover at the end of a long trip, I'd walked into the fields around the airport at Narita. Then, too, it had been rice-harvest time, and the roads had been lined with wooden racks, rice spread out on them to dry in the sun. The rice had been cropped off close to the ground with a sharp blade, then gathered in bundles, sheaves, that had been bound at one end and parted at the other, so that each sheaf hung on the rack like a towel over a waiter's arm. All this was so beautifully done that at first I'd thought it purely decorative, beautiful rice-sheaf screens along the road. Discovering them to be a functional part of the harvest, I was filled with admiration for these careful farmers. Then on the shoulder of the narrow road I saw a photograph torn from a magazine and picked it up. It was pornographic, a picture of a naked young woman tied up with ropes, a lighted candle inserted into her vagina. The setup and lighting of the shot, the knots, the candle, all showed the same exquisite care as the cropped sheaves of rice by the roadside.

Horrified again, I noticed I was lying in a pink room. There was a pink floral print on the wallpaper, and a pink bedspread. The bed frame was delicate wrought iron, the metal flourishing with a motif of flowers. This place was ludicrous, I thought. Where was she, anyway? Her travel items littered the bedside table: her Colette, which I'd looked into and found ludicrous as well. "Let's give the young mimosas something to drink" began one story. Also nearby were her suntan lotion and brush, and her purple velour snood, retrieved from the ocean, dry and soft again, but retaining something of its transformation into a sea monster, and now a little sinister.

The morning went on as I mounted up evidence against life. Outside my window, beyond the courtyard somewhere, applause rose in bursts, a crackling sound at that distance, like a heavy wheel rolling on a sandy floor. Something to do with the festival, I thought, or simply the local men giving L a hand as she passed by in her shorts. Finally I slept. In a dream, I was eating in a French restaurant when a black dog, like a terrier, jumped into my lap. At a nearby table a family looked startled and then began to laugh. They loved their dog, no matter what.

Just then L unlocked the door and came in. "We're incredibly lucky," she announced. "This has got to be the best weekend of the year, and this was the last room in this hotel." The whole town had been transformed for the festival, she said. In the square they were making a feast for that night.

She'd gone out into the crowds to look for van Gogh here in the town where he'd painted, but she hadn't found much of him. The small museum evidently couldn't afford any of his paintings, which had all gone to big cities. She'd gone down to find his house, but even that was gone. He'd lived in a poor quarter, she said, outside the gates of the old town. There was a traffic roundabout there now, and in the middle, a new, out-of-nowhere fountain.

She'd bought a guidebook with some of van Gogh's paintings reproduced in it, and she showed me one, of the yellow house where he'd lived. It was night in the picture. Van Gogh's place was a tiny house, like a single square apartment with two stories. The other apartments in the background had their windows lit already, but the yellow house in the foreground was dark. Its crazed occupant was out late, recording the scene. Yellow was van Gogh's life-force color, L said.

Plus, she said, there's a Roman arena. She showed me a postcard of it, the picture an old illumination from the Middle Ages. In those days, the whole town had taken refuge in the arena, and the postcard showed the stone arches of the coliseum, built with rows of tiny houses and apartments, like an Anasazi cliffside. This picture of the whole town, withdrawn into the arena like a snail into its shell, for some stupid reason melted my heart. What was I doing, lying in bed, nursing my anger against her for something—perhaps simply not fulfilling my expectations—and looking at postcards of a town in France that was right outside the window?

"What else is going on?" I asked.

"Something you can't miss," she said. "There's going to be a running of the bulls." It turned out to be the only word she got wrong the whole trip.

So I got up and dressed, thinking I'd at least see young men gored. We went out into the sunshine and walked down the street, past the very arena she'd shown me in the postcard, and through a plaza where a crowd milled, and finally coming to a railing, where we stood above an alcove in the lower street. Down there two ambulances and a crowd restrained by a police fence waited. Next to us stood an old gaunt Frenchman, looking a little like the farmer from the TGV, though he was now wearing a white polo shirt. L asked him, I took it, if this was where the bulls came out, and he spoke, barking out a curt, frank *"Oui."*

I looked down at the crowd of dark Mediterranean faces, all of them knowing what they were about to see—the rites of their festival were, after all, as inevitable-seeming to them as the fireworks finale on the the Fourth of July would be to me. We couldn't see the gate they faced from above, though they clearly expected something to emerge from it.

But they didn't look right, for a crowd awaiting the running of the bulls. There weren't enough of them, for one thing, and they were sedate. There were cheers and whistles, but these rose from somewhere behind us. L seemed to sense the same thing, and spoke again to the farmer-turned-tourist.

I didn't understand her question, and didn't have time to work out his arch answer, as just then the gate beneath us slammed open and the crowd reacted. Two horses in belled harness came out, pulling a low cart, chariot-style, on which two men in blue and white stood, one holding the reins. On the cart lay a bull's big body, black with blood, the flesh loose and jiggling with the beat of the horses' hooves. In an instant they appeared, rolled past the ambulances—for the bullfighters, of course—and were gone around the bend in the narrow street and around the arena, in which cheers for the next matador were already rising.

Bull*fighting*," said L, correcting herself.

The sight of the dead bull returned me to my previous distance as we wandered around. On the street circling the arena, where vendors sold hats and tapes and food, a display of stuffed bull's heads lined one stall. These varnished objects had been given a glazed look of focused rage, like a cat's for a bird. Looking at their sharpened horns, I recalled Hemingway and Picasso, ballsy old bulls themselves, and Ferdinand who only wanted to smell the flowers. L asked if I wanted to go in to see the bullfight. It would be an experience, she said. But now the whole thing seemed too close to home. I'd want to call 911 as soon as it started.

That evening I started to feel actually sick, as though my excuse had humorously conjured up the real symptoms of a cold. I went with L to the festival anyway, though I was out of it, and we didn't talk a lot. We walked through narrow crowded streets, buffeted with gusts of warm wind, the sky beyond the rooftops bright with twilight. The market square was filled with tables set with linen and wineglasses under the trees. On the braziers lay steel platters, broader than the reach of the cooks. Saffron paella crackled and steamed. It was going to be all right, I hoped, though when we sat at the table, I had to close my eyes. L ordered sangria.

Somewhere from speakers the strains of a slow march leaked into the plaza, a faint bass drum beating once per measure. We drank our sweetened wine as the crowd gathered, voices slowly rising beyond recognition into hubbub, when I could hear the strings in the march music no more, only the drum, which had quickened beneath the crowd noise. Waiters already bore trays to the tables.

"Am I getting drunk or are they getting louder?" said L.

"Both," I said. We got more punch anyway, and ordered food,

amid shouts of greeting and barks of laughter, as bells rang the hours and the cutlery jangled. The paella was hearty and hot and I felt whole again for the first time in days, certainly drunk as well. The streetlights, by then brighter than bits of sky showing in the slots and notches of the rooftops, illuminated the canopy of leaves over the square, and the gusts of wind rocked the boughs. Amid the uproar someone whistled and a baby cried. By then music rose from several directions at once, from the bars and the bodegas around the square. I could hear from one a strummed guitar, robbed of its pitch by the crowd and so sounding like a high hat, playing flamenco while some other bar played funk. "The Commodores," said L.

She'd been watching a trio of young girls in the crowd, all in short dresses and makeup for the festival. A single guy strolled up and they talked. One of them seemed to jest with him a little. Her friend chimed in, and the third girl stood apart, seeming a little shy. "Which one will get him?" said L. I couldn't say, though I figured the shy one might. What was it to get someone? I thought wistfully. L pointed out the way that the talking girl threw back her hair from time to time, with a flip of her head. She remembered being sixteen, she said, and doing that. I could see her suddenly, as the talker, whose like I had never chosen before for a mate. The boy kept his hands in his pockets, seeming awestruck. Maybe the talker would get him, after all. I'd been like that myself in France, mute, having to give in to situations and be explained for, being the other guy. Across the little table L was still entranced by the festival and its cast of thousands. She and the crowd in the square were calling me back into life, and on simple terms. Maybe I could be that other guy.

When we finished dinner, we walked again, sideways sometimes through the crowded streets and into the festival night. Every third house, even places that were mere garages the rest of the year, had become a bodega, a kind of open dance floor and wine bar. Now the music competing in the square was unraveled, strand by strand, as each bodega radiated with its own clean, loud song. We went into one place and danced, to Little Richard's "Lucille," bumping around in the crowd as we did our spin-around jitterbug, and for a moment I was released from myself and happy. We pressed out into the crowd again and worked our way for a long time to the outer streets, where a car parted the crowd with a rhythmic beeping of its horn as it crept along.

As this car passed a curbside table, a dog barked angrily at it. A big guy without a shirt—evidently the dog's owner—jumped up furiously from his seat and pursued the car down the crowded street. He slammed the back window with his open hand and shouted some threat, instantly stilling the talk. The car jolted to a halt, and the driver began to get out, though he thought better of it when he saw the big shirtless guy coming at him. He'd gotten almost all the way back into his car when the big guy caught his left leg in the door and crushed it there with all his weight until it cracked, loud in the silence of the crowd. I reeled at the sound, feeling sympathetic pain in my leg.

Satisfied, the big guy went back to his place at the table and patted his dog. The driver withdrew his leg, sat in the car a moment and then drove slowly down the street, the crowd letting him through. Not taking it seriously and seeming like an invincible member of this other species, L said, "Young bucks." My wave of dizziness came back and this time didn't leave.

Back in the room, I fell asleep quickly but awoke later from a horrible dream. A bad gang said they'd come to fill me in. "We got you," they said, "and we can get her." I was plunging a sharp stick under the collarbone of one of them when I awoke. I went down the hall into the strange bathroom and sat in there in the brightness with my notebook, waiting to be able to see so that I could write down some things about beautiful, cruel life.

.   .   .

In the morning she took me to a store she'd discovered, which sold a dozen kinds of honey—sunflower honey, lavender honey, clover honey and others, the flavor differing according to what sort of blossoms the bees had found near their hive. L bought me honey from bees who'd harvested oak pollen, which was strong and bittersweet and brown. Then we walked to a café for an infusion of hot mint tea. She put the oak honey in the pot, and I drank the strange, potent brew, obedient.

We still had an hour before checkout, and so went to the cloister, where big-eyed beings from the Middle Ages stared from the carved capitals. The priest taught from the rooftop; the devil crouched beneath the floor; the saint was stoned by two sinners, each of whom raised a rock as big as a breadloaf overhead. Also, the Virgin and Child posed, headless, a man and a woman rode lions, and what looked like two sphinxes, also female and male, squinted into the stony distance. We found a small, square garden framed by the pointed arches of a colonnade and looking like an ornate box of green daylight. In the far corner was the well, its mouth utterly dark, its marble cap gouged by the ropes that had for centuries brought up water. I found a pebble and dropped it in, and we waited for that musical blip in the depths.

25

THE EXILE OF LOVE

....

Fleeing the debacle at Moscow, Napoleon made the colossal error of scrambling in the direction of his stores, never mind that it was already October and the land between his army and Vilna—fifty days away—had already been laid to waste. His troops, Henri Beyle—he who would be Stendhal—among them, were driven west like a vast herd pursued by wolves onto an ice pack. They died of exhaustion or hunger or violence at the hands of the cossacks at their heels or the local resistance ahead of them, ready this time, with what Tolstoy called the cudgel that broke the French rapier. Only 20,000 survivors of the 600,000-man Grande Armeé came home.

Henri survived, buoyed up by his enormous vanity. Even reduced to extremes, he insisted upon shaving and keeping his last uniform pressed. His concerns were aesthetic. He confessed to his journal that he feared he was being "turned into a barbarian" by the ordeal, "a barbarian lost to the arts." Though his commander assumed that his behavior showed bravery, and commended him as "a man of stout heart," Henri was in large measure simply out of it. A wiser, older Henri would recognize the role of his own self-absorption in his survival, though he would wrap the truth with a boast. "The good side of a character like mine," he said, "is that I take a retreat from Moscow like a glass of lemonade."

Still, even egotism has its limits, and the catastrophe that he endured was enormous. Elsewhere he notes that at Vilna the troops had to fortify the wall with frozen bodies, and that he himself fell to his knees before a pile of tiny, dirty potatoes, wept and thanked God. Even this, though—from his own report of it, written later and so for other purposes—shimmers that Stendhal shimmer, once Henri has won our belief.

On his return to Paris, he found neither Paris nor himself the same. Tolstoy might have his fictional Russian principals in *War and Peace* turn to new lives in families—even Pierre married off—but Henri and Napoleon came back to a France that would be ripped apart for decades. Emaciated from his ordeal, Henri was soon back in striped trousers again, a mending impecunious dandy out on the boulevards on the day that he heard a crackle of gunfire from the heights of Montmartre and recognized the sound of Russian muskets. The burning of Moscow, which Henri had so appreciated as an aesthetic spectacle, now fully revealed itself as a disaster on an epochal scale, marking a change that would drastically alter his life ever after. Afterward, he knew that he had been defeated personally there, that the blaze he'd witnessed had manifested some climax for France and—of course—for himself. The kings returned, leerier than ever, promoting their own prince, Metternich, and requiring proof that their defeated subjects hadn't stood with the mobs.

Henri's political behavior had never been what it appeared. He had always acted out his own inner drama, merely appropriating the external situation as a kind of metaphor. In this he was like the gentle bull in the children's story who, stung by a bee, only seemed ferocious. But reasons didn't matter to the king's agents, who took him at face value and blacklisted him as a subversive.

So he was shut out of the new old France. His former way of life—clothes, the theatre, dining out in Paris—vanished, along with his former income, as the royalist state, revived and reactionary, buried the republic with thirty stuffy years, during which Henri became the flamboyant stranger, an onlooker at home and abroad, the exile of love who called himself Stendhal. His only consolation was imagining a future when his works might be read, and when some ember of the revolution might revive.

It was at this point that Henri began to write about the French as if he were not a Frenchman. Above all the French were vain, he decided, and after all, he was an expert on the subject. Parisians were hypocrites, people with short memories. "Here I feel obliged to lie every day," he wrote to a friend. The French, for their part, responded in kind. At last Henri with his severed connections and not-even-questionable past spurned his native land and went into exile, like his hero Napoleon. Or so he claimed anyway, making the best of a bad situation. His rejected job applications were recently discovered in old government files.

He took the stage over the Alps, his dwindling books and wardrobe down to mere luggage, and went to live in romantic Italy, where they knew how to live and where they still had passions other than vanity. There he could pose among the crowd in the baroque lobby at La Scala, hear Mozart's *Don Giovanni* and *Così fan Tutte* and afterward go to a late supper, and all this for a few francs a day. In Milan he tried to forget the war and think about art. He'd visited the city before, as a young officer, but on his return found it altered, like everything else in Europe. Milan had fallen under Metternich's Austrian regime, authorities so reactionary they had outlawed streetlighting in the Papal States as subversive and Napoleonic. In Milan, as in every Italian city, an underground resistance had developed. Here they called themselves the Carbonari, their banner the red, black and blue. They met in secret, small units at night in the forest outside the city and debated around the charcoal fires that had given them their name.

So on his return, Henri found a Milan full of spies and suspected spies, and was instantly suspected himself. For his part, he reveled in the role, having read Machiavelli. He went about in a cape and wrote his letters in a code not so difficult as to obscure his style. "Gionreli," he wrote, for "religion." "Philadelphia," he called his own notion of freedom. He gave new names to everyone—and several to himself. As for actual spying, though, he declined. The romance of the Carbonari attracted him, but he thought them indiscreet—a disadvantage of the passionate natures that he otherwise admired. They were dangerous, he thought, and liable to implicate him. So he gossiped but kept his distance, and spied for himself only, as he had always done.

The secret police in Milan, no more attuned to nuance than those in France, considered him a spy anyway, and a double fake, so obvious he might be dismissed in some less dire time. In this they were partially right. Henri's lifelong flamboyance had always been a ploy to avoid notice by attracting it. The secret police started a file on Henri almost immediately upon his arrival, opening his mail and not being fooled in the least by his pseudonyms or his code.

Despite the terror of the regime, Henri and Milan managed, nonetheless, to carry on with style. The opera at La Scala remained the central focus of high society, although those gatherings were tinged with circumspection. Certain persons appearing in the splendid lobby cast a hush over the intriguing crowd. Henri basked in the scene all the more for its drama. It was extravagant, passionate, romantic, dangerous, in short, Italian, felt Henri who took for his models of ideal Italian lives the Borgias and de'Medicis. Under this influence, he mended in Milan, gaining back—

even on his reduced income—the weight he'd lost in his Russian ordeal. He lived on five francs a day, didn't mind being poor in Italy, where he could return again and again to sigh before the great art—of Botticelli, Leonardo—that he loved.

Art became his life at this point. When he heard of his beloved Napoleon's final defeat at Waterloo, he thought only of the young artists in the army who would now not have to die. So in Italy he tried to live a life of beauty and leisure, however threadbare his coat. He made travel notes, but didn't tax himself with too much writing. He started a small book on music, stylish but rather reliant on its sources. And when the time was right, and he might fully return to the spell, to the themes and glittering dark ladies of the opera, he fell in love, casting an obsession upon a woman in the romantic, dangerous and, in short, Italian manner.

Again he first glimpsed her in a dramatic setting. Métilde appeared above him at La Scala, in her box. Thin and dark, gorgeous and sincere, she was an authentic heroine of the revolution, still bearing—as she would always—the surname of her ex-husband and enemy. Henri, big-eyed in the cheap seats, couldn't watch the opera for gazing up at the fluted box where she sat between two friends, Teresa Confalonieri and Madame Frecavalli, Milan's fierce graces of the Carbonari. Henri sensed the moment as the opening of a "great musical theme." She was, he thought, a perfect Lombardian beauty—a type he recognized from a Renaissance painting he'd seen in Florence of the fatal Salome.

From the start, the romance was doomed. For here was a woman whom life had placed beyond him. At sixteen she'd been given in marriage to the Count Dembowski, a Polish general and ally of the conqueror Napoleon. The Count had received as tribute from her father 150,000 francs and his daughter besides. She, who had no say in the matter, determined not to be possessed simply because she had to be married. She bore him two sons, but never gave in to him, and in the end, when he tried to beat her into submission, she fled—still in her early twenties—to Switzerland with her sons.

There, chastened and consumed with the suit for separation she brought against the count, she attracted a poet. The young romantic Ugo Foscolo made her his ideal, and pursued her with poems, in vain. His verses had no effect upon her, though they fed rumors back in Milan and were used by her enemies, who said that she fled to Switzerland not to escape her husband but to take Foscolo for a lover. When she finally won her separation—keeping her husband at bay, though she had to retain his name—she brought her sons home to Lombardi, walked the streets and went to the opera with dignity, and took up the cause of the resistance.

Singular, serious, Italian, where he was multiple, frivolous and French, she was everything that he was not. She was ten years his junior, and he was awestruck by her. She was life as drama, as grave as her cause—possessed, he wrote, of a noble candor. In her gaze, there was a deliberate slowness, "as if she knew in advance that nothing she regarded could render her happy again." This he found especially irresistible. He was determined to render her happy, or at least to render himself miserable in trying. When he finally met her, he summoned up his courage, seized her hand and kissed it passionately.

But for an instance or two, we view Métilde entirely through Henri's multifaceted reportage. So we can't know how exactly she felt at first. Perhaps big and fancy Henri with his broad, plain face managed to charm her, though certainly she would have been alert to charm, having experienced various would-be conquerors—her husband, Napoleon, Metternich and Ugo Foscolo among them—and never having been in a position to appreciate the subtle differences between them. By then her life was simple, based on a few verities—that she hated tyrants and loved her country and her people and her sons, whom she had not chosen but had given life. And there, where there was no room for romance, appeared buoyant, deer-eyed Henri. Still, she did not refuse him. When, after kissing her hand, he asked if he might call on her at home, she agreed, though she could have had no idea what this entailed—months, years even, of the man's attentions.

Some days of fierce imagining passed before Henri arrived at her house. On this first visit, he was on fire, all wit and ardor, courting like mad. He conducted what would be their liveliest and friendliest conversation. An early hurt makes a later love sweeter, he argued. You, she said in effect, have no idea. In the end he again won her promise that he might call on her, and this further permission was certainly all his fertile imagination needed. Confessing all this later in his hypothetical guidebook for lovers *De l'Amour,* he notes that the merest hint of hope at the right moment will suffice to make a man fall in love, and that an even tinier trace may do "in a decisive, bold and impetuous person, with an imagination whetted by misfortune," in other words, in Henri himself.

In the following nights he could no more sleep than could Romeo or Dido. By day he tried to recoup by indulging in other pleasures, but found them inane, and when the trance overtook him he pledged himself ready to die for her. He burned for his appointed hour, yet feared for courage and his cause. His very furniture seemed to reproach him, "for the happiness I had dreamed in their presence." He went to the mountains at Varese for relief, but found none, only able to think of Métilde, dark-eyed in the town below. He wrote her florid letters and got no encouragement at all. Back in Milan he went to a ball, watched her dance with another and wept. He became a spectacle to his friends; to her simply a speck.

Still, she did not entirely turn him away. She agreed to his continued visits, though she imposed a limit on them. She banished him for two weeks at a time, giving him only an evening every fortnight. If she sought to discourage him with this, she was mistaken, for having more time to reflect simply inflamed him the more. In the long blank between his visits, he could hatch his fervent designs unencumbered, and so her rejections only fed his castle-in-the-air obsession, his *amour fou*. The visits themselves, not surprisingly, became "pinnacles of utter madness."

At first, in her presence, words poured from his mouth, and the hour passed "like a searing flash." But as the visits continued and his defenses failed, otherwise verbose Henri lost the power of speech altogether and sat mute and adoring before her until his time was up. He felt split in half. "It is as if you had two beings," he wrote of the Lover in *De l'Amour*, "one to act and the other to reproach you for acting." When he found others present during his visiting hour, he first enraged her by speaking over them to her, and then—to ingratiate her, to win her by seeming not to want to—sat silently and endured their drivel and wanted to kill himself afterward. "If some assassin had shot me in the head with a pistol," wrote pistol-obsessed, hyperbolic Henri, "I would have thanked him before I expired."

This condition between Henri and Métilde—his drama of their lives—went on through 1818 and into 1819, feeding on the impossibility of its consummation. "Always a little doubt to calm," he writes in the margin of a book, "this is what gives life to passionate love." His kind of love—not just existing in the face of doubt, but created by it—he believed was "modern," a kind of erotic correlative of the philosophical spirit of his age. "Whatever you do," he writes to her, "will not change the idea that has seized me, the idea of the happiness of being loved by you." Henri had appropriated this irresistible "idea." It was the pursuit of happiness, made coequal in America's Declaration to life and liberty itself. Encyclopedic Henri applied it to his own erotic life and then turned it back to the world in general terms, as his ego universalized in *De l'Amour*. There, in a profusion of identities and various pronouns, Henri played in all guises Man in Love.

Reading *De l'Amour*, one may begin to assume that Métilde saw the situation in the parlor on Henri's enormously projected scale. But in her actual life in the context of that time, Henri was most probably a distraction, and a minor one at that. Métilde endured a year of his visits (and in what spirit, we may only imagine). It was a year of declining fortunes for the Carbonari. The arrests continued. The secret police shipped their suspects north into Moravia, to the dreaded Spielberg citadel, a vast, Gothic torture chamber in the mountains, from which most never returned. Métilde and her two companions kept a vigil for those who had been imprisoned. As the numbers of the faithful dwindled, those remaining rose automatically to prominence, in the eyes of the populace and in the eyes of the police. As Métilde herself was besieged by paralyzed Henri in her parlor, she came into the glare.

To him, she was Athena in judgment. He had professed his love in more and more dire terms, and finally by his silence itself. He assumed she had learned of his reputation as an artiste, up all night with theater people, a whoremonger. He knew she knew, and felt her reproach before it came. Her cool gaze may have taken in Henri's passions as not so important, given the situation, but he made much of it, even if she saw Henri as Henri, not as he saw himself—as romantic, systematic Henri, Stendhalesque Henri at the center of the universe.

Conspiracy-ridden Milan had nothing on his intriguing brain by then. At night he haunted the moonlit piazza near her house. By day he searched her out in the street. If at a distance he saw a woman in a white satin hat—like hers—he had to lean against the wall until his heart began to beat again. In his own terms, things had completely crystallized. There was no more world—

just the endless, ambiguous proof of their love, and all of Milan reduced to signs and omens.

Finally, she suggested that he return to France. Grandiose, yet ironic, yet grandiose nonetheless, Henri refused. "I could never consent to place mountains between us," he jested, as if he had the Alps at his command. Then, in May, she journeyed to the hill town of Volterra to visit her sons at the seminary there. Henri could not be alone in Milan without her. The next day he undertook the two-hundred-mile journey after her, first going to Genoa, then by sea to Leghorn, then on horseback inland over the ridges into Tuscany. He wore a long cape and dark green glasses and considered his large, conspicuous foreign person incognito.

On the afternoon of his arrival in the little fortress town, Métilde passed him in the street and didn't discover him, though she noticed the strange man in green glasses. The sheer unlikeliness of his being there was apparently adequate to disguise him. Evidently unsatisfied by the success of his anonymity, he went at sunset to the piazza overlooking the gorge, where as it happened she had the habit of walking in the evening. There Henri struck up a conversation and removed his shades. Perhaps he imagined she'd be delighted to see him, but when she came into the square with two friends, she walked on, furious and saying nothing. That night she wrote him a cold, clear letter, addressing him as "Monsieur," accusing him of failing in delicacy and demanding that he leave Volterra. Thus recognized, he sent in return a long, florid and self-indicting message. "This passion," he wrote as if in explanation, "is to be the great concern of my life." He claimed to reject every stratagem, every calculation, even the idea of seduction itself, and asked that she merely love and not despise him.

But he did not leave town; rather he wrangled an invitation to a reception at her sons' seminary, and intruded upon her there. She mostly ignored him, as she leaned on the arm of a certain handsome Signor Georgi and Henri died a thousand deaths and failed to pass himself off as an expert on Etruscan art, the local specialty. The following day she granted him a brief audience so that she might demand again that he depart. They met in the gardens of the school, and he agreed finally to leave town. He went from there to Florence, where he visited her image as Salome and wrote to her daily and at length. She sent two of his letters back, unopened, with this note: "Sir, I do not wish to receive any more letters from you and I will not write to you."

But of course it didn't end there. Back in Milan, through the fall of 1819 and into 1820, he pursued her, her brief reprieves scarce now, her annoyance blooming into rage. In March, as good weather finally arrived, he was still in the full clutch of his obsession, envisioning her image before his window. But by the end of that year she had worn him down, and he had to admit his failure. The thing had reached "a dead blank," he wrote. He began to spend more and more of his day writing, as his consolation, at first to her, then for her, then of her, then of others as her. This last turn he discovered on "a day of genius," when he decided to turn his first-person confession into a third-person treatise. He would alchemize torment into an "anatomy," transform his disease into a discourse. He would compose a system of his love, within which he might hide from love itself. There was nothing in nature like it, he decided. It was a "wonder of civilization."

Milan proceeded toward its own crisis, the forces of repression and rebellion slowly encompassing everyone's personal life. Henri came to be suspected and shunned by both sides. "I have not been admitted to a certain circle," he wrote, "because an impartial person said, 'If he comes several people will leave.' . . . This is the most shattering blow I have ever had in my life." By March of 1821 open rebellion had erupted in Turin and Naples, and the police in Milan cracked down in anticipation of rebellion there as well. The two best-known leaders of the resistance were captured and sent to the Spielberg. Métilde herself was called to testify before a secret grand jury. Finally, the authorities advised Henri to leave the country.

It was, he says, "the most painful resolution of my life," this decision to return to Paris. He crossed the mountains on horseback, devastated, "hoping that I would have a fall, and take off so much skin that I would be distracted from other matters." He reported that she had asked him, in their last words together, when he would come back to Milan. "Never, I hope," he recalled himself replying. He later spoke of her as "one who loved me but would not admit it."

Back in Paris and contradictory as ever, he finished and published *De l'Amour*. He augmented its first book—about Métilde and himself, coded into generalizations and stories—with a second, a sort of travel guide surveying the customs of lovemaking in various times and places, including Provence in the twelfth century. Of love in the United States, he wrote that the defeat of tyranny had delivered its people only into a vague sense that they were missing something. The habit of reason makes the crystallization of love impossible in America, he wrote, and the place was anyway totally devoid of writers and artists, having not supplied the world as yet with so much as a single scene of tragedy.

Though *De l'Amour* is Henri's first great and original work, it did not prove popular. A Parisian reviewer called it "most bizarre," and this judgment was generally shared by the ages. The work defied definition, taking up one form only to shake it off and assume another. He himself described it in one of several prefaces—each an effort to elucidate what followed—as merely the compilation of "certain facts of which I have been an involuntary witness during my prolonged stay in the country of the orange tree." It was a work recalling—for him anyway—"so many of the fine shades of feelings I'd experienced in Italy."

He never saw Métilde again, and no woman would ever again

inspire him so deeply. After he left Milan, she fell under the power of the authorities. We see her clearly at last, in other reports, declining to name names under duress, showing the same steel she'd shown to Henri, branding the regime an inquisition and an insult to her female dignity. When she refused to answer any further questions, the secret police set her free, kept her under surveillance, finally arrested her again, this time deporting her to the Spielberg Citadel, where in May of 1825 she fell ill from her lifelong tuberculosis and died, at age thirty-five, in the arms of Madame Frecavalli. "What goodness," wrote her friend, "what sweetness in that noble heart."

Henri would continue to recreate her in his art. Some part of her was reflected truly in him, and this part became the fierce and independent heroine in his novels, which are his lasting work. Métilde transmogrified is Madame de Renal in *The Red and the Black* and Giulia Rinieri in *The Charterhouse of Parma*. Though his true and only subject was finally himself, his enshrinement of the "Stendhalesque" heroine would make her famous, and make him seem even feminist, as he is called by Simone de Beauvoir and others.

Obscure in his own lifetime, his writings would strike various chords in later centuries. Universally, he is seen as some kind of original. His separateness, his buoyancy, his tourist's eye, these would be recognized—as Henri himself predicted they would—as quintessentially modern. His aesthetic dissociation, his appropriation of everything in the name of the self, these would be hallmarks of the new age. He seems like a contemporary of Warhol, rather than of Jefferson, when we see him reading something he likes in the paper and remarking, "It is pure Stendhal."

One might imagine that, being so inward and ready to assume the world, he would at least have come to understand himself. But for all his self-absorption and his explanations, at last he found himself opaque. In the short, sharp, final book, *Memoirs of an Egotist,* he wrote that though he was perfectly capable of giving good advice to others, as for himself, "I've acted according to my mood, blindly."

Ten years after her death, Henri still thought of her often. "Métilde absolutely occupied my life from 1818 to 1824," Henri wrote then, "and I am not yet cured." When he heard of her death, he wrote in the margin of one of his copies of his failed little book, *De l'Amour,* "1 May 1825—Death of the Author." Yet he lived on, reminded of her, or at least of his feeling for her, by anything beautiful. He would live to see the Bourbons finally expelled in 1830. Then in favor again, he would obtain a secure—if boring—sinecure in his beloved Italy, though not in Milan, but in the hot and desolate port of Civitavecchia, which he found *"un trou abominable."*

We see him at last old, visiting Florence again, still solitary and jarred and passionate, as he comes out into the light after gazing upon the tombs of Michelangelo and Machiavelli in the Church of Sante Croce. He feels agitated, haunted, upset. To calm himself, he sits at a little bench in the sunshine and opens his favorite volume, the poems of Ugo Foscolo.

26

North

....

After breakfast we walked to the river with our luggage. I had the oddest feeling looking at the town, as if every appearance—the shirt display in a shop window, the pot of geraniums on a balcony, the French flag—was an invitation to a future that never arrived. I remembered how our trip had seemed before we'd taken it, and how gorgeous and meaningful the France that I'd imagined had been. That was a France we'd never get to, no matter how authentic the real France was. It was hazardous to cling to one's dream life, I saw, but I couldn't help it. I'd be the guy to put out geraniums so that he could live a geraniums-on-the-porch kind of life. So, too, the city gate, set between enormous and ancient stone turrets, looked like a huge tab, holding down its old intentions.

I'd awoken first again in the pink room on that day of our departure from Arles. She slept deeply, too, I'd thought. I was overmatched. I'd been charming, I'd been wounded, I'd tried to explain and none of it had worked. Now I couldn't count on the magic of the South, either. That morning we were heading north. She wanted to visit her friend in the Loire, which was closer than Paris, though farther west. We'd discovered, though, that traveling by train in France one had to return to Paris, to the hub of the system, and then set out again to reach the farm country of the Loire. This made it seem as if we had failed to achieve orbital speed in the South and were succumbing to the gravity, to the reality of Paris, where she had hated me, she'd said.

The Loire would be our last stop in France, and my last chance. Probably it would be our last "our" as well, I thought. Since my swim in the sea, I was no longer sure of "us." Actually, it had been a brief stay in the first person plural. In the notebook dedicated to her, I'd mostly written in that most poetic of numbers, the second person singular, and in the most poetic of tenses, the present. Whole libraries of poems have been written in this moment-by-moment address: "Lovely, you go to the corner to buy sunflowers for the apartment. You are fine."

The trip had stripped me, layer by layer. By then I felt detached from my faith in the power of language. For days, weeks, I'd been inundated with French: French from L, French from strangers, French from waiters, French pouring from open windows—even at that moment—until my brain had to singsong the jingle of it, turning up nonsense phrases on its own. By then, all language, not just my own private tongue but also the meterless French all around me, seemed like a mere fume. Worse, it was a trap. It was what love had to fall into, to exist in the world. So by then I wasn't saying much to L, for fear I'd blow it further.

Despite this, though, I was still writing like mad in my notebook, having hypothetical English arguments with myself. It was a comforting habit. That morning at breakfast, as L composed her trip notes, I'd remembered something of Stendhal's, that sincerity was the antidote to the I, though still unsure of everything,

I had avoided even the first person. I'd written abstractly, about jet lag. I was having a grand theory about jet lag at that point. It was psychic dislocation on the face of the earth; disphasia with old sol, the source of all life; a metaphysical malady of the first order. Even then I knew why I was enlarging it. I wanted it to be what was wrong. Only that, as bad as it was, I prayed, and not a permanent burn from falling—like a Mercury space capsule, scraping into the atmosphere—in love, too late and too hopelessly. Across the table, writing in her own notebook, L looked burnished and as if ripened by France. She was beginning to seem beautiful to me again, and I didn't want to see that. Thank God we were going home soon. Home to America and my apartment, where I could hide, where I would be back in sync with the earth. And thank God, too, I was a writer. I had writing, no matter what, to remind me of what I was.

Outside the town gate of Arles was the clean, modern, American-looking traffic circle L had described to me as I had lain Miss Havisham–like in the pink room. The traffic circle seemed to pose, displaying itself as if it had managed to ward off the unforeseen once and for all. In its center, perhaps where the yellow house had been, was the fountain that rose from nowhere, as L had said, its jets springing from the surface of its pool. It was doing what we require of fountains, making water defy itself. At the river's edge nearby was a wrecked bridge, which we passed as we circumnavigated the roundabout. There was even less of this bridge than there had been of the old pont at Avignon. Here stood just a single white foot, the rest blown up by the resistance in World War II. The foot still had stone lions flanking it, though they were bullet-pocked. Juxtaposed with the new traffic circle and fountain, it looked like Europe. They made me wonder if we could think anything that we didn't badly imagine from the first.

Maybe the whole mechanism of thought was an evolutionary misstep, consciousness itself a failed adaptation.

We arrived at the station and walked through it to the modern quay, where we waited among a crowd for the big train north. "You're being really quiet," L said.

"Just observing," I said. I pointed out a couple near us. "They're Americans," I said. For one thing, they had no American-seeming slogans on their clothing. They seemed to be trying to appear unmarked, incognito, though the little commercial flares of their labels gave them away.

"They match," said L. They both wore white T-shirts and sunglasses and fannypacks and Nike street-hiking shoes and khaki shorts, though his had bulging zippered pouches down the thighs. Both had ties for their sunglasses draping the napes of their necks, as I did, I realized, suddenly feeling American myself and understanding that need to be unmarked. I had a *tête américaine,* I remembered.

As we watched the American pair, the guy said something the woman didn't like, and she pounded his meaty shoulder several times, in play. The guy spread his *Herald Tribune* on the quay and knelt to read, while she watched for the train. First a TGV express went by, bullet-nosed, roaring like a jet, its huge orange bulk ethereal with speed, as on the quay I held my ears and glimpsed, for an instant, a woman sitting calmly in the big train looking out, that condition of speed the norm for her, and the crowd on the quay blurred, wheeling past. Then another TGV came in, this one slowing smoothly to a halt, and we got on. We got real seats this time, in the tall car that seemed to have the proportions of French writing paper. In my seat I got out my notebook, conscious that eight-and-a-half by eleven was the American size, as the train slipped from the station. I didn't look up until we were out in the country.

Then it was agricultural out there, with far towns like ships in the delta. Crowding the track in the low, square fields were sunflowers, their big flowery heads lopped over, all in the same direction, south, where the lost sun had gone. Their faces were unanimous, resigned, mournfully groundward, exposing the undersides of their flowers, which were a creamy color, a delicate yellow.

I let the silence reign for a while before I spoke. "You could tell the people running the hotel in Arles were new at it," I said. "They seemed rushed."

There'd only been three of them, said L, the husband and the wife and her sister.

"Her sister?" I said.

"She made the beds," she said. "The wife did the kitchen and the guy did the desk." They were going crazy. It was a festival weekend, she reminded me.

"You can always act as if you had time," I said.

"Besides," she added, "they'd just bought the place." She'd talked to the guy while I'd been sleeping. "The French aren't born with savoir faire."

I was sick of savoir faire, I thought. Out the window France went by, triumphant and ordinary and large as life. The Rhône withdrew. The quiet, huge, speeding train again seemed to reverse the context of travel, the country seeming to move as we stood still. I glanced at L's calm, elongated face. Since La Ciotat, she'd looked different, though I couldn't say how, only that she looked like herself, a woman. And I could see in her face that I had shielded myself from her with her age. She was young, I could say, avoiding everything. But she'd turned out to be formidable, and now that made her age worse.

Then Lyon began to assemble itself around the train, which seemed to slow slightly as it did, though it was still moving so fast that a man in whites in mid-serve on a tennis court made his toss but not his stroke as the scene whipped by. The town thickened into being. I didn't want to see it. Another French town. I was sick of the trip already. *Je le déteste,* I thought, wanting to impugn it in its own tongue, the place, the innocent drivers flashing by on streets full of morning traffic. Impenetrable streets, awash with impenetrable language. Again I was glad to be going home.

Lyon felt like the land's last drag. After the town released us, the open country plummeted past the train, a high rolling plain in free-fall. In a forward seat, two girls began talking brightly and quickly in Italian, their speech as light and pummeling as the land falling by outside. I looked out the window, concentrating on the continuous, engineered features of the track that held a line in the blur beside the train: the concrete rim generalized into a single ongoing beat.

In a field a red-and-white cow leaped butt first to its feet as we went by. Evidently the noise of the train had startled it. Inside the car, the train's only sound was a soft, continuous ringing, like steel swords drawn together. But outside, the train was loud. Loudness was like a condition of its being. As far as the train was concerned, the roar might just happen to be there, wherever it went, and cows happened to be a leaping species. I watched a raven land in a field of stubble, hop once and take off again, maybe spooked by the train, maybe not.

I was thirsty, and asked L if she wanted water. Then I got up and walked back down through the train to the club car, where the air was warm from the crowd and tangy with French cigarette smoke. There was a sort of line at the counter, not an American sort of line exactly but a quasi-linear crush, each face in it full of the sense of being nearly next. *L'eau,* I practiced mentally. Nearby in the crowd an old French couple argued. He was insisting on something in his crushed and gravelly voice. *"Dis moi oui,"* he demanded, several times. And she, tired of it, so tired of it, but never giving in, saying, *"Non,"* that short, matter-of-fact

French refusal that seemed merely to acknowledge some natural order of the universe. A young woman in line saw me listening and gave me an ironic smile, as if I knew what the argument was all about. I'd be in on this, back in America. As it was, I was smiling back and faking it, feeling that familiar ineptness, around me like an atmosphere since I'd come to France.

Thinking of its apostrophe, I bought *l'eau,* a big bottle, and wandered around the car a moment until I heard English being spoken. Thinking just to bask a little in it, I found a place for my elbow at the counter, and listened to the group of American college kids, two guys and three girls. They were telling gross-out stories, it turned out. The guy who was holding forth at the moment, comfortably and loudly as if no one in the car knew English, had peed in some guy's VCR once, for revenge. What a dweeb, I thought, using one of L's words.

So, feeling further stripped, I got out of the club car after that, and took my water back to my seat. There was L. She hadn't wanted water, but she'd have some now, as long as I had gotten it. She was all right, I thought. She was there. I didn't have to be advancing my cause, carrying a chalice every minute. Whether or not she was in love with me, she was all right. As soon as I thought this, though, I recognized it as wishful thinking. Why couldn't I just be in her presence? I recalled visiting Cézanne's studio in Aix, where I'd asked about the tiny wooden models, like marionettes, that we'd seen there.

He'd used them as models for figures, it turned out. "He wouldn't have any woman in the studio," the young French female guide had said, meaning a real woman, instead of a puppet.

"Wouldn't?" I'd said.

"Couldn't," she'd said, carefully correcting her accented English. "He was too emotion."

·   ·   ·

This, too, I wrote in my notebook as Paris fell toward us. I wrote with a sense of finding various points that might bear me, like footholds on a rock face. At that point in the trip, I'd almost filled the notebook, a thin-lined school tablet with a plain tan cardboard cover and a spiral wire binding. What would it be worth to me, when it was done? I'd written most of it as a pretense. Then, after the Best Western, the writing had composed a deeper alibi. The notes had been evidence for me, notices, at least, of my chaos. But these weren't exactly writing either. Just more language, heaps of it. I'd almost filled the book. Now that I looked at the notebook, it seemed to go everywhere and nowhere, serving no cause finally and more often than not memorializing something I'd rather not have recalled.

I put the notebook in the seat pocket in front of me on the train, to get away from it a minute. Outside, the country began to modulate toward the urban, as the mouth of a vast bowl that held Paris enveloped the train. The city quickened in industrial sheds and houses, small new commuter stations that flicked past, then in cemeteries, then in a phalanx of high rises that rose up and fell away, as the heart of town finally opened and the river materialized and the train slowed, releasing the inside-out feeling of the journey, until we were what was moving, riding along the river and suddenly in silver Paris again.

We pulled into the same station from which we'd departed, the Gare de Lyon. Back at zero, I thought. The South of France hadn't transformed us into anything, as I hoped it might. No, it was just us, still doing the Everything Dance. Some of the passengers in the car were already standing up in the aisle, eager to be done with the journey, and when the train slid up beside the quay, we stood up with them. The train stopped. I wrestled with the luggage as the other passengers pushed by, filing out, and then we were down the steps and within the echoing station, hurrying with the bags and eager to make our next connection.

And it would be the following morning before I had any thought of my notebook, when I would reach habitually for it, to go on regardless with my construction of our trip to France, and would find it gone, with a shock instantly recalling having left it on the TGV, and then vividly imagining it borne off by the big orange train—all that work, the last evidence of myself, lost.

27

Cheops

....

I veered close to finding out when we arrived at Chaumont at sunset, the castle on a bluff above the river, its pointed turrets backlighted, the orchardy plain of the Loire beyond. It was gorgeous, and I recalled later the moment when I'd considered writing down something about the crowned towers and the twilight, there amidst my other impressions in the notebook.

But I rejected the scene. It was too poetic, even if it were actual. That was the problem with places like Chaumont, with castles and sunsets. No matter what you tried to write about them, it got purple. You'd want to paint it or be a poet anyway for a second, and then if you had any sense you'd have to refrain. How great in the old days—in the sixteenth century for Chaumont—when you might have been just there with it, the way I was there with San Francisco, when it might be black spires over a sky going-to-rose like that, and it wouldn't occur to you that it was romantic. I'd been a poet; I'd written down the beautiful things. But by the time I got to L, I was avoiding anything like that. So I dismissed the

Gothic weathervanes outlined in amber and didn't look for the notebook in the shoulder bag, where it wasn't.

At the castle we unloaded the car. L's schoolgirl friend Sylvie took up her tiny, swaddled-in-yellow infant, and we grabbed the luggage. In the car I'd felt unsure that this was the right moment to be visiting them—with the new baby and all—but that afternoon Sylvie had made us feel welcome. The family lived in third-floor apartments in the castle, like the old nobility. Her husband was the concierge. He had left the drawbridge down for us.

Behind the wrought iron gate at the far side of the drawbridge, a huge dog leaped and squealed with joy. He was to be my last dog in France, a mottled, bristle-haired animal, slobbering with happiness that Sylvie was home. Inside the gate, in the castle's courtyard, she quieted him with a command, and the animal led us up the flights of stone stairs to their apartment.

Sylvie and L took the baby into the back rooms, to take care of it, and I sat in the living room with the dog and Pierre, Sylvie's husband. We tried to make new conversation with our fringe of a common language. *"C'est grand,"* I said, meaning the dog. It is, he said, seeming to refer to something else—the room, the place, the country. I couldn't remember the word for dog for a moment, and there was a pause until I came up with *chien* and by then he seemed to have lost the thread, until, at last, I simply pointed at the dog, and he told me its name, Cheops. *"Briard,"* he added, which I'd never heard of. He pointed again at the dog and said something that I finally understood to be about Napoleon, with whom this dog was somehow associated. Then, after even more work, we could agree on Charlemagne as well. An old breed, I took it. The dog himself, Cheops of Briard of Napoleon of Charlemagne, lay seriously on its forepaws and watched the man. When he began to whine, his master gave me to understand that it was time for the dog's walk. Would I like to go? "Yes," I said, leaving it at that. The dog, prescient, reached the door before we'd gotten up. There he yawned nervously, concluding with a low squeal, a plea. When Pierre opened the door, the dog bounded down the stairs.

I felt comfortable with Pierre, now that we had the dog for a subject. We called his name as he ran ahead, stopping to look back at each landing and then, let out at last onto the grounds of the castle, racing off under the trees. Of all the dogs I'd seen on the trip, this was the most amazing. He was a huge fast creature in the open, and fierce. He ran ahead and circled back, blasting past us.

It was dusky and cool, compared with the South. As we walked, the path forked and the grounds broadened into a rolling field, the trees planted there in a wide grid across the knolls. The low places, even that early in September, were full of fallen leaves. When the dog came back, he came up behind us and leaped one of these hollows as he went by, his face full of speed and animal joy, his huge body airborne a second, flung out like wordless intention itself. The path ran along a stone wall—the castle's boundary—and then turned away, looping back. There was still some light in the sky behind the towers, though it was deep blue and couldn't be called daylight. High on the black castle wall, the windows of their apartment glowed. The women were up there with the baby, I wanted to say to Pierre, but I couldn't, and so just pointed. He nodded.

Back inside the place was bright and redolent with dinner, roast chicken. The dog lay on the floor in front of the fire as we ate. The baby was sleeping in a back room, and we listened to him breathing via a walkie-talkie by his mother's plate. The baby's presence gave me an intimate sense of being in a home. With a baby, it seemed to me, you responded, you didn't consider, and so existed in life, not hovering over it. Again I wondered if we should be there.

He carved the chicken as she spread the rest of the dinner before us, and the two of them were *charmant* at the table. L spoke her French for both of us, and I hung in there, trying to get the gist, so that she wouldn't have to explain everything. Only once did she pause—to try out *écouter* for *entendre,* which they discussed. I didn't quite get the difference, and asked. I could *écouter* without *entendre,* they told me, but not vice versa. The baby didn't awaken during dinner. The silence in the infant's room stood as a steady hiss—white noise—enveloping the meal.

That night L and I slept as we had since La Ciotat, as roommates. We were given Pierre's office, and slept on the convertible couch there, beneath a huge Renaissance tapestry crowded with fabulous creatures, unicorns and peacocks and a creature with the body of a bull and the head of a cat. In the broad stone chamber one door led to a spiral staircase, which ascended and descended inside a tower. Pierre had shown us these stairs and given us a heavy, old-fashioned key to the door at the base of the tower so that we might come and go in the morning as we wished. That night, we just went to bed. L was quiet again, I noted. I'd write something about it, about my assumptions and the varieties of her silence, in the morning.

We awoke to hear the baby crying next door sometime around dawn. Though its cries seemed far off through the stone wall, the sound was clear in the silence of the place, a wail and a grabbing of breath and a wail again. I couldn't go back to sleep and so eventually got up to write, to inscribe some hope before the day poured its new load of phenomena upon me. Then the notebook was gone. It was not there in the shoulder bag, and I realized immediately where I'd left it. I knew with a sick certainty that it had blasted across France overnight and was probably lost forever. I searched anyway, performing a ritual in which the notebook might magically return. L woke up as I was going through the bags. "I can't find my notebook," I said.

"I'll kill you," she said calmly, "if you've lost those notes." This suddenly felt like a double grief, for I could tell by the way that she'd said it that she'd loved those notes, which had enshrined us. The entries had been my love poems, a record of my feelings for her, which, since I couldn't express them outright, had crystallized into descriptions of France. She took their loss like a blow, and was angry, and in that moment showed that she cared for the notes and for us in France more than she'd let on. She got up, and together we looked through everything and found nothing.

Then I descended the tower to the thick door at its base. I crossed the grass to the parking lot and peered into the windows of the empty car. On dozens of trips, my notebook was almost the only thing I'd never lost. So I couldn't take refuge in considering its loss accidental. Too much was signified by it. For two days, since the Best Western, I'd been out of it, looking at the earth as if it were the alien thing, and in that reversal of the truth, something I had refused to see in myself had risen in rebellion against my construction of things and my courtship of L. My unconscious—so much smarter than I was—wasn't going to let me dodge my hurt and anger. I'd sabotaged myself, and I could never have done it this well on purpose. In one simple gesture, I had destroyed us, obliterating my ideal image of the two of us in France.

And I had knocked off my last excuse for having taken the trip. I was a writer, I would write. It had become a sort of mantra. I would make the trip into material, if nothing else, so I could stand apart from it, as if measuring its proportions with my thumb. But that wasn't going to work this time. I'd arranged for the writing to disappear. I felt like crying, like going home.

When I got back the family was waiting, worried for my lost *cahier*, and it was terrible, at breakfast, to have to act nonchalant about it. I'll get it back, I assured everyone. But I knew I wouldn't. I tried to steady myself, drinking my bowl of coffee with both hands. I could remember what I'd written, I told them, though I didn't believe it. In the past I'd written whole stories without glancing at my notes—only checking them afterward. But I could only do that, I knew, with faith that the notes existed. If they'd existed, I probably wouldn't have needed them. That morning I could remember only utterly inconsequential things, like a piece of an envelope on the red stairway of Phillipe's apartment building, or things that seemed merely to reflect me and my fears, like the dead bull in Arles. Of the good parts, the parts with L, I could remember only very little. What had we been? Why hadn't I paid more attention to that? I brooded on this as life went on around me at the breakfast table.

Pierre went to work, taking the dog, bidding us good-bye and saying *"désolé"* to me, and Sylvie and L made plans to take the baby to town and do some shopping. I would stay home and read, I volunteered. Before they left, L made a call for me, to the Gare de Lyon in Paris, to find out about their lost and found. That they had one gave me some dim hope. L's blue eyes as she told me this looked then like something else I'd lost.

I went back to our room and found a small blank sketchbook in my bag and tried to write down everything I could recall of our trip, but I filled only three pages, two of which consisted of items on a list I titled "Outline of Feelings." My feelings I could remember. There turned out to be twenty-four of them, just my feelings and the towns they occurred in, beginning with Big Shot in Airport Lounge and ending with Alienated in Arles and *Désolé* in the Loire. Two dozen emotions, and some of the big ones: love, hope, fear despair. But it was meager, compared to the actual trip—a list, for a life.

. . .

After that I took the big key and the tiny notebook and my Proust to distract me, if it could, and climbed the tower. The spiraling staircase was a well of dark, lighted only from above by slots in the stone of the turret. I climbed up there, leaning into the smoothed outer wall to get my footing on the steep, radial stairs. At the top I panicked some pigeons, who flapped madly against the stone and were gone, out the squared slots around a narrow circular walkway. In the dust the birds raised, beams of sunlight shot through the chamber, like swords. I was looking out as the old castle guards must have. Some guard, I thought. I watched the countryside appear, vantage by vantage as I walked around the turret. There was the empty parking lot; there, the long vista of the valley; there, a cluster of other towers and turrets and the slate roofs of the place. The mad among the nobility had been locked up in the tower, and Rapunzel with her unlikely hair.

I descended the stairs to the blackness of the tower's base, the keyhole a single bright point at the bottom. I was noticing again, I noticed, composing, but for what? For whom? I came out into the light and found myself at the top of a bluff. Outwitted by my own unconscious, I thought, I was faced with what I'd really wanted all along. Which was what? To be with her, helpless. To cast out this observer, this imposter. To stop composing. Below was the river, and across the valley, orchards. This family in the castle didn't seem to have to keep a grip on the concept of their lives. They seemed to have responded to the simple demand of generation, and it had taken over. Now thinking about purpose was the last thing they had to do. For thousands of generations we'd found mates, had families and, effortlessly it seemed, brought forth this present. The far trees seemed to express that old concentration. Had the whole thing failed in my time, or was it just me?

I made my way around the walls and found a garden of red roses, ornately planted on an overlook. The broad view felt focused on me. I shuddered and sat at a white bench among the roses and opened the Proust. This would be my last try with this guy, I thought. I had struggled through the tortuous relations of Swann and his Odette, proceeding on the basis of the challenge—by now a diminishing concern—and the possibility that things might work out between the lovers, thus shedding a little decent foreshadowing on me and L. Old varnish-sniffing Marcel, though, was no help. When I opened the book where I'd thought I'd left off, bad text jumped to my eye: "This new manner, indifferent, offhand, irritable which Odette now adopted with Swann undoubtedly made him suffer, but he did not realize how much he suffered." This wasn't what I needed, but I plunged on. "This change was his deep, secret wound." I felt this wound, which hurt not just for her, but with a loneliness I hadn't let myself feel for years.

Across the river was a fringe of trees, and beneath them was a train track, and I noticed a train moving on it, miles off and downwind, so that it couldn't be heard. It was an older train, a provincial freight. Its momentary progress was tiny at that distance. It was awful to stand among the moments without marking them. To have them arrive and leave unnoticed, unmarked, in person or in writing. I was putting the lovers on the urn, I thought. I was hopelessly romantic without even thinking about it, acting out of some wordless hope that I could control things by making a code or a currency to buy love. Which couldn't be bought by anything, or even earned. Love didn't have anything to do with control—that was the terrifying thing about it. You either had it or you didn't, and I didn't. Beyond the river, the train took its long moment to disappear, and I watched it the whole time, hanging on.

.   .   .

When L returned with the baby and Sylvie, I noticed some sadness in her face that I hadn't seen earlier. And when Sylvie took her baby back into the bedroom to change him, L came to me. "Let's go walk," she said, and we went out, through the gate and onto the grounds where Pierre and the dog and I had walked the night before. We left the path where it forked and proceeded into the field, saying nothing, just walking over the dry grass together and crunching the leaves underfoot in the low places. We found a little knoll and sat down.

She was sad, it turned out. She began telling me about her morning with Sylvie and the baby, then her voice caught a little, and I realized she was on the edge of tears.

"What's wrong?" I said. She gasped and began crying openly.

"What, what is it, what?" I said, holding her and holding myself.

"It was all baby, baby, baby, baby," she said. "Taking care of the baby. Telling stories about the baby." She burst into tears anew. I had my own reasons for tears, and so I thought to let myself cry with her. Part of me still didn't want to, though, and it hurt my throat as I held her, ostensibly for her comfort, actually for my own.

For an instant I thought she was sad because she wanted a baby of her own, and suddenly it seemed as if my moment had arrived. I had to do it, I was thinking. I didn't care. I had taken this whole trip to do it, I had come halfway around the world and run all over France. Even if she was going to say no, I had to say it. So I took her shoulders in my hands and said, "I want to get married."

This interrupted her in her tears, and she looked at me, as if discovering me there. After a moment she said, in a kindly voice, "I know that's what you what."

And it would be months before I recalled my words exactly— with her help—and before I realized my proposal hadn't included her, that my question hadn't been a question, that her answer—which was no, I thought—hadn't been intended as an answer.

So we sat there a moment, overwhelmed. Then she went on. "I feel as if I've lost her," she said. Dismissed, I was eager to continue. With all my shredded attention, I tried to fathom what she was feeling. Was it that she was for once as unsure as I was, and as distant from this warm home, into which her friend—now a mother—had vanished?

"People change," I ventured, wanting to live. "You have to hang on to them." I reminded her of all the years she'd known Sylvie since grade school. Besides, I argued, this baby isn't even a month old. "I'm amazed she even invited us here, right now," I said. L said she guessed I was right.

"Remember those innkeepers in Arles, with their festival?" I said. "You understood them. A baby is ten times worse than a festival."

She considered this. "Were you crying?" she asked. I didn't know.

Then we walked. We found a gate in the far wall and fields beyond planted in sunflowers, and walked out among them. They had nodded, like those we'd seen in the South, though these were further gone, their black, warped heads loaded, the seeds packed in interlocking spirals. *Tournesol,* she said.

That night we had a last dinner with the family. It was a regular night for them, a dinner of squid and rice and no wine and the baby crying on the walkie-talkie. We helped with the dishes, knowing it was time to leave. Later we lay in bed and talked over our plans, looking up into the dark ceiling with its darker beams. By then we'd gotten into a rhythm of decision about what we'd do next. We'd go back to Paris in the morning, we decided. We'd be a day early for our flight and we had no reservations anywhere, but we'd see what happened.

"Trip's almost over," she said, as we settled.

"Seems like it passed in an instant," I said.

"Well," she said, "it had its long moments." She laughed and I laughed.

28

*O*BJETS *T*ROUVÉS

The next morning, while somewhat strenuously making the bed, I dislodged the tapestry. I must have lifted it off its hooks. As it fell, it folded over me: the fabulous animals, the peaceable kingdom, I experienced at that moment as darkness and dust. L, who was packing the bags, had to dislodge me, and then I had to tell our host, the curator, in my broken French: "*C'est tombé,* the tapestry." When it was remounted and L and I were finally alone again, it seemed funny, in a rueful sort of way. We'd been through hell on this trip.

Dropped at the train station in Blois, we sat on one end of a long bench, L teary again at bidding her friend good-bye. I had never considered that the trip would reveal so much of us. We'd spent almost all day every day together, and at that point I was thinking that we'd seen everything. In San Francisco, we'd been able to present a certain aspect. But in France, we'd been through the round.

And we hadn't been to one France, but dozens, the one at the moment superfluous. Big, slow, loaded trains on that workday track clanked through the station, their tank cars dusty with crushed grain. It had been summery in the South. I recalled sitting in the shady, open-windowed silent train at Aix, waiting to go, when out of the massive green bramble against the car that hummingbird had flown in. Iridescent, the bird had passed through, calm and level in the air, sounding like a struck guitar string.

There in the working station, L sobbed at intervals, her breath intake sharp every little while. Even that morning I still wasn't sure about the cause of her pain, about what was so upsetting to her about Sylvie and the baby. I assumed Sylvie's preoccupation had frightened L with a prospect of having to sacrifice girlhood to motherhood. As if women had to part from the world of women to be with a man, to have a family. If that was it, it wasn't the same for men, at least for me. When L showed up, I'd been waiting for years.

When I looked at L then, I knew things about myself that I hadn't known before. How frightened I had been of her, for one thing, of her of all people. Her youth made my own age apparent. She'd been so right, but even that was a challenge I had to stand up to. It was reassuring to be with the wrong person.

Now, stripped by France, I didn't know who I was, but I didn't know who I'd been afraid of, either. I'd known I could fall hard, and I had, and now it was done. France and everything else, I'd concocted to protect myself. If things were really romantic, I didn't have to feel everything, but merely play my little part, as in a puppet show.

A priest in his white robe and rosary beads sat down at the other end of our bench. He took a piece of bread from a plastic bag and began to eat. L and I both noticed him, pulled from our quiet moods. The priest ate quickly, yet gingerly, as if there were a thousand courtesies to be observed, even if one were really hungry. The priest finished the bread, licked one fingertip and dabbed away the rest of the crumbs, eating them one by one, and when he was done, wiped his mouth with the plastic bag. He was an old man.

Courtesies, manners, conventions—I'd hidden in them, partial and protected. Having been through the round, one recognized what was left out of a given moment. I recalled, in that context, being under the dusty tapestry, and her sweet face, laughing despite the damage, as she extricated me from it. Then, among the freights, our train arrived.

On our way back to Paris, we decided to save time by splitting up. She would go on to the Métro station called Cardinal Lemoine to see if she could catch a cancellation at a nice hotel she knew. I'd check the lost and found and meet her later. So returning again to the Gare de Lyon, we set off with curt good-byes in opposite directions, our bags on our shoulders. We'd gotten used to carrying the luggage. With the sentence L had taught me, I asked for the *Objets Trouvés* department, and the man answered in English, telling me to follow the blue signs. The first of these took me up a flight of stairs, and the next, over the tracks and onto a backlot of buildings and trucks, which went on for acres. At each turn appeared another small blue sign with an arrow and the words *Objets Trouvés*. I wandered back there, still thinking about L and the round. Out back of the station was a Dickensian brick workplace, complete with iron-wheeled carts. The last sign directed me toward one of the large warehouses, where even at a distance I could see that the door had a blue sign on it upon which were words I knew but couldn't read yet.

Maybe being with L was going to require some distance, the way one had to consider a whole country from a map. That meant, of course, that a few characteristics had to stand for the whole, that boundaries had to be agreed upon, though in some sense wouldn't be real. All maps were wrong to some degree.

Projection was one choice, color another, and always most of what could be, left off—just the road it was deemed you'd need, the place something happened to happen. That was the trade-off, though. Without a map you were immersed in the world, going from one sign to the next, just as when you got close to people they got more and more vast, became a multitude of appearances and feelings, many of them contradictory. Vast and complex L, gone off with her accustomed luggage into vast and complex France. Even as I thought this, though, I feared I couldn't be in love with her, if she was vast, or not as I'd wished to, anyway.

The sign on the door to the *Objets Trouvés* department was bigger and had no arrow, indicating that I'd arrived. Inside was a counter with shelves beyond it like stacks in a library, illuminated with long white florescent lights. Two men worked there, or rather one worked for the other. One asked me in French what I wanted and I repeated the other sentence that L had taught me on the train, *"J'ai perdue mon cahier."* *J'ai perdue* like jeopardy. I held my hands at right angles to show its size, then made a spiraling motion with my finger. The counter guy told the other guy to go get it, or something.

But he brought back a big box full of notebooks, two or three dozen of them, all kinds and sizes. So thoroughly had I imagined my lost notebook, its dull physical attributes, that I could tell in an instant that mine wasn't in the box. I looked through the notebooks anyway, hoping against hope. I looked at three with tan cardboard covers, not exactly like mine, I knew, but maybe I'd been wrong. All three had been written in, in French, which communicated in script was truly indecipherable, except that one was obviously in a child's hand, and one full of equations and mathematical symbols—square roots, less than and greater than. I put them back in the box and shrugged and the two men shrugged and I left.

I walked back through the complex brick station, occasionally having to find the blue signs and do the opposite, and still without my notebook, though less pained about its loss. Seeing all those other notebooks had given me an impression of furious human scribbling, and of the absurdity of writing things down, of putting one's feelings down within an event, as if one impression—one's own of course—helped the world along, the world that packed each moment with impressions, that tiny forest of script in the notebooks the merest part.

Love poems, those variations on "Come hither, my love, to me," seemed particularly absurd. First of all, I wondered if any-one ever really wrote a love poem. By the time you thought of writing anything down, you weren't in love, but were rendering it, in a sort of crystalline variation, making a shelter—like a glass house, I imagined—in which one might live afterward, safely out of love's direct beams. That courtly lady, the knight on bended knee. You read the poem and tried to act it out, and then wrote your own poems about it. Love poems were finally always self-portraits that pretended not to be, projections of one's own image onto someone else. The funny part was that love poets always wanted out of love poems. In quatrains and couplets, they cried out for real love to come and shatter the edifice. Unbelievable, I thought. All that energy, and the same little dance every time, like a spinning prayer wheel. All of the notebooks in the box, even the math book, all the notebooks everywhere, were love poems in this aim, hoping to move things by manipulating symbols for them. Greater than, less than, the square of, equal to, infinity.

Finally the Gare de Lyon disgorged me into a funky and crowded neighborhood compressed into irregular blocks around the train station. I took whatever street confronted me, and got lost—I didn't feel like getting out a map at that point. I tried simply to sense the direction to the river, and go more or less downslope. The next block had been demolished. The corner lot lay open, white rubble bright in the sun. Beyond it, the wall still showed the signs of the old inhabitants. Each apartment—there were three on each of the five floors—was still outlined on the remaining adjacent wall. Exposed to the morning sun, various tattered wallpapers still marked the individual units, the rooms reduced to two-dimensional boxes of faded patterns, fans and flowers, grids and shields. One of the upper rooms was mostly yellow, and I had to look awhile before I could tell vertical stripes, interrupted by sunflowers.

Those faded flowers were in full bloom, the way we'd never seen them on our trip. I felt with chagrin the old urge to write this down and—not in the sketchbook but inside the back cover of the Proust, where it might stand tinily next to the evidence of his lifelong obsession to reproduce the past—sketched the scene anyway, and L saying *"Tournesol."*

I remembered a friend who'd lost everything in a fire, telling me that having lost everything, she felt nothing, though in the ensuing weeks, as she needed things and found them gone, she recognized the depth of her loss. You could find things like this, too, as I had retrieved *Tournesol.* Maybe I would come across our whole trip again like this, finding everything in the lost notebook as single, associated moments.

The river appeared where I thought it would be, beyond the boulevard at the end of that street, and up the block I found a bridge that led me onto the grounds of the Jardin de Plantes, the botanical gardens. I cut through it, wandering a little in the menagerie they have there. I saw gazelles and thought of L and her Everything Dance, which by then was the dance that everything did. I wrote this down, too, retrieving it in the back of the Proust. By then I knew I was going to buy another notebook.

I walked up the hill on the Rue Cardinal Lemoine. I'd been there, I realized, on my first trip to Paris. That trip had been embarrassing, too. Maybe there was something intrinsically em-

barrassing about Paris to American men like myself. On that trip
I'd been wowed, and back home had written an article like an
instant expert. My editor, a frank woman on the other coast, had
just asked, after reading it, "Jim, have you ever been to Paris
before?"

"No," I had to say.

Let's just put that in the lead, then, she said. I agreed, embarrassed, and the piece came out headlined PARIS AT FIRST GLANCE.
But the ingenue angle made it a better story, I had to admit.
Acknowledging the gee-whiz tone of the thing made it tolerable.
I was still an American ingenue, I thought, walking up Hemingway's street, toward the address he had in the memoir called *A
Moveable Feast*. I'd gone there on a pilgrimage during that first
trip, and had walked from there along the route he described,
across the Luxembourg Gardens to Gertrude Stein's on the Rue
de Fleur. Then I'd thought Hemingway romantic, but walking up
the hill at that moment, I thought of Hadley, auburn-haired Hadley, ditching all his stuff in the Gare de Lyon, where it might have
ended up in *Objets Trouvés,* with all those other notebooks full
of script, all that writing like the tracks of needles, each minute
and exquisitely sensitive. You could think you loved someone,
and really only love the way you saw her, the words you found to
frame her. Finally, I thought, you had to choose.

L sat at a white table in the courtyard of the little hotel called
Grand Ecole, her journal and pen out, her luggage at her feet.

"We didn't get it," I said.

"We got it," she said. "Somebody canceled their reservation
just as I walked in the door."

The room was tiny but cute, she reported. It was on the top
floor, another dormer. The maid was still cleaning it. L pointed to
the little window, and I could hear the vacuum humming up
there. I sat down, and would have gotten out my notebook, had

I still had it. We'd done that so often—every day for three weeks, being writers. But my journal at that point had been reduced to the blank page at the back of the Proust.

"You're writing in that?" she said, when I opened it.

I'd never finish the book anyway, I said, and thought I'd use it for something.

"It'll be harder to lose," she said, pointing out that it weighed about a couple of pounds.

And as a note to myself only, I thought that the single available page would keep me in line. Then the room was ready, and we went up. Our window looked out into the plane trees, their broad burnishing leaves just out of reach. The room was mostly taken up by the bed, which was not a big bed at that, with a brass bedstand.

In the morning, birds woke us up.

29

HOME

....

I wish I could say that I maintained that feeling, of clarity and light, of having found more than I expected in L and in France, of noticing without naming, or at least being concise about it. I wish I could say that L and I continued in the easy togetherness that had graced us the day before. But on the last day, I lost it again. And we ended up sitting apart on the airplane, coming home. Such understanding is not—for some reason—a lesson I learn and so know, ever after. I arrive and pass on through, afterward as benighted as before.

That last morning of our last day in France, we rushed around Paris, engaging again in the sheer effort, the labor of international travel. I felt that we hadn't seen it, hadn't done it and now were about to be gone. I was waiting at the Galeries Lafayette when it opened, clinging to a list of gifts for friends at home, but once inside was so dithery that I ended up buying only clunky gold earrings for L, then rushing back to the hotel to meet her before checkout time. She had hurried out into Paris by herself as well, to bid good-bye to friends. When we met again, there wasn't time for conversation—we had a plane to catch.

L's old babysitter, Thérèse, back from her *vacance* in Seguret and back in her more ferocious Parisian mode, picked us up in her car and drove us on a heart-stopping ride across Paris, heading out of the city to the airport called Charles de Gaulle. It was hardly the leisurely, sentimental, farewell-laden departure. Thérèse squealed the tires and shouted complicated French insults— *"Espèce de con!"*—at the other drivers as she careened down the boulevard, and at the same time quizzed L nonstop about our trip. Their French flew in the wind in the front seat as I rocked in the back among the luggage and tried to hear. Thérèse grimaced as L told her about our train travel and about getting around Paris on the Métro. With her jet pilot father and her job as a flight attendant, she hated trains.

"Dangereux," she said, of the Métro. She yelled at another driver and hurled us around a traffic circle, nice as anything when she turned back to chat.

By the time we reached the airport I was anxious to be off and hoped Thérèse would just drop us at the curb, but still being the babysitter, she parked and walked us in, insisting we couldn't possibly find our way without her. That rankled L a little, I could tell. Again at the security check I thought to say good-bye to Thérèse, and again I was wrong. She produced an airport worker's pass and insisted on escorting us to the very door of the plane. Then the guard at the X-ray machine confiscated my Swiss Army knife. I'd get it back in San Francisco, he said. I didn't like this—it was a tool, not a weapon—and got a little outraged about it, arguing with the security man. L looked at me like I was an idiot and said, "Just come on."

We proceeded toward the gate. By the time we reached the duty-free counter, where I was asking L if she'd like perfume and Thérèse was insisting that she pick it out if L did, L was beginning to get genuinely angry, though Thérèse, now all sweetness and solicitude, didn't notice, and waited on and on with us, chatty and oblivious at the gate. Finally, we were called on board, and at the very door L said good-bye as nicely as she could to her old babysitter, but still was snorting with rage when we were safely into the steel tube of the plane. For an awful moment, I'd thought Thérèse was going to put us into our seats and buckle us in.

There was more trouble on the plane itself. The attendant told us that they'd overbooked the business class and didn't have seats for us. We had to get back off the plane as they worked it out. I was furious until I understood that they were upgrading us to first class. My relief, however, was momentary. There was a hitch—they couldn't seat us together. When we were shown the seats, one on each side of the first class cabin, yards of space and other people in between, it was too much. It seemed to sum up the whole trip to me: everything would be fine, so long as we remained a safe distance apart.

"That would be impossible," I said defiantly to the attendant, who simply looked at me and shrugged. L was furious with me, though.

"Don't be such a baby," she said, loudly enough to alert the other passengers. "You sit over there, and I'll sit over here. It's no big deal." I just sat down in my single seat by the window, hurt and angry. It was a big deal, I thought. It was a big deal.

Across the cabin L took her seat, paired there with a tall, young, elegant European man who had long black hair, a perfect gray suit, black tassel loafers and no socks. They struck up a conversation right away.

The big plane took off as I fumed, and we were out of the country before I thought to notice, consumed as I was by my jealousy and rage. I hissed to her across the cabin, but she refused to acknowledge me. By then she was in animated conversation with Mr. Suavo. Finally I called her name, and she couldn't ignore me any further, and pausing in her conversation, just looked at me and said, "Not now," then turned back.

I knew I should stop. If I had learned anything from our trip, it was that my need drove her off. How to not need, though, that was the question. I called her again. This time, angry by now, she said, "Wait a minute."

Seated next to me was a woman I hadn't noticed, but who had witnessed my attempts, as I had been shouting over her. Now she spoke up. "I'll change seats with her," she said, "if it will help." It would, I told her gratefully.

I called L again. She just tried to wave me off. "She'll switch," I said. "Go ahead," I told the woman. Once my seatmate was in motion, L had no choice, and she came over indignantly, not speaking. She stowed her stuff angrily around her seat, as across the plane my former seatmate was already happily exchanging greetings with Mr. No Socks.

"He was a film director," L said at last.

"Big deal," I said, still mad.

Slowly and emphatically she said, "You are *such* a baby." As this was manifestly true, I couldn't think of anything to say. I pretended to look out the plane window. We were over water already, France gone like a swallowed pill.

It was late afternoon by the time we took off, but for a long time, as we stayed angry, the sky beyond the window remained bright. We appeared to be chasing the sun, though we weren't actually, only more or less maintaining our position relative to the turning of the earth. Why did I always think of outer space as night? It would be more like this, endless daylight, the sun glaring all the time.

The attendant came around, she, too, attending me coldly for my outburst. I was asked perfunctorily if I'd like champagne, as if, since I had a seat there with the others, I was entitled to imbibe

with them, outcast though I was, an exile, like the Old English
Wanderer bemoaning his lost hearth. So be it, then, I thought,
looking grimly around the aircraft.

Some of the passengers lowered their shades as we flew on
toward dinner and Greenland, though we remained in daylight. I
alone seemed to recognize that we were more or less stationary in
the sky. Dinner and Greenland were proceeding toward us. The
cabin grew dim, anyway, as if with evening, as the blinds drew
down, and the filet mignon arrived with three kinds of wine. It
wasn't dinnertime. We'd eaten on the turning earth, and so would
seem to turn the earth, that we might eat. Miserable, I made a
point of praising the California wine to the attendant, who
looked down at me as I did, keeping her perfect French balance.

"*D'accord,*" she said.

After dinner I spread my blanket and arranged my pillow and
shut my own window shade against the still-bright sky. When I
woke up the whole cabin was dark. L lay in her seat wrapped in
a blanket and sleeping. Everyone else on the plane seemed to be
asleep, too. I lifted the tight plastic shade and saw red light, sunset
finally just about over out ahead of the plane somewhere.

On a trip once, an airline industry PR guy had told me that big
jets like this one were programmed to home, like elephants, toward a specific place to die. If everyone on the plane, including
the pilot, passed out—or was taken up by the rapture, he'd
said—the plane would turn at last, empty of other commands,
toward the zero-zero: the Greenwich Meridian at the equator,
which was somewhere off the coast of Togo. I didn't know
whether to believe this or not, but even if it were just a story, it
was just like human beings to come up with this, expressing their
hope for completion, their desire that everything end up somewhere.

I watched L breathe a while, tried not to care and couldn't.
Then I got up and moved around her, careful not to touch her, lest

she wake. I went to the tiny stainless steel bathroom and on the way back walked around the darkened cabin in my transcontinental booties. Even among first-class seats, some seemed better. The best of all, I thought, were a pair at the point of the central bulkhead. Two enormously fat people, a man and a woman, snored away, fully reclined in these seats, which seemed like the most spacious of all. The symmetry of the cabin arrayed the whole sleeping plane around these two bundles, their thick bodies like those of the king and queen, borne up but utterly still, as if nothing active were required to maintain their rule. Around them the darkened plane was like a sleeping hive.

L slept on and on. Finally it was dark enough for me to raise the shade and look out without disturbing her. There wasn't much to see, though. I cupped my hands around my eyes, pressed them to the window and looked down, but could only pick out the rare web of light, dim as radium, glowing as if from the lost sun, a little grid that was a town somewhere on the Canadian prairie. Then, much later, the little grids seemed to gather and join, and at last the plane changed tones and began to descend. Now I could see what I thought was California, the blank, black, rugged, innocent land strung with the glowing fringe of human network, people in their illuminated homes, connected by smooth streets that were lighted all night by headlights and streetlights, so that no one had to proceed anywhere in the dark. Beyond a last ridge, this network overlaid everything. Thin, brilliant, unbroken, it looked like circuitry and loomed closer and closer until it had almost enveloped us, after which our lights would glow tinily among the others.

Then I woke L up gently, saying "We're almost home," and she sat up groggily, just as the attendant made the announcement— in English, then in French—to prepare us for our landing. L was no longer angry. Thérèse had driven her crazy in the airport, she said. "And then you drove me crazy on the plane," she added. I was sorry, I said, though I wasn't.

So much for simple proximity, I thought. We'd been to France together. When everything was said and done, this would still be true. No matter what, there would be that trip to France with Jim.

It wasn't enough. Life seemed automatic, that way. So people might become close, just by being around each other, the way honeysuckle tendrils might overwhelm a chain-link fence. Big deal. I wanted eternal love, proclaimed and proven every second.

We took a long time to get through customs, waiting in lines with our carts and our documents beneath the gaze of a crowd who stood at a railing high above us. People in the line waved to people up there, who waved and beamed back in our general direction. I searched their faces, expecting, as always, to see people I knew as soon as I got back to San Francisco. But no one waved to us.

I asked the customs agent about my Swiss Army knife, but nobody knew anything about it. "I knew this would happen," I told L.

"Be a man, not a boy," she said, just wanting to get out of there. "Forget the knife."

Then we went out into the traffic, into the California evening, and at a curb landed a cheap airport shuttle, a white van with FRANCISCO'S ADVENTURE written on it in big red letters. In the van she told me that she wanted to go home to her own apartment. Fine, I said, hurt again. Still, I didn't want to say good-bye to her in Francisco's Adventure. I resented adventure, at that point, and romance, which was worse. Who thought of these things, and how had they gotten us so far from ourselves?

I talked her into getting off at my place and letting me drive her home. Then in my own car I drove down Guerrero Street and across Market and up the hill to her place, as if we'd simply been out on a three-week date. I helped her get her luggage into her lobby, then kissed her quickly and got out of there.

I'd gotten as far as the curb when she opened the front door again and called my name, now that the trip was over, and there was nothing left to prove.

"What?" I said, half-fearful.

Flatly and frankly she told me she loved me, then disappeared back into the lobby.

I drove home, afraid to think anything. Back in my old apartment, things were the same. The cat, fed by a neighbor for three weeks, was wild to see me, and circled my ankles and purred. Because it was time, I went to bed, though I slept fitfully. Once I woke up and couldn't compose my dark apartment into anything. I stared out, lost among columns, in a garden somewhere.

Then in the morning L woke me with a phone call. She'd been dreaming, too, it turned out, of posing for photos as a bride.

BIBLIOGRAPHY

FOR STENDHAL

Cameron, Norman. *To the Happy Few: Selected Letters of Stendhal.* Westport, Connecticut: Hyperion Press, 1979.

Hazard, Paul. *La Vie de Stendhal.* Paris: Librarie Gallimard, 1927.

Josephson, Matthew. *Stendhal.* New York: Doubleday & Co., 1946.

Stendhal. *Love.* Gilbert and Suzanne Sale, trans. New York: Penguin Books, 1957.

———. *Memoirs of an Egotist.* David Ellis, trans. New York: Horizon Press, 1975.

FOR THE SONG OF SONGS

Adler, Cyrus, Isadore Singer, et al., eds. *The Jewish Encyclopedia.* New York and London: Funk and Wagnall's Co., 1925.

Falk, Marcia. *The Song of Songs: Love Lyrics from the Bible.* New York: HarperCollins, 1990.

Finklestein, Louis. *Akiba: Scholar, Saint and Martyr.* New York: Covici, Friede, 1936.

Gollancz, Hermann, trans. *Targum to the Song of Songs.* London: Luzac, 1908.

Gottwald, Norman K. *The Hebrew Bible: A Socio-literary Introduction.* Philadelphia: Fortress Press, 1985.

Graves, Robert. *The Song of Songs.* New York: Crown Publishers, 1973.

The Interpreter's Bible: The Holy Scriptures in the King James and Revised Standard Versions with General Articles and Introduction, Exegesis, and Exposition for Each Book of the Bible. New York: Abingdon Press, 1956.

Jones, Alexander. *The Jerusalem Bible.* Garden City, N.Y.: Doubleday, 1966.

Johnson, Paul. *A History of the Jews.* New York: Harper & Row, 1987.

New American Standard Bible. Reference ed. La Habra, CA: Foundation Press Publications for the Lockman Foundation, 1973.

Roth, Cecil, ed. *Encyclopedia Judaica.* Jerusalem: Ketter Publishing House, Ltd., 1972.

Notes: "Holy of Holies:" *Yedaim* 3:5. "No place in the next world:" *Tosephta Sanhedrin* 12:10; cf. also the parallel passage *Babylonian Talmud, Sanhedrin* 101a. "Make way for her:" *Nedarim,* p. 50a.

FOR PETRARCH

Bishop, Morris. *Petrarch and His World.* Bloomington: Indiana University Press, 1963.

Fusilla, Joseph G. "Petrarchism." *Princeton Encyclopedia of Poetry and Poetics.* Alex Preminger, ed. Princeton: Princeton University Press, 1965.

Petrarch. *Letters from Petrarch.* Morris Bishop, ed. and trans. Bloomington: Indiana University Press, 1966.

———. *Petrarch: Selected Poems.* Mortimer, Anthony, ed. and trans. Tuscaloosa: The University of Alabama Press, 1977.

Wilkins, Ernest Hatch. *Life of Petrarch.* Chicago: The University of Chicago Press, 1961.

ABOUT THE AUTHOR

JIM PAUL'S poems have appeared in *The New Yorker, The Paris Review,* the *American Poetry Review* and elsewhere. He holds a doctorate in medieval literature from the University of Michigan, and was a Wallace Stegner Fellow of Creative Writing at Stanford University. He is the author of *Catapult: Harry and I Build a Siege Weapon,* published in 1991 by Villard Books.